ENGLAND'S ASHES

THE STORY OF THE GREATEST TEST SERIES OF ALL TIME

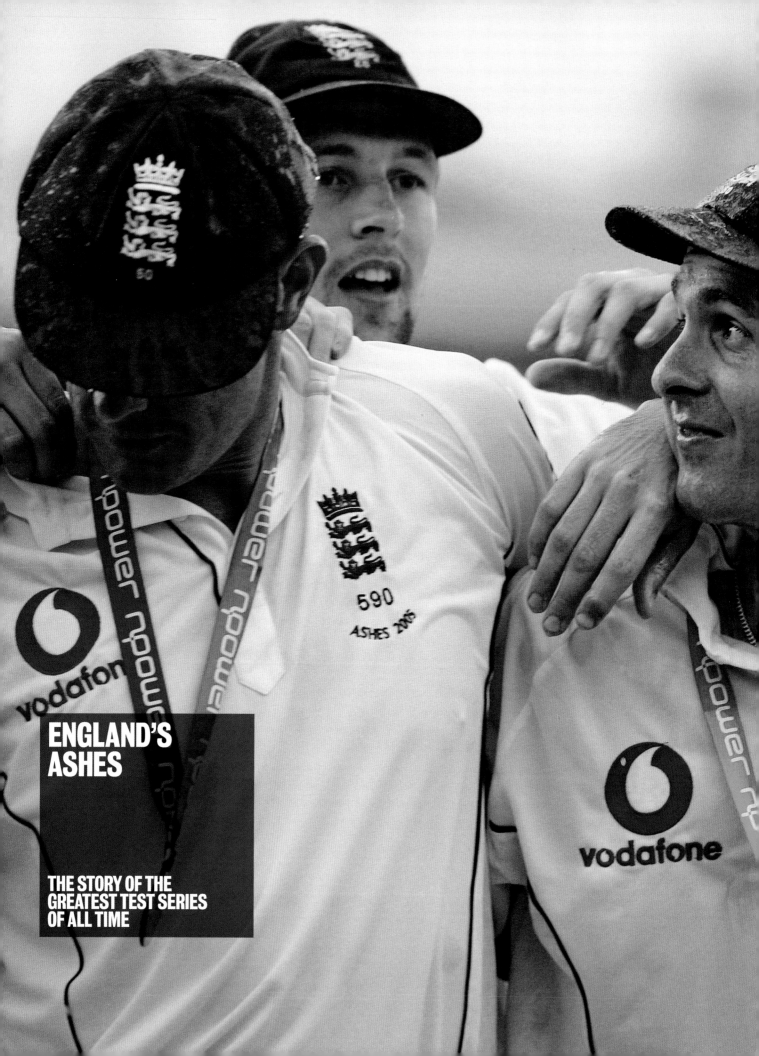

ENGLAND'S ASHES

THE STORY OF THE GREATEST TEST SERIES OF ALL TIME

First published in UK in 2005
by HarperSport an imprint
of HarperCollins*Publishers*
London

© Telegraph Group Limited 2005 and
Hayden Publishing Ltd 2005

A CIP catalogue record for this book
is available from the British Library

ISBN 0 00 722728 0

Colour reproduced by PDQ Digital Media
Solutions Ltd, Bungay, United Kingdom

Printed and bound in Great Britain
by Butler & Tanner

Produced by Hayden Publishing Limited

The HarperCollins website address is
www.harpercollins.co.uk

HarperSport
An Imprint of HarperCollins*Publishers*

England's Ashes

Foreword
Michael Parkinson

At its height, eight million tuned into the Ashes series. That's as maybe. But how many were looking? This Test series had an epic grandeur capable of making all other big sporting events seem puny by comparison.
To this seasoned observer, only the three fights between Muhammad Ali and Joe Frazier compare.

Then, as now, the opponents were stretched to the very limits of their resources, both physical and mental.

Then, as now, the spectators were involved in a relationship with the participants which made watching as unbearable as turning away was unthinkable.

In the end, even the most clunk-headed partisans were forced to concede that if Andrew Flintoff had been born in Sydney he would be perfect, and that if Shane Warne played for England we would be invincible.

Extraordinary encounters produce genuine heroes. Flintoff is the real thing. Not only is he a greatly gifted athlete but also an agreeable young man. He is an implacable adversary, a ferocious competitor, yet respectful of worthy opponents. Flintoff consoling Brett Lee at Edgbaston will remain in the memory like Bobby Moore and Pele's embrace at the Mexico World Cup. Fact is, as this series proved, the greatest sporting battles are fought between opponents who understand that respect is a much better ally than contempt.

Flintoff now joins the likes of Jonny Wilkinson and David Beckham as both superhero and tabloid fodder. Nowadays, the consequence of hero worship is as corrosive as it is lucrative. They will come at Freddie from all sides offering this and that and he must learn to sift their temptations. He must understand he is living under the closest scrutiny. He must pick his way carefully, a difficult job for any young man, particularly one as exuberant as he, always bearing in mind that the consequence of not doing so defines Warne.

Warne's indiscretions cost him his marriage, not to mention the captaincy of his country. It tarnished him in the eyes of some, particularly those who live in glass houses. The paradox of Warne is how a cricketer of such intelligence, strength of mind, genius even, could be so careless and silly in private. On the field of play he has few qualms and no equal. He is the greatest spin bowler there has ever been, but more than that, much more. He is a consummate entertainer, an alchemist, a master of illusion, an impresario.

Proof, if needed, came in the last overs at Trent Bridge. There was no one in the watching millions, nor indeed in the England dressing room, who didn't believe he could bowl his side to victory, that even with England needing two to win with three wickets in hand, he wasn't capable of settling things with a hat-trick.

In any sensible reckoning of sporting achievement he belongs in the most select company along with the aforesaid Ali, Jack Nicklaus, Pele and, dare I say it, Don Bradman. Warne has redefined the art of spin bowling every bit as much as Bradman demonstrated his mastery of batting.

In spite of the virtuosity of Flintoff and Warne, the series turned on planning and team spirit. There is no doubt Duncan Fletcher, the coach, should take a bow, if ever he could be persuaded. He can be proud of what he accomplished.

This is now a formidable England team with a tough, intelligent captain and an appetite for a scrap. They are united with a team spirit and common purpose which England's football coach and players can only envy and hope to emulate.

This great Australian side were challenged and found wanting. They were out-thought and outmanoeuvred by a team capable of giving the Aussies a hard time for many a year to come.

The television images of the series reflected the real meaning and purpose of a sporting event, demonstrating that no matter what Bill Shankly said, and however tough and uncompromising the contest, no one dies.

The importance of sport is that it doesn't matter, except as an antidote to things that do.

What I took from this summer was a belief that cricket is in safe keeping not just because Freddie Flintoff hits big sixes or bowls like the wind, or Brett Lee might become one of the great fast bowlers, but because neither man has forgotten how to smile.

The lesson is an important one. It's not so much about having a sense of humour as possessing a sense of proportion. ●MP

AFTERWORD
Marcus Trescothick

I first started to get a sense that something might be in the air during the one-day international at Bristol. The Twenty20 had been great, sure, but Australia had only been in the country for a few days and were completely underprepared, so I couldn't take it all that seriously.

At Bristol we saw a reversal of the normal roles. Normally when we play Australia in a one-dayer we get into a winning position then lose it. This time we were losing the game before Kevin Pietersen came in and just took it away from them. I had played in two previous series against Australia but I had never seen that happen before.

It was clear that Australia weren't in great form. The day before they had lost to Bangladesh, for goodness sakes. And even at that early stage we got the idea that Jason Gillespie and Michael Kasprowicz might not be the players we had seen in previous years. A few chinks were opening up in their armour.

Given all those positives, it was pretty crushing to lose the first Test in the way we did. I remember leaving Lord's feeling worried sick, especially about the way we had dropped all those catches. That only seems to happen against Australia, and I knew it had to be a mental thing, because we catch everything in practice. I came back to Taunton and told the Somerset lads that if we didn't win the next match we might as well give up and go home.

Lord's was an example of us reverting to old-school England. We fell into the trap of standing off and not getting into Australia like we had in the one-dayers. Even though the bowlers hit people on the head and there was not a lot of mateyness between the teams, we were still a bit shy. We conceded a big lead and just capitulated on the Sunday.

That finish was such a contrast with how Australia played the series. They never gave us a single inch. They were miles out of the game in the next three Tests, yet they refused to lie down. The only time I thought we had the match wrapped up was going into the last day at Edgbaston, and look what happened there ...

The performance was out of character for us, especially at the end, because we normally fight all the way down to No. 11. We were copping it in the media and starting to think negative thoughts, worrying that if we messed up we would get more grief. It was a relapse into bad habits, because over the previous two years we had managed to chuck that old-school approach out of the window. Our whole game had been based around saying: "The hell with it, if we mess up we mess up, but let's go out there and enjoy ourselves, be aggressive, and that way maybe things will happen."

Looking back, I regret not going up to Ricky Ponting to see how he was when Steve Harmison hit his helmet and cut his cheek. Especially as Ricky is a friend and Somerset team-mate. I didn't realise how bad it was at the time. But we had also set out to be a bit tougher than in previous Ashes series.

Australia were making a big thing about playing in the best spirit and being fair and respectful. That's all very well, but in that first Test we had to make a statement of intent. And I think we did manage to wind them up a little. We made them realise we didn't give a damn about how they wanted to play the game, we were going to do things our way.

But as the series went on, all that stuff was forgotten. We all sat and chatted together in the dressing-rooms at the end of every match. That created a lot of mutual respect, which was then taken out into the field.

Personally, I learned so much from the gracious way the Australians dealt with their wins and losses. I think the people who followed the series appreciated it more because of the good feeling between the teams.

The only other point when things got a bit tetchy was after Ponting was run out by Gary Pratt at Trent Bridge and stormed off in a rage. But that was pretty quickly resolved. We saw Ricky afterwards and took the mickey out of him. In the end, Ricky gave Gary a pair of boots as a souvenir.

Back to the aftermath of the first Test, and we were still struggling mentally with the challenge of the Ashes. Then there were a couple of things that happened in the ten days before Edgbaston. The first was that Ashley Giles had a bit of a rant in the press about how jealous former players didn't want us to win – which definitely wasn't part of the plan.

We had sat down before the series and talked about the media, and how we expected the Aussies to say a lot of things and try to manipulate the press against us. We agreed that we just wanted to stay professional about it. Then Ashley had gone totally the other way.

Okay, he felt he needed to do it, and in the end maybe it was the right thing for him. But when he got to Tuesday's nets at Edgbaston we could see he wasn't his normal self. He seemed shy and worried that everyone was looking at him.

This needed sorting out. We sat down in a couple of team meetings, got the team psychologist involved and told Ashley that everyone was behind him and it would all turn out right. We knew we had to keep him in the bubble of the team, because if we lost him he would cop it from all sides. By Wednesday Ashley was his normal self again, then he went out and picked up Ponting's wicket at a big moment. That helped him relax and he bowled well for us throughout the summer.

The other thing that happened between the Tests was that Freddie Flintoff and I played in the Twenty20 finals day for our counties. That may not sound like a big deal, but I watched Freddie's innings for Lancashire and it was a turning point for him. When he came out he was awful at first, just couldn't get going. But he started knocking it around, picked up a few singles, then suddenly went bang-bang and he was past 40 and a totally different player. It was almost as if he was back in the zone.

Freddie ended up coming out to bat in a pressure situation on that first day at Edgbaston and again it was a similar thing. He looked at sea early on against Shane Warne, toe-ended one just over mid-off, but then he hit one out of the ground and he was away.

We were over the moon on that first morning when Ponting put us in. I had woken up at 7am, turned the TV on and seen BBC news at the ground with Gus Fraser and Geoff Lawson who were both saying: "It's overcast and a bit green, definitely win the toss and bowl today." I thought it must have been a different pitch to the one I had seen the day before. But Ponting went along with them and we were delighted, especially with Glenn McGrath out of the reckoning.

I had been feeling good in practice and when I got out there everything felt in slow motion. The pitch was very slow and easy and Brett Lee bowled me a few half-volleys which I just timed. At Edgbaston the outfield is so good that the ball races away.

That was a crazy day of batting. I have a vivid memory of sitting with Andrew Strauss on the balcony, doing a Sudoku puzzle, while boundaries were flying everywhere. We agreed that it was like watching a benefit match. Australia managed to bowl us out by the close but we were scoring at five an over, and they looked shell-shocked when they came off.

Freddie had to bail us out in the second innings, and his batting with the tail made the difference. The way he smashed Kasprowicz everywhere, moving across to whack two over the onside then stepping back to cut, it was as if he knew where the next ball was going.

You might think that a Test-match seamer should be able to deal with a guy who is premeditating his shots, especially someone like Kasprowicz who bowls a good one-day yorker. But it is a different game bowling yorkers at No. 9 or 10 to bowling at someone like Freddie, who you know will nail it every time you get one slightly wrong.

There were some great bowling efforts that evening. After Freddie had picked up Justin Langer and Ponting together, I turned to him in the slips and said: "That's the best over you'll ever bowl." He was buzzing, the crowd were buzzing, and I thought we had won it when Harmey did Michael Clarke with that fantastic slower ball.

But then we came out the next day and the total just started ticking down so fast. I remember saying to Straussy, "I hope we win by 100 because that was the deficit on first innings and that will highlight their mistake in putting us in." It was down to 60-odd by the time we got Warney, and I thought: "Okay, I'll take 50 runs, that's pretty comprehensive."

I couldn't imagine that Kasprowicz would get to 20-odd, I just thought he would miss one or nick one or punch one. But then the lead came down to under 20 and I started thinking, "How are we going to cope with this?"

Going 2-0 down, in that fashion, in the middle of back-to-back Tests, was just too horrible to contemplate. We'd be nailed in the press, we'd be out of the series – we'd be absolutely crucified.

When Simon Jones dropped that catch, I thought "That's it, game gone." Then the final ball from Harmey seemed to go in slow motion. I could hear myself shouting "Catch it!" And the next 20 minutes were a bit of a blur. It was a great match, but you don't like winning games like that – it's just too painful.

One of my main memories of the Old Trafford Test is of getting caught, via the glove, the back of the bat and Adam Gilchrist's leg, when I was on 60-odd and feeling good. I couldn't believe it, especially as I had just become Warney's 600th Test wicket!

Australia played McGrath despite his ankle injury. After the way we had gone after their seamers at Edgbaston, that didn't surprise me. His second ball was a beauty: it reared up, hit the top of my handle and sailed over the slips. But you could tell he wasn't quite himself. A fully-fit McGrath groups his deliveries perfectly, while on this occasion he bowled a couple on the legs and a couple to cut.

Vaughany's innings was a joy to watch. Some of his shots, especially off Gillespie, were reminiscent of the way he played in Australia on the last tour. We bowled well in that Test too, reverse-swing on the button from Freddie and Simon Jones, but the rain meant we never quite finished them off. When McGrath came in with four overs to go, I thought they would never make it, especially as Freddie was getting the ball to reverse-swing away – always the hardest skill. But Lee kept it out somehow.

Despite the disappointment, we were also feeling pretty good about ourselves. We had just dominated a Test against Australia's first-choice side. Our cricket was getting better and better throughout the summer. We went from thinking "Hang on, we can beat these," to "We are beating these," to "Blimey, we're ahead!"

The win we were looking for duly came up at Nottingham. Freddie was magnificent again, playing a different kind of innings this time. It was a big step forward for him to be so controlled, more like a batsman than an allrounder. I got pretty worried when we were chasing 130-odd on the last day, because I knew Warney would make life hard for the tailenders. But then Matthew Hoggard came out and hit that fantastic off-drive for four. I had been talking to Hoggy about his bats before the match, and he was saying "I've got a beauty at the moment, I just haven't had much of a chance to use it." He used it then alright.

It was a strange feeling that night. The first thing was a sense of relief, that we couldn't lose the series now, and that was a big step forward for us in an Ashes summer. But then when we sat back we realised that if we drew 2-2 it would mean absolutely nothing. Losing the last game would have felt just as bad as a 5-0 hiding.

We got through somehow. We were
delighted to win the toss, but then Warney
bowled brilliantly to take six wickets. It wasn't
spinning much, so he almost had to con us out,
but he is a master in any conditions. The good
news was that Straussy's hundred and another
70 from Freddie meant that we got to 370,
which would take a long time to overhaul.

How long we could never have guessed. I
was amazed that they went off for bad light on
the second evening. Maybe not the third: they
only had six overs then, and Damien Martyn
wasn't seeing it too well. But the day before
they could have had an extra 90 minutes in
the middle. As it was, they only got close to
our score on Sunday morning, then Freddie
bowled them out to give us a small lead.

Duncan Fletcher sat us down before the final
day of the series and told us that he had been
surprised and delighted with the way we had
gone about the whole summer. He hadn't
thought we were mentally ready to challenge
Australia, just like he hadn't thought we were
ready to beat South Africa away from home in
the winter. But we finished 2-1 up there and
we were 2-1 up again here. Now we just had to
fight for every run to get over the line.

The final day was set up for KP. The biggest
Test we'll ever play, the biggest occasion, the
most pressured day: it all suited him down to
a T. I was watching from the other end, and he
started out by faffing around against Warne.
Then suddenly he went six, six. I walked down
and said "Well played", and he said "Yeah I've
had enough of blocking, I'm gonna smash it."

Fair enough, that's the way he is. The
selectors picked KP because of his aggression.
Instead of trying to bat out for a draw he took
it to them. A hundred from 120 balls while
saving the match! It was magnificent.

The celebrations were tremendous. I
crashed out at 3.45am the next morning, then
got up early for the open-top bus parade. I felt
a bit ropey but a glass of champagne perked me
up. It was an amazing procession – something
I will remember happily for the rest of my life.

The best thing about all this is that we have
finally got a monkey off our backs. Everyone
used to say "Same old story" whenever we lost
a wicket or dropped a catch against Australia.
But now, when battle resumes next winter, we
know we won't have to worry about all that
"old wounds" rubbish. ●MT

AFTERWORD
Matthew Hayden

Cricket tours are memorable for a range of reasons and throughout my international career, I've been lucky enough to take away more than my fair share of great memories.

The 2005 Ashes series has to go down as one of the most memorable series I've ever played in. Sure we are all feeling the disappointment of losing the Ashes, something that is going to take a good while to get over. However, being part of the epic, see-sawing contest that the series became over two months as it captured the imagination of not only Australians and Englishmen but cricket lovers around the globe was a privilege.

From the dressing room it was amazing to see how cricket fever swept the nation, knocking football off the back pages, and enticing thousands of people through the gates. Talking to family and friends back home, we heard how thousands were heading to work bleary-eyed, after being glued to television sets all night.

I was told that television ratings for midnight in Australia had never ever been so good and the free-to-air network, normally known for showing Eastern European movies with sub-titles, who had acquired the rights to show the series had pulled off the programming coup of the year – leaving rival television executives completely red-faced.

On the tour coach, in shops and restaurants, and in the team hotels it was obvious that cricket had completely taken over – we're used to that in India where the passion for the game is unique, but in England?

For a generation of players who grew up with the one-day game as the sport's showcase event, attracting big crowds and big corporate dollars, the hysteria surrounding the tradition game of Test cricket transported us all back to another time.

People sitting on rooftops, or taking turns at standing on their mates' shoulders just to get a peep over the fence was something I never thought I would see during my time as an international cricketer.

And even more promising for the health of the game was the fine spirit in which each match was played.

While Michael Vaughan and his team proudly celebrated with what seemed like half of London, and the bulk of our team were boarding an Australia-bound 747 at Heathrow Airport, I wrote that cricket administrators should use the spirit in which the 2005 Ashes Series was played as the text-book example when teaching young players how to handle themselves both on and off the field.

This spirit wasn't at all manufactured. It came from the mutual respect that existed between the sides; something I had never experienced before. Like so many things in the series, it was reminiscent of an earlier period when cricket was played hard, but fair.

Perhaps the best example of the genuine warmth and respect which had pervaded the series after Lords, and scenes I will forever carry with me, occurred in our dressing room after the umpires had finally removed the bails at The Oval. The England side, still in a euphoric state, joined us to share a few beers and swap stories about what we had all experienced over the summer.

Despite the fact that our group was pretty flat, if there had been a fly on the wall, it wouldn't have been able to distinguish between losers and winners that night. Everyone was just relieved that the extraordinary roller-coaster ride had come finally to an end.

Sitting deep in the corner of the dressing room was the Hampshire connection of Shane Warne and Kevin Pietersen both still fresh from their amazing solo performances; at the other end of the room was Jason Gillespie in deep conversation with Matthew Hoggard; the two captains, Ricky Ponting and Michael Vaughan, were, astonishingly, still talking tactics.

My opening partner, Justin Langer, and I found ourselves deep in conversation with the England new-ball attack of Andrew Flintoff and Steve Harmison. Very rarely do you see an opening batting pair and a set of opening bowlers in Test cricket talking socially.

This Australian side admires Andrew for what he achieved throughout the series – he was incredible. He embodies so many of the traits that Aussies respect, because he has a heart as big as the sun. We toasted him with a few cans of Foster's, saying that anyone who bowls 18 overs straight at that pace and quality deserves nothing other than respect.

I'm sure that the England lads then moved from our rooms on to far bigger celebrations. But why wouldn't they have celebrated? They outplayed us, and given it had been 18 years since they had held the Ashes, they had every right to enjoy the moment. ●MH

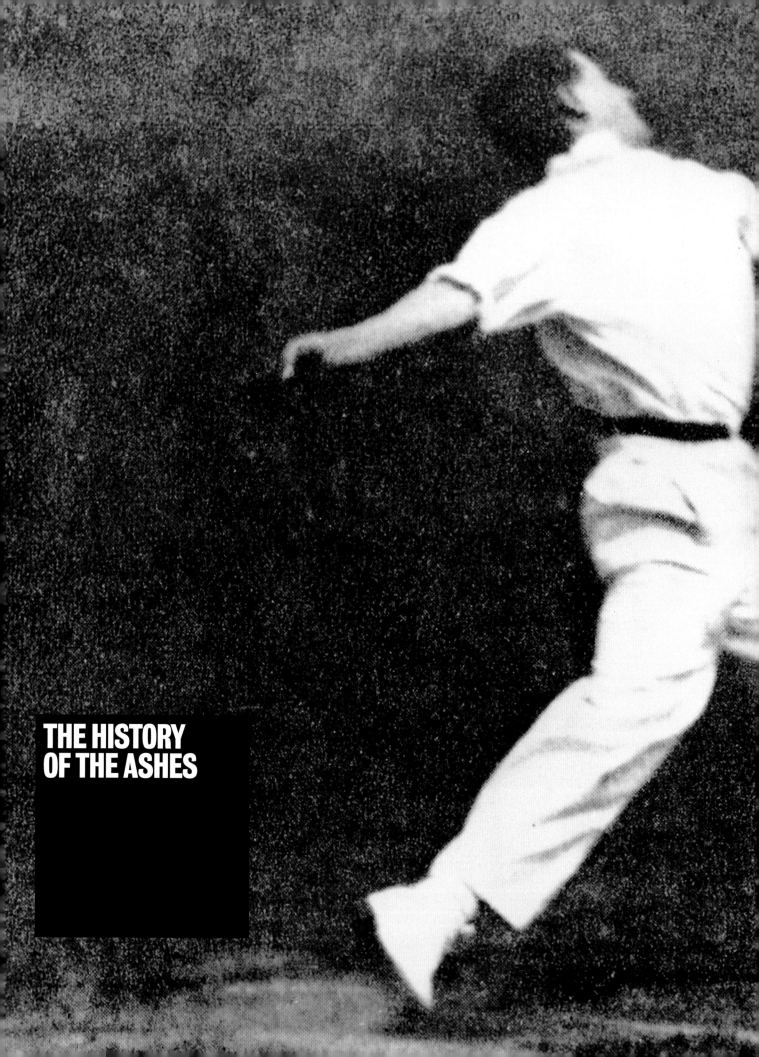

**THE HISTORY
OF THE ASHES**

out in front of thronged stands and packed roofs at the Oval. Defending a meagre victory target of 85, Australia were bowled to victory by Frederick "The Demon" Spofforth – a tall, spindly, metronomically accurate fast bowler who must have been the early prototype for Glenn McGrath.

Shocked by England's first Test defeat on home soil, the nation resorted to navel gazing – as it does after every great sporting or military defeat. Shirley Brooks, editor of Punch, was looking for answers when he published the following verse:

Well done, Cornstalks, whipt us
Fair and square.
Was it luck that tripped us?
Was it scare?
Kangaroo land's 'Demon', or our own
Want of devil, coolness, nerve, backbone?

lamented by a large circle of sorrowing friends and acquaintances R.I.P.
N.B. – The body will be cremated and the ashes taken to Australia."

Brooks's message ensured that the following winter's tour – captained by the tall and blue-blooded Hon. Ivo Bligh – would be billed as England's mission to recapture the Ashes. Indeed, Bligh mentioned them in an early speech at the Melbourne Cricket Club pavilion, saying: "We have come to beard the kangaroo in his den – and try to recover those Ashes."

Though few Australians would have had any idea what Bligh was going on about, he had spent much of the two-month steamship journey from England explaining the concept to Sir William Clarke, president of

1882

The most prized of possessions: sport's most famous urn contains possibly the ashes of a bail, or a burnt ball or even veil, but to the cricketers of England and Australia it means everything

In Affectionate Remembrance

OF

ENGLISH CRICKET,

WHICH DIED AT THE OVAL

ON

29th AUGUST, 1882,

Deeply lamented by a large circle of sorrowing friends and acquaintances.

R. I. P.

N.B.—The body will be cremated and the ashes taken to Australia.

Death notice: Reginald Brooks' mock obituary as it appeared in the Sporting Times on the Saturday after the fateful Oval Test

Melbourne Cricket Club, plus his family and staff. One member of the entourage who received particularly close attention was Florence Morphy, a beautiful but near-penniless music teacher.

Once the Peshawur had docked at Adelaide, the Clarke estate at Rupertswood in Victoria would become a regular retreat for Bligh's men. It was here – after England had won the second and third Tests to claim the series – that a group of ladies including Morphy, Janet Clarke and Ann Fletcher are said to have presented him with the original Ashes urn.

The details of the story are often contested – as indeed are the contents of the urn itself, which are variously described as the ashes of a ball, a bail, or even Morphy's veil. Neither does anyone know who wrote the feeble doggerel inscribed on the side of the urn, though Morphy is again suspected. It reads:

When Ivo goes back with the urn, the urn;
Studds, Steel, Read and Tylecote return, return;
The welkin will ring loud,
The great crowd will feel proud,
Seeing Barlow and Bates with the urn, the urn;
And the rest coming home with the urn.

If all this was part of an elaborate courtship game, it worked a treat. By the time Bligh left Australia, Morphy had agreed to marry him, and the ceremony was conducted at Rupertswood a year later. They were married for 43 years, and when Bligh finally died in 1927, his widow – now Florence, Countess of Darnley – presented the urn to MCC.

THE WG YEARS

England's first great cricketer was already 34 and a qualified doctor by the time the Ashes were born. It is a mark of WG Grace's durability that he was still only halfway through his unparalleled career. But even at that early stage, the contrasting aspects of his character had made their mark on Anglo-Australian cricket.

Grace's supreme batsmanship proved irresistible at the Oval in 1880, where 65,000 squeezed into the ground to see him carve 152 – England's first century in Test cricket. He later described it breezily as "one of the best I ever played". But his equally peerless gamesmanship turned the All-England team's 1873-74 tour of Australia into a public relations disaster.

Grace demanded a fee of £1,500 – at least £50,000 in today's money – to lead that tour, then proceeded to fall out with everyone: promoters, local dignitaries, even the professionals in his own team. "He sowed many of the seeds of mutual hostility and suspicion that intermittently soured Anglo-Australian relations in the years ahead," wrote his biographer, Simon Rae. "Not until Jardine led the Bodyline tour of 1932-33 was there a more unpopular and vilified English captain in Australia."

Both sides of the Grace coin were again present at the definitive 1882 Ashes Test. His second-innings 32 was England's highest score of the match; but equally his under-hand run-out of Sammy Jones was the spur for Australia's furious rearguard. Grace waited for the batsman to leave his crease and pat down a few divots before whipping off the bails and appealing.

In a fore-echo of Devon Malcolm's "You guys are history" outburst – supposedly delivered after Fanie De Villiers had clonked Malcolm on the helmet at the Oval in 1994 – Spofforth was reported to have gone "into the Englishmen's dressing-room and told Grace he was a bloody cheat and abused him in the best Australian vernacular for a full five minutes. As he flung out of the door his parting shot was, 'This will lose you the match'."

Spofforth was as good as his word. His figures of seven for 44 made sure that England fell seven runs short, even if it was Harry Boyle who took the final wicket. It was a finish to match any of the glories of 2005: folklore has it that one spectator gnawed through the handle of his umbrella, while another died of a heart attack. To

Lionheart: Fred "The Demon" Spofforth was Australia's first true fast bowler. His first-class career spanned the period between 1874 and 1897

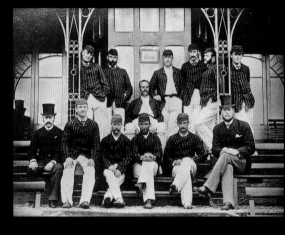

Kangaroo land's finest: the Australian touring party of 1882 captained by Billy Murdoch who is seated rear centre

modern sensibilities, it seems only proper that Australia should have prevailed; an England win would have been forever tarnished by WG's gracelessness. In a similar situation at Old Trafford, Matthew Hoggard omitted to run out McGrath, even though the batsman was standing several inches out of his crease.

Grace's England appearances were restricted to home Tests, at least until his belated promotion to the captaincy in 188. Then he set out on his second great Australian adventure, in 1891-92. The worst of his previous misdeeds had clearly been forgotten, judging by some of the eulogies that greeted his arrival. Here is Grace's former opponent Tom Horan, and by now Australia's leading cricket reporter: "As he walked from the MCC pavilion to the practice nets, he looked what he is, the king of cricketers, and the personification of robust health and manly strength and vigour."

Some of the same adjectives could have been applied to England's batting in the first Test, which was as entertaining as it was careless. Grace's team went down by 54 runs, then lost the second match as well despite the captain's hard-nosed refusal to let Australia use a fielding substitute for the injured Harry Moses. Even a consolation win at Adelaide was soured by a row over the umpires, and by the time Grace left

Australia he was almost as reviled a figure as he had been 18 years earlier. Even a chastened Horan had to admit that "Grace is ... a bad loser, and when he lost two of the Test matches in succession he lost his temper too, and kept on losing it right to the finish."

THE GOLDEN AGE
Cricket historians know the years from the turn of the century to World War I as "The Golden Age". This was an era of teeming talent, of exhilarating performances from such all-time masters as Sydney Barnes, Kumar Ranjitsinjhi and CB Fry. But if there was one man who captured the debonair spirit of the age, it was the ultimate dasher – Australia's Victor Trumper.

While Trumper's statistics – 3163 runs at 39.04 – may not seem exceptional, his worth can be measured in the admiration of his peers. AC MacLaren, not a man lacking in self-esteem, once said with a snort: "My best innings compared with one by Victor was shoddy – hack work!" Len Hutton commended Trumper's character too, recounting the story of how he once refused to play any attacking strokes at a young collier making his Yorkshire debut. Afterwards, he admitted that he hadn't wanted to "spoil that lad's chance of getting a living in an easier way than heaving coal".

Trumper's debut coincided with WG Grace's final Test, at Trent Bridge in 1899,

when the old master was 50 and the young gun 21. His first innings was a duck – something of a recurring theme for a man who refused to play the percentages – and his second mustered only 11. But in the next game at Lord's, Trumper struck a scintillating 135 not out as Australia won by 10 wickets. It was the only result of a five-Test series, and good enough for Joe Darling's team to retain the Ashes.

Trumper returned to England three years later to make another classic hundred in another classic Test. This time his 104 at Old Trafford set up Australia's first innings in a match they went on to win by three runs. England responded with 128 from the Hon FS (Stanley) Jackson, perhaps the finest amateur batsman of his day. But poor Fred Tate, father of the more famous Maurice Tate, was cast as England's villain. In his only Test, he dropped a crucial catch off Darling and was then bowled by Jack Saunders to settle the match. The young Maurice remembers his father calling a hansom-cab, drawing the blinds and weeping.

After four series of Australian rule, England finally regained the Ashes in the following winter of 1903-04, under the captaincy of Pelham (Plum) Warner. The first team to tour under the banner of MCC, this was one of the great England sides. The batting was led by RE (Tip) Foster, still the

1883

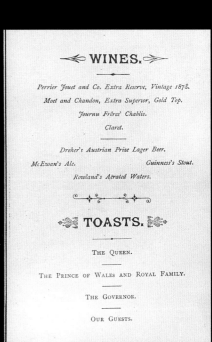

"We have come to beard the kangaroo in his den and to try and recover those Ashes," said the Honourable Ivo Bligh, but not until after a good dinner apparently

only man to captain England at cricket and football. Foster made just one century in his eight-Test career, but it was a big one: 287 in the series opener at Sydney. He still holds the record for the highest score by any tourist in Australia and the highest by a debutant in Tests.

England's bowling, meanwhile, was given extra sting by Bernard Bosanquet, whose new mystery ball – known variously as the bosey, the wrong'un, and the googly – was a controversial addition to the spinner's armoury. When Bosanquet ran through the Australians in the fourth Test, wrapping up the series with six second-innings wickets in less than an hour's play, Warner was able to hit back at the "unkind people [who] said ere this that I 'ran' Bosanquet into this team because he was a friend of mine ... When he gets a length he is, on hard wickets, about the most difficult bowler there is."

Even in a disappointing series for Australia, Trumper was again a shining light. He answered Foster's 287 with 185 brilliant runs at Sydney, then played another sensational innings on a "sticky dog" in the second Test. Some 10,000 miles away in London, Fry rose to his feat at a dinner and announced: "Gentlemen, I give you a toast. It is to Victor Trumper, first in, last out, 74 runs out of a total of 122, on a vile pitch against the best bad-pitch bowlers in the world."

THE BIG SHIP

One of England's victims in that 1903-04 series was a fledgling allrounder by name of Warwick Armstrong. Tormented by Wilfred Rhodes's left-arm spin, confounded by Bosanquet's googlies, the 24-year-old Armstrong was dropped for the final two Tests. Yet this tall, slim figure would return – in an altogether different incarnation – to inflict the only 5-0 whitewash in Ashes history.

Armstrong's rehabilitation began just 18 months later in the 1905 series. Though he failed to score a Test hundred, his first-class figures over the summer – 1902 runs at 50.05 and 122 wickets at 18.2 – have never yet been surpassed by an Australian cricketer on tour.

As his place in the side became more secure, Armstrong's frame swelled to WG Gracian proportions – hence his nickname "The Big Ship". He had some of Grace's other characteristics too, being suspicious of authority and prone to sharp practice. One of his favourite tactics was to dry up the scoring by sending his slow top-spinners well down the leg-side. The novelist AA Thomson remembers attending one match where "Armstrong was bowling practically at the square-leg umpire".

Armstrong's most audacious piece of gamesmanship came in the final Test of 1909, and outdid even Grace for sheer cheek. It was the second day at the Oval,

and England were pressing for the win that would square the series. On the fall of the fourth wicket, the great Kent allrounder Frank Woolley strode out to play his maiden Test innings. Remarkably, he was forced to stand around for a full 19 minutes while Armstrong made use of a rule permitting an indefinite number of looseners.

Many historians feel that Amstrong heralded a sea change in Australia's sporting attitudes. The fair play of the Darling era segued into something far tougher and more pragmatic – a "win at all costs" mentality. But whatever the rights and wrongs, there is no doubt that when Armstrong took on the captaincy for the 1920-21 Ashes series – the first to be held after the Great War – he wiped the floor with JWHT Douglas's England.

Armstrong was tactically ahead of his time in the emphasis he placed on fast bowlers. He found two good 'uns, too, in Ted McDonald and Jack Gregory – the latter ironically spotted by Pelham Warner during a wartime match between the Artillery Officers' School and the Red Cross.

Deploying his twin spearheads in short bursts – another strategic innovation – Armstrong scattered his opponents in all five Tests at home, then extended his winning sequence to eight matches in England the following summer. The power of pace was brutally evident when Gregory

1891/92

WG Grace: his supreme batsmanship and peerless gamesmanship during the 1873-74 tour combined to sour Anglo-Australian relations for years to come

1899

Victor Trumper: he visited England on four occasions, but 1902 was the year he reached his highest point when, in a summer of wretched weather, he scored 2570 runs in thirty-five matches with an average of 48. He was the most popular Australian cricketer of his time, dying at the tragically young age of 37

knocked out Ernest Tyldesley at Nottingham with a bouncer. To add insult to injury, the ball rebounded from Tyldesley's skull onto the stumps.

Selectorial panic, of the kind familiar from recent years, was soon evident. England made six changes for the second Test of 1921 – prompting Douglas to exclaim: "What's this damnable side of picnickers they've given me?" – and seven for the next game. The Honourable Lionel Tennyson, grandson of the poet laureate, was appointed captain just in time to bid the Ashes farewell at Leeds.

Surprisingly, though, Armstrong seemed content to sit on his 3-0 lead for the last two Tests. He confounded Tennyson's hopes of an early declaration at Old Trafford by a lawyerly dissection of the Laws, then angered the Oval crowd with his lack of interest in a rain-blighted finale. Both matches were flaccid draws, prompting calls for English Tests to be extended beyond the usual timespan of three days.

Armstrong's final act of the tour was to slam England's professional batsmen, such as the ultra-defensive Phil Mead, for their selfishness and lack of initiative. And with that parting broadside, the Big Ship – now aged 42 and weighing more than 20 stone – sailed into a stately retirement.

REIGN OF THE MASTER BATSMAN

Jack Hobbs, known simply as "The Master", was the only player to bridge the eras of Trumper and Bradman. He played against Grace too, making 18 and 88 on first-class debut in 1905. Fielding at point, Grace stroked his beard and announced: "He's goin' to be a good'un." Good enough, as it happened, to break Grace's own record of 126 hundreds.

Hobbs took 18 innings to make his first Ashes century – a veritable drought by his later standards. But when it finally came, at Melbourne in January 1912, he proceeded to reel off tons in the next two Tests. With Sydney Barnes and Frank Foster collecting 66 wickets between them, JWHT Douglas's 1911-12 tourists enjoyed a supremacy – and a 4-1 scoreline – that England could only dream of after the war.

Hobbs's great decade, though, was the 1920s. After the selectorial bloodletting of 1921, when England used a record 30 players, his rock-steady opening partnership with Herbert Sutcliffe would be the biggest single factor in restoring national pride. Notching up 15 century stands in 38 attempts, their 87-run average outstrips every other pairing in history.

The young Hobbs was an impish dasher who used quick feet and whipcord wrists to dazzle opponents and spectators alike. The post-war model was sober by comparison, yet equally productive. Wisden's encomium, delivered to mark his appointment as one of the Five Cricketers of the Century, notes that Hobbs "switched the emphasis away from gentlemanly Victorian off-side play to a more pragmatic approach, with an emphasis on the businesslike pull, plus an acute judgment of length, footwork, and, where necessary, pad play". In later life, the modest Hobbs was often heard to play down his achievements, pointing out that the prevailing lbw law disallowed any ball not pitching on the stumps.

The great Hobbs-Sutcliffe alliance encountered Australia for the first time in 1924-25, and immediately flourished. Hobbs averaged 63 in the series, Sutcliffe 81. As England were also introducing Maurice Tate, who took a record 38 wickets, one might have expected them to run off with the series. But Australia were ferociously strong too, and while Tate had virtually no bowling back-up, the home side combined Gregory's pace with the leg-spin of Arthur Mailey and Clarrie Grimmett to retain the Ashes 4-1.

The next two series continued the theme of batting supremacy. Five Tests in 1926 produced only one result, an England win at the Oval. Then, in the first match of 1928-29, two immortals made their Ashes entrance simultaneously: Wally Hammond for England, Don Bradman for Australia. It

1930

TEST MATCH—LEEDS, JULY, 1930.

ENGLAND v. AUSTRALIA, at Headingley.

Fri., Sat., Mon., and Tues., July 11th, 12th, 14th and 15th, 1930.

AUSTRALIA.

		1st Innings		2nd Innings
1 W. M. Woodfull b Hammond ...		50	...	... ...
2 A. Jackson c Larwood b Tate		1	...	... ...
3 D. G. Bradman c Duckworth b Tate		334	...	... ...
4 A. Kippax c Chapman b Tate		77	...	... ...
5 G. McCabe b Larwood		30	...	... ...
6 V. Y. Richardson c Larwood b Tate		1	...	... ...
7 E. L. a'Beckett c Chapman b Geary		29	...	... ...
8 W. A. Oldfield c Hobbs b Tate		2	...	... ...
9 C. V. Grimmett c Duckworth b Tyldesley		24	...	... ...
10 P. M. Hornibrook not out ...		1	...	... ...
11 T. Wall b Tyldesley ...		3	...	... ...
Extras b 5; lb 8; w 1.		14	Extras	... ...
Total		566	Total	... ...

Total runs at fall of each wicket
2 194 423 486 491 508 519 544 565 566 |

Bowler	Overs	Maidens	Runs	W'kts	Overs	Maidens	Runs	W'kts
Larwood	33	3	139	1				
Tate	39	9	124	5				
Geary	35	10	95	1				
Tyldesley	33	5	104	2				
Hammond	17	3	46	1				
Leyland	11	0	44	0				

Umpires:
Messrs. Bestwick & Oates

ENGLAND.

		1st Innings		2nd Innings
1 Hobbs c a'Beckett b Grimmett		29	run out	... 13
2 Sutcliffe c Hornibrook b Grimmett		32	not out	... 28
3 Hammond c Oldfield b McCabe		113	c Oldfield b Grimmett	35
4 K. S. Duleepsinhji b Hornibrook		35	c Grimmett b Hornibrook	10
5 Leyland c Kippax b Wall ...		44	not out	... 1
Geary run out		0	...	... ...
6 A. P. F. Chapman b Grimmett		45	...	... ...
8 Tate c Jackson b Grimmett ...		22	...	... ...
9 Larwood not out ...		10	...	... ...
10 Duckworth c Oldfield b a'Beckett		33	...	... ...
11 Tyldesley c Hornibrook b Grimmett		6	...	... ...
Extras b 9; lb 10; nb 3.		22	Extras lb 8. ...	... 8
Total		391	Total for 3 wkts. ...	95

Total runs at fall of each wicket
53 64 123 206 206 289 319 370 375 391 | 24 74 94

Bowler	Overs	Maidens	Runs	W'kts	Overs	Maidens	Runs	W'kts
Wall	40	12	70	1	10	3	20	0
a'Beckett	28	8	47	1	11	4	19	0
Grimmett	56·2	16	135	5	17	3	33	1
Hornibrook	41	7	94	1	11·5	5	14	1
McCabe	10	4	23	1	2	1	1	0

Scorers:
Messrs. Ferguson & Brownfoot

HOURS OF PLAY—1st day, 11-30 to 6-30; other days, 11-0 to 6-30.
Luncheon Interval, 1-30 to 2-15 each day. Tea, 4-30.

The Don: Sir Donald Bradman was, beyond any argument, the greatest batsman who ever lived. In the 1930 Ashes series he scored 974 runs, 309 of them in one amazing day at Headingley

remains a historical curiosity that Australia lost Bradman's first Test by 675 runs – the highest figure ever recorded.

BRADMAN AND THE BODYLINE CRISIS

The most famous words in Ashes history, barring Brooks's obituary notice, are probably those spoken by Bill Woodfull in the Adelaide Oval dressing-room on January 14, 1933. "There are two teams out there on the oval," he said. "One is playing cricket, the other is not."

Woodfull was lying on a massage table at the time. He had just been struck on the ribs by Harold Larwood, the Nottinghamshire coal-miner turned fast bowler, who was bowling short-pitched, physically threatening deliveries to a packed leg-side field. This was the method that came to be known as Bodyline. Conceived by England's patrician captain, Douglas Jardine, the tactic was intended to tame Bradman's genius. It succeeded – Bradman averaged a mere 56 in the series – but only at the cost of creating an international incident.

To understand the thinking behind Jardine's ruse, one has to look at the context. Hammond's 905 runs in 1928-29 had already heralded a shift in the balance between bat and ball. But when Australia came to England 18 months later, Bradman – still a 22-year-old stripling – upped the ante with the most astonishing sequence of individual performances ever recorded.

Bradman made 131 in the opening defeat at Nottingham, then 254 – an innings he always described as his finest – at Lord's. Headingley produced 334 (including 309 in a day) and Lord's 232. His series tally, which has never been beaten, added up to 974 runs at 139. It was a tribute to England's own excellence that they only lost the series 2-1.

Bradman, clearly, was a marvel of the modern world. Yet he was curiously hard to love. Neville Cardus said he was that rare combination, "a genius with an eye for business". Certainly he had a remorseless approach to cricket and life that could exasperate more romantic souls. After his retirement in 1948, Hobbs wrote: "I think the Don was too good: he spoilt the game ... I do not think we want to see another one quite like him. I do not think we ever shall."

These reservations may explain why the Bodyline saga is often recounted as a morality tale – sport's answer to the Great Fall, in which cricket's innocence is lost through the greed of one over-mighty batsman and the pride of his ruthless opponents. In Jack Fingleton's definitive study Cricket Crisis, the Australian opener-turned-journalist wrote: "Not even a Bradman had the divine right to pre-suppose that he could indulge himself in gargantuan feast of runs and not pay the penalty of something like bodyline indigestion."

Considering how carefully England had prepared their anti-Bradman missiles, it was somehow ironic that he should miss the first game of the series through illness. Still, Australia were overwhelmed, despite the spectacular display of pulling and hooking that brought Stan McCabe an unbeaten 187. Bradman then returned at Melbourne, to be greeted by a massive ovation. But the first ball, delivered by the lumbering Bill Bowes, found him skating across off-stump and somehow glancing the ball into his stumps.

This was a portent of things to come. All through the series, Bradman could be spotted dancing around the crease or chasing after Hedley Verity, England's only spinner, with uncharacteristically risky shots. Warwick Armstrong, now a columnist on the Evening News, expressed a typically trenchant view: "To put the matter bluntly he was frightened of fast bowling."

Bradman did his best to refute such criticism, claiming that "my method of playing Larwood exposed me to considerably more danger than the orthodox way". But, in this pre-helmet era, no-one could be blamed for blanching at England's methods. The flashpoint finally came in the third Test. Woodfull was hit, uncontroversially at first, by an off-stump bouncer bowled to an orthodox field. But when he groggily returned to the wicket, Jardine

1932/33

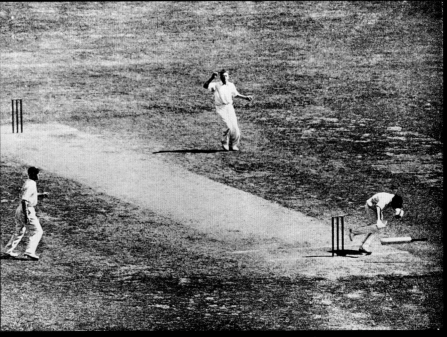

Leg theory: captain Douglas Jardine has already designed a tactic to restrain Don Bradman before leaving England. It will result in the most controversial cricket tour in history

The consequences: Bert Oldfield, top-edging a delivery from Larwood, is hit on the head and has to be carried unconscious from the field. When Larwood settled in Australia, the two became close friends

leg-side and Larwood let fly with a sustained barrage – much to the anger of the crowd.

That was the day of Woodfull's solemn dressing-room pronouncement to England's manager Pelham Warner, who had visited to enquire after his health. The very next afternoon, Bert Oldfield had his skull fractured by a ball that came off the top edge of his bat. The Australian Board of Cricket sent this telegram to England: "Bodyline assuming such proportions as to menace the best interests of the game, making protection of the body by the batsmen the main consideration. This is causing intensely bitter feeling between the players as well as injury. In our opinion it is unsportsmanlike. Unless stopped at once it is likely to upset the friendly relations between England and Australia."

But the English government stood behind Jardine, who threatened to boycott the final two Tests if the accusation of poor sportsmanship was not withdrawn. In the end, Australia's Prime Minister Joseph Lyons talked the ABC into backing down, on the grounds that trade relations could be damaged. England proceeded to win the final two Tests – mercifully on slower pitches at Brisbane and Sydney – and claim the most infamous 4-1 victory in history.

"I do not think there was one single batsman who played in most of those bodyline games who ever afterwards regained his love for cricket," Fingleton would write. "Bradman never regained his 1930 poise, and his batting in the early games in England in the 1934 season made people wonder whether he was identical with the Bradman of four years before."

FROM ILLNESS TO INVINCIBILITY

There was another reason why Bradman struggled at the beginning of that 1934 series: he was suffering from ill health. Every innings he played was a drain on his resources, and at the end of the summer he developed near-fatal appendicitis. As he lay in a hospital bed, tended by his wife Jessie, even King George VI was demanding constant updates on his condition.

Tired and out of sorts, Bradman made a mere 133 runs in his first five innings. Yet Australia still won the first Test thanks to 11 wickets from Bill "Tiger" O'Reilly, a hot-tempered leg-spinner whose mutual antipathy towards Bradman catalysed a dressing-room rift between Protestants and Catholics. (Their feud was posthumously resolved on O'Reilly's death in 1992, when Bradman described him as the best bowler he ever saw or faced.)

Verity replied with 15 wickets in England's win at Lord's (a ground where the home side have yet to claim another Ashes victory despite 18 attempts). Then, after two draws, the teams arrived at the Oval with the series poised at 1-1. Bradman and Ponsford promptly buried English hopes under a 451-run stand.

England stuck remarkably close to Australia's might through the 1930s, though they never quite managed to regain the Ashes. The 1936-37 series – Bradman's first as captain – was a titanic tussle, much of it played in bad weather on "sticky dog" pitches that negated the great man's gifts.

Fingleton wrote that his "repeated failures on wet wickets must forever remain the mystery of his career."

Bradman must have felt under enormous pressure after defeats in the opening two matches. But in the pivotal third Test at Melbourne, he proved a more cunning tactician than Gubby Allen, reversing the batting order to make best use of a drying pitch. He then ended the series with a more typical sequence – 270, 26, 212, 169 – to claim a startling 3-2 victory. Even now, Bradman remains the only Test captain to win a rubber from 2-0 down.

The 1938 Ashes not quite go to the wire. Australia won the fourth Test to reach the Oval 1-0 up. Yet it was that "dead" final game which went down in cricketing legend. Presented with the ultimate featherbed pitch, Hammond told his team "No score is too high," and they listened well. Schoolboys across the land learned to recite such

1932/33

Hero and villain: Harold Larwood spearheaded England to a 4–1 series victory, taking 33 wickets at just under 20 apiece. Batsmen ducked and danced while a concentration of voracious leg-side fielders hunkered down to catch defensive prods and jabs. Larwood's classical action culminated in a side-on delivery, the ball's velocity amongst the highest ever recorded

"The rarest of Nature's creatures": by his own unparalled standards, Bradman was discomfited by Jardine's Bodyline tactic, nevertheless he still averaged 56.57 for the series

statistics as the highest individual score (Len Hutton's 364), the highest team total (903 for seven declared) and the biggest victory margin (an innings and 579). Australia's cause was hardly helped when Bradman broke his shinbone in a fall while bowling.

The first post-war series, 1946-47, introduced a host of new Ashes heroes: Denis Compton, Bill Edrich and Alec Bedser for England, Arthur Morris, Keith Miller and Ray Lindwall for Australia. But it will also be remembered for those who weren't there, notably Hedley Verity, who died of his wounds as a POW in Italy.

Australia were soon taking belated revenge for their Oval thrashing. England's first-Test reverse, by an innings and 332, was the harbinger of a chastening tour for Hammond, who averaged 21, lost 3-0, and never faced his nemesis Bradman again.

Perhaps that was a mercy, as the summer of 1948 produced the most famous squad of touring cricketers ever to land at Tilbury. Bradman's "Invincibles" won 25 of their 34 first-class matches, and were never defeated. They only fell short of Armstrong's 5-0 whitewash because of the drawn third Test at Old Trafford.

No-one can say what would have happened without Manchester's habitual rain, which washed out the fourth day of that match and then terminated Australia's

pursuit of 317 on an ominous 92 for one. But it was a magnificent Test anyway. England led by 142 on first innings thanks to Compton's heroic batting and outrageous showmanship. Suffering a cut forehead from a top-edged pull at Lindwall, he staggered off the field for plasters and two large slugs of brandy, then returned to strike an undefeated 145. "Great as Compton is, never has he been greater," intoned Leslie Mitchell over the famous Movietone News footage.

Given a full five days, England could have set Australia anything up to 600 to win. Yet even the hugest totals were no bar to a Bradman-inspired chase, as witnessed by the very next match at Leeds. This time England were 404 runs ahead when the declaration came from Norman Yardley (one of the least remembered English captains). Australia got them in under five-and-a-half hours for the loss of just three wickets. Morris made 182, Bradman 173 not out.

There was more high drama, of a more personal kind, at the Oval a fortnight later. In normal circumstances, Morris would have taken the plaudits for his 196, especially as the next-highest score in the match was just 64. Yet this game will always be remembered for Bradman's poignant failure in his last Test appearance. Needing just four runs to average 100 in Test cricket, he propped forward to his second ball and was bowled by Eric Hollies's googly. "It's not easy

to bat with tears in your eyes," said Bradman afterwards. The man, it seemed, had finally triumphed over the machine.

But England's close fielders were not convinced. "Get away with you," was the view of Jack Crapp at first slip. "That bugger Bradman never had a tear in his eye throughout his whole life."

FROM SPIN TO PACE AND BACK AGAIN

"All England feels that now, at last, we may be able to fight for the Ashes on more equal terms again," said Bill Edrich after Bradman's retirement. Though the 1950-51 tour was a disappointment, Edrich was at least partly right: England would hold the Ashes for the middle part of the 1950s.

Their first obstacle came in the unlikely shape of Jack Iverson, an artless fellow who took up cricket at the age of 30 after discovering an entirely new way of spinning the ball. Iverson had huge hands, and while on army service in New Guinea he found that by flicking the ball out from between his thumb and bent middle finger he could totally befuddle his comrades in their parade-ground games of French cricket.

On his return home, Iverson enlisted to play for Brighton thirds in Melbourne, and within four years he was up against England. He was still something of a cricketing idiot savant, a man who struggled to remember the names of fielding positions, but he could

1948

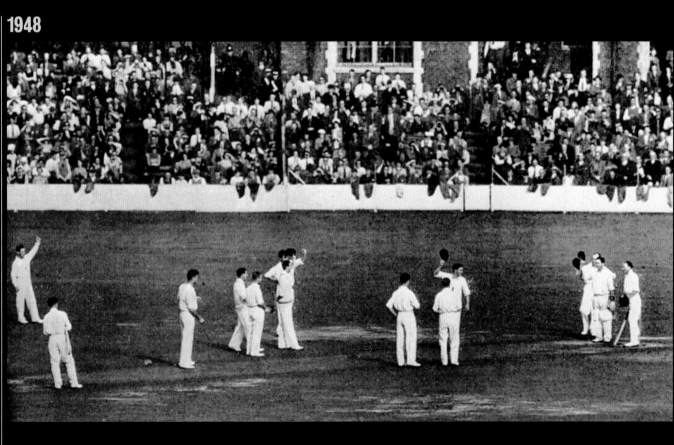

Bradman's last Test: Bradman was out second

bowl both leg-spinners and googlies without offering the slightest clue about which was which. England had no more success in unlocking Iverson's variations than his wartime mates, and he took 21 wickets at 15.23 in Australia's 4-1 win.

Oddly, those five Tests were all that Iverson would ever play. He left representative cricket as suddenly as he had joined it, took over his father's real estate business, and became one of the sport's many high-profile suicides in 1973.

The summer of 1953 produced some dour old matches, deservedly overshadowed by the conquest of Everest and the coronation of Elizabeth II. Australia – and the crowds – were regularly frustrated by Trevor Bailey, who lingered more than 17 hours over 222 runs in the series. On the last day at Lord's, with England listing at 73 for four, Bailey and Watson added 163 in four hours to claim a famous draw.

Len Hutton (443 runs) was now installed as England's first professional captain. Putting that metronomic medium-pacer Alec Bedser (39 wickets) through an exhausting 264 overs, Hutton took a thoroughly pragmatic approach to regaining the Ashes. But it was all worth it when England snatched an eight-wicket win at the Oval to claim the series 1-0. Thousands of ecstatic fans flooded the outfield to celebrate the urn's return after 19 long years.

For Hutton, the 1954-55 tour brought perhaps the greatest triumph and disaster of his career. But at least he got the disaster out of the way early. On the first morning of the series, Hutton won the toss and put Australia in – Nasser Hussain-style – at Brisbane. By the close, Australia were 208 for two, Compton had broken his finger while crashing into the boundary fence, and the captain was so depressed he was unable to speak. "Upon Hutton will fall the odium of an unsuccessful gamble," pronounced EW Swanton in typically Old Testament tones.

England lost by an innings, then Hutton further annoyed Swanton by dropping Bedser for Sydney. This was a nerve-jangling match. England overhauled a 74-run deficit through Peter May's first Ashes hundred and Colin Cowdrey's first Test fifty, setting Australia 223 to win. But it was Frank "Typhoon" Tyson, bowling at the kind of pace that is given to very few, who won the match with figures of six for 85. Only the previous day he had been rushed to hospital after ducking into a Lindwall bouncer.

Though the hulking shoulder-heave of Tyson's delivery stride bore little resemblance to Iverson's deft trickery, his impact on the Ashes was similarly explosive – and short-lived. He won this series 3-1 for England, taking 28 wickets at 20, before gradually fading from the scene. Even now,

Richie Benaud reckons Tyson to have been the quickest he ever saw, "fractionally shading Jeff Thomson".

Off-spin, a type of bowling rarely seen in Australia, was the trump card that claimed a 2-1 English win in 1956. This was Jim Laker's summer. In the fourth Test, Laker produced the immortal figures of 19 for 90. When you consider that no other bowler, Test or first-class, has taken more than 17 in a match, this must go down as a statistical freak. Yet Laker was not just a one-match wonder: his series haul of 46 wickets remains an Ashes record.

Laker had a score to settle with Australia. His career had been badly dented by the Leeds Test of 1948: after failing to take a wicket in 32 overs on a helpful pitch, he would hardly feature in the next three Ashes series. But at Old Trafford he had his revenge. Jim Burke was the only batsman to elude him, falling in the first innings to his regular Surrey and England spin-bowling partner Tony Lock. The other batsmen were confounded by Laker's accuracy on a crumbling pitch. Their collective technique of stepping forward and across was designed to combat leg-spin, and when the ball broke back at them they tended to lunge across their pads and pop the ball to the close fielders. Laker became the first cricketer to win the BBC's new prize of Sports Personality of the Year.

1950

The last of the Corinthians: Dennis Compton with help from his friend, opening partner and joint captain of Middlesex Bill Edrich, helped return cricket to its pre-war place in the nation's affections. Until the summer of 2005 only Ian Botham had ever come remotely close to matching this achievement

1953

BRIGHTER CRICKET?

The 1958-59 tour was the most controversial since Bodyline. Two of Australia's fast bowlers, Ian Meckiff and Gordon Rorke, pushed the Laws to the limit in different ways. Meckiff appeared to bend his left arm on delivery – a quirk that eventually led to umpire Colin Egar calling him for throwing four years later, and so terminating his career. Rorke also had a suspect action, and on top of that he was a 6ft 5in giant who took advantage of the back-foot no-ball rule to encroach some three or four yards down the pitch.

England lost 4-0, and afterwards England captain Peter May maintained that he had done well to keep a lid on his team's dissatisfaction. Yet England can hardly claim to have been cheated out of the Ashes: while Meckiff and Rorke claimed a total of 25 wickets, leg-spinner Richie Benaud – in the first of three winning series as captain – and left-arm seamer Alan Davidson took 55 between them without the faintest hint of a bent elbow.

In 1960-61, Australian cricket was given a boost by perhaps the only Test series that can match the 2005 Ashes for drama. Played against the West Indies, it featured the first tied Test, and raised hopes of a new era of "brighter cricket". Yet such expectations were short-lived. In terms of entertainment, the 1960s proved to be the low point in

Ashes history. An astonishing 13 Tests out of 25 were drawn, despite the presence of such free spirits as Ted Dexter and Fred Trueman. Though Australia won only two of the five series, they drew the other three 1-1 and so hung on to the precious urn until 1970-71.

Benaud and Davidson – friends, clubmates and training partners – were a dominant force at the start of the decade. The Shane Warne and Glenn McGrath of their day, they somehow managed to haul Australia out of the mire whenever England threatened. The classic example came in the fourth Test of 1961: with the series poised at 1-1, England were 150 for one in pursuit of 256 when Benaud made the unheard-of decision to bowl around the wicket. Dexter was instantly caught behind, May bowled off his backside for a duck, and Benaud finished with six for 70 in a 54-run win.

Safety-first tactics returned in 1962-63, despite more protestations of "brighter cricket" from both captains. Again the series was level going into the fifth Test, but Dexter's sporting declaration – 241 to chase in four hours – found Australia unmoved. Craggy opener Bill Lawry was 45 not out at the close.

The emphasis was on individual feats in 1964: Bob Simpson turned his first Test century into 311 at Old Trafford, while Fred Trueman claimed his 300th wicket at the Oval, in the same match as Geoff Boycott's

own maiden hundred. Yet the only rest of the series had come at Headingley. For once, American bemusement at the futility of a five-day draw seemed well placed.

Back in Australia, Bob Barber's match-winning 185 at Sydney gave England the unfamiliar feeling of being ahead in an Ashes series, but Simpson's double-hundred in the next Test soon restored normal service. Jeff Jones, father of Simon, took the only five-for of his 14-Test career at Adelaide.

At least this dullest of decades reached a compelling conclusion in 1968. As so often, England reached the Oval already 1-0 down, but a bloody-minded hundred from Edrich and a brilliant one from Basil D'Oliveira helped them stick Australia in on the fourth evening against a rampant Derek Underwood. By lunch the next day, England were halfway to victory, but then a sudden downpour flooded the pitch and prompted a call for spectators to help mop up the water with towels. Australia were eventually left with 75 minutes to survive, and there were just six of those left when Underwood defeated stubborn opener John Inverarity – padding up to his deadly arm ball – to finish the match.

If Underwood's figures of seven for 50 represented the high point of his first-rate career, D'Oliveira's 158 was the innings that changed the world. It led to his selection for

1973

The Oval: the scene as the crowd celebrate England winning the Ashes, August 1953

Yorkshire's son: Raymond Illingworth's greatest gift as a captain lay in creating the illusion that he had 14 or more players on the field, so expertly did he block a batsman's favourite scoring strokes. Leading England to an Ashes series win, he was much helped by the accuracy of his own offspin, giving away a miserly 1.91 runs per over in his 61 Tests

the following winter's tour of South Africa. And when Prime Minister John Vorster cancelled the tour, arguing that it was unthinkable for a South African emigre of Cape coloured origin to play against his all-white champions, the concept of a sporting boycott was born.

THE CHAPPELL ERA

England finally got their hands on the urn at the start of the 1970s, after a furious battle in the only Ashes series to be played over seven Tests (the third match at Melbourne was washed out). Ray Illingworth decided to stack his batting order with three specialist openers in Boycott, John Edrich and Kent's unheralded Brian Luckhurst. The plan worked brilliantly as the three men piled up 1760 runs between them at an average of more than 70. But it was John Snow's venomous fast bowling that sealed England's 299-run win at Sydney. His favourite tactic was to push the batsman onto the back foot with bouncers, often delivered from around the wicket, then clean them up with the fuller ball.

The series reached a turbulent conclusion as Australia dropped Lawry – their captain for four years and still arguably their best batsmen – and appointed the unflinching figure of Ian Chappell as the team's new leader. England still went on to win the final Test, despite ugly scenes after Snow sent

Terry Jenner to hospital with a blow on the head. As the umpires warned Snow for intimidatory bowling, the crowd hurled beer cans onto the outfield. Snow then returned to the boundary where a drunk spectator grabbed his shirt, prompting Illingworth to take England off the field. Only after the umpires threatened that he would forfeit the match did Illingworth agree to return.

Like Tyson before him, Snow hardly fitted the stereotype of the brutish fast bowler. Both men were highly literate: Tyson liked to quote Shakespeare and Wordsworth at batsmen, while Snow published two books of poetry. Their triumphs, taken together, gave rise to the theory that the best way to win in Australia was to turn up a matchwinning fast bowler. And that 1970-71 series marked the entrance of two other pretenders to the title: Bob Willis for England, Dennis Lillee for Australia.

Illingworth held onto the Ashes in 1973 despite an individual performance to rank alongside Laker's 17 years previously. Bob Massie, on his Test debut at Lord's, swung the ball like a boomerang to take eight wickets in each innings. Yet he would play only two more games after that halcyon summer, and even dropped out of his state team within 18 months. England were then accused of doping the pitch at Headingley, where Underwood made the Ashes safe with

ten wickets on the driest of surfaces.

It was hard to tell whether any ill-feeling remained by the time Mike Denness led the 1974-75 team to Australia. Because Lillee and Jeff Thomson would have bounced the hell out of them anyway. In the most physically intimidating display of fast bowling since Bodyline, England were not just beaten, they were beaten up. Both Edrich and Dennis Amiss suffered broken hands in the first Test, prompting a call-up for the 42-year-old Cowdrey. When he introduced himself to Thomson at the crease, with the typically English words "I don't think we've met – my name's Cowdrey", the reply is believed to have been unprintable.

England limited the damage to 4-1, picking up a consolation win in the final Test thanks to a shoulder injury sustained by Thomson while playing tennis on the rest day. But the series was measured as much in bruises as runs and wickets. Thomson struck the future England coach David Lloyd one fearsome blow that split his box in two, and forced him to be carried from the field. Years later, when Middlesex seamer Mike Selvey incapacitated Lloyd in similar fashion, he popped into the dressing-room to commiserate and was told: "After Thommo, you were a pleasure."

The return series in England next summer started in equally humiliating

1975

Ode to a batsman: John Snow was the son of a clergyman, a published poet and a strong-willed and difficult man. But for eight years from the mid-1960s he was, by some margin, England's best fast bowler. In 1970-71, he was one of Ray Illingworth's main weapons in winning back the Ashes

1977

HM Queen Elizabeth II meets Ian Botham during the Trent Bridge Test of 1977

Captain's table: Greg Chappell may have lost the Ashes series of 1977 to Mike Brearley's side, but his feat of scoring centuries in each innings of his captaincy debut is unequalled

fashion, with Graham Gooch bagging a pair on debut in an innings defeat. But the selectors brought Tony Greig in as captain to replace Mike Denness, summoned 33-year-old David Steele from Northamptonshire, and saw their side fight out three creditable draws (the series was reduced to four Tests because of the inaugural World Cup). The third Test at Headingley would surely have reached a result but for the protesters who broke into the ground on the fourth evening, dug up the pitch, and cut the message "Free George Davis" into the turf. The captains had no alternative but to agree a draw, despite Australia's tantalising position of 220 for three in pursuit of 445. Davis, a convicted armed robber, was in fact freed the following summer after a review of the case. But he would serve plenty more time after two further convictions in 1978 and 1987. Meanwhile Steele, memorably described in The Sun as "the bank clerk who went to war," finished the summer with 365 runs at 60 and emulated Laker by winning BBC Sports Personality of the Year.

A one-off "Centenary Test" was played in 1976-77, though the Ashes were not at stake. Still, this match more than lived up to its billing. Derek Randall made a splendidly quirky 174, debutant David Hookes smashed Greig for five successive fours, and Lillee's 11th wicket earned Australia victory in the final hour. Spookily, the result – an Australian win by 45 runs – was exactly the same as in the first Test match 100 years earlier.

The disruption caused by Kerry Packer's World Series Cricket was England's biggest ally at the end of the 1970s. With WSC busily signing players on both sides, the 1977 Ashes were something of a farce. Recruited by Packer as a consultant and figurehead, Greig had to give up the England captaincy to Mike Brearley. The Australian squad, meanwhile, was riven down WSC lines and succumbed to a 3-0 defeat.

England's highlights of a summer were provided by a 21-year-old tyro and a 36-year-old veteran. Ian Botham stormed onto the scene at Trent Bridge, immediately establishing his golden-armed reputation when he took his first wicket with a long-hop. In the same match, Boycott was finally restored to the England team after a self-imposed absence of 30 Tests in protest at Denness's captaincy, Boycott hit 107 and 80 not out in the third Test followed by 191 – his 100th first-class hundred – at a tumultuous Headingley.

By the time England arrived in Australia in 1978-79, stocks were running appallingly thin for a home team captained by Graham Yallop. The visitors dominated the series 5-1, only faltering in a third Test notable for Allan Border's debut. Led by Hurst, Hogg and Higgs, Yallop's attack sounded like it might have been picked by a selector with hiccups. But Rodney Hogg proved to be the team's one success story, claiming 41 wickets at 12 with his very fast, very skiddy torpedoes.

After a reconciliation between Packer and the establishment, a similar England team returned to Australia a year later to face full-strength opposition. This time, the only thing Brearley won was the argument over Lillee's notorious aluminium bat. Perhaps surprised by the sudden hike in quality, England lost all three games, and must have felt grateful that the Ashes – thanks to a quixotic TCCB ruling – were not at stake.

BOTHAM'S ASHES

The rise and fall of Ian Botham was well underway by the summer of 1981. His upsurge had made him the best allrounder in the world within a year of his Test debut, then England captain at 24. But his pressure of office seemed to wreck his form. After successive series defeats against the West Indies, he came into the Ashes series under attack from every side.

The nightmare lasted another two Tests, the first of which was a low-scoring defeat on a terrible pitch at Nottingham, and the second a draw at Lord's. Botham bagged a pair, then resigned within an hour of the finish. When he walked through the Long Room after his second duck, bowled

1980

100 years: in 1980 a one-off Test was held at Lord's to commemorate the centenary of the first Test match played in England. In a game decimated by poor weather, tempers became frayed on the Saturday when, despite glorious sunshine, play did not start until late afternoon. The time lost consigned the game to a draw. Ian Botham, in the year before his apotheosis, scored a less than memorable duck

sweeping at Ray Bright, the MCC members maintained a disrespectful silence.

So to the fateful Headingley Test, surely the most famous of all Ashes contests. Brearley was back as captain now, but lost the toss and watched Australia pile up 401 for nine declared, despite Botham's revitalising six for 95. That was a big score on a tricksy Leeds pitch, as was evident once England had been rolled for 174 in reply. Once again, the only positive was Botham, who now struck 50 from 54 balls and could be seen laughing and joking with Lillee in his old manner. "Botham's change of mood was obvious to everybody," Graham Dilley would comment. "It was almost as if you'd taken a child, made him an adult for a while, then allowed him to go back to being a child."

As England went back out on the third evening to follow on, the electronic score-board flashed up the Ladbrokes prices: England 500-1, Australia 1-4. In a two-horse race, these odds looked far too good for Lillee and Rod Marsh to resist, and they got their bus driver to place £10 and £5 respectively on an England win.

The procession continued on the fourth day, and England were 135 for seven, still 92 behind, when Dilley arrived. The game was over, to all intents, so the pressure on the batsmen had eased and they simply decided to have a dash. The result was a maiden Test fifty for Dilley and a barrage of boundaries for Botham, who smashed the ball every-where in what Yallop called "an educated slog". Even his mishits – and there were a fair few of those – were nearly going for six. His final total was 149 not out from 148 balls, with 27 fours and a straight six that gave rise to Benaud's classic line: "Don't even bother looking for that one. It's gone straight into the confectionary stall...and out again." England were finally bowled out on the fifth morning for 356, 129 runs ahead.

The final act belonged to Willis. Beset by illness and knee trouble, his place had been in doubt, and he only just made this team ahead of John Emburey. But he found an unstoppable rhythm downhill from the Kirkstall Lane End, with the wind at his back. His figures of 8 for 43 were won through sheer pace, hostility, and – according to his team-mates – a bizarre trancelike state. "I looked into his eyes and it was like there was nobody here," said Dilley.

Australia should have won the fourth Test as well, in the sense that they only needed 151 in the fourth innings. But it was a low-scoring match on a seaming pitch, in which the highest score was Brearley's 48. Botham had a quiet match, for the most part. As the game neared its conclusion, Brearley brought him on to keep the City End tight. Emburey, who had just taken two quick wickets to leave Australia 106 for five, was supposed to be the match winner. But Botham had other ideas: he zipped through the tail with five wickets for one run in 28 deliveries and charged off the field holding a stump as if it was an Olympic torch.

The stuffing was finally knocked out of Australia at Old Trafford, where they conceded a first-innings lead of 101, then had to put up with another Botham master-class as he slammed a hundred from 86 balls. This was a far superior innings to Headingley's game of roulette. It contained six sixes, two of them hooked off his eyebrows against Lillee, and virtually every shot was sweetly middled. Australia made a good fist of their theoretical target of 506, thanks to centuries from Yallop and Border (batting with a broken finger) but they fell 103 runs short. The Ashes were England's – or, rather, they were Botham's. And after an anti-climactic sixth Test, Botham followed Laker and Steele as BBC Sports Personality of the Year.

BORDER TAKES CHARGE

Terry Alderman had set a new Ashes record for Australia with 42 wickets in 1981, but he was an early casualty of the 1982-83 series when he rugby-tackled a streaker during the first Test and dislocated his shoulder. England, meanwhile, had lost a major tranche of their team, including Boycott, Gooch and Chris Old, to the rebel South Africa tour of 1982.

1981

Phoenix of the Ashes: Ian Botham, with not a little help from fast bowler Bob Willis, wins the Ashes in a series widely held to be the most enthralling ever – until the summer of 2005 that is

With a defence that appeared to be impenetrable, Geoff Boycott's value to England is shown by the fact that only 20 of his 108 Tests ended in defeat, mainly when he failed

Rather ironically, the second Test began with a battle of South African-born batsmen: Allan Lamb made 72 for the visitors, Kepler Wessels 162 for the home side. But the man of the series was Australia's strike bowler Geoff Lawson, whose high pace brought him 34 wickets. England went away frustrated, despite a memorable win in the fourth Test at Melbourne where Norman Cowans took six for 77.

The conclusion of that match ran in close parallel to the great cliff-hanger of Edgbaston 2005. Border shepherded the tail towards Australia's target of 292, and a last-wicket stand of 70 with Thomson took them to within four runs of victory. Then Thomson edged Botham, Chris Tavare palmed the ball backwards over his head, and Geoff Miller stooped to conquer.

Border's unique tenacity had made him captain by the time the 1985 series came around. But in a glorious summer for English cricket, he was forced to surrender the Ashes to the contrastingly languid David Gower. England's rebels were now back in the fold, having served their three-year ban, and both Gooch and Emburey flourished. Australia, meanwhile, had lost three senior players, including Alderman, down exactly the same plughole – a rebel tour to South Africa.

Poised at 1-1 after four Tests, the series was settled by the introduction of Kent swing bowler Richard Ellison: he took 10 wickets at Edgbaston to set up innings victory, then seven more at the Oval. Australia cried foul over Wayne Phillips dismissal in the fifth Test, when he looked like saving the match before being given out caught off an alleged rebound from Lamb's boot. But to no avail. After a good-natured but ultimately unsuccessful series, a disconsolate Border vowed that next time he returned to England, it would be a case of "No more Mr Nice Guy."

Thanks to a West Indian bombardment, Mike Gatting had replaced Gower by the time the 1986-87 Ashes came around. The omens weren't great: England, missing Botham for much of 1986 thanks to a drugs ban, had just lost series to both India and (for the first time at home) New Zealand. Their early efforts in Australia hardly inspired any more confidence. After a broadside from the Telegraph's own Martin Johnson, Gladstone Small recalls: "We became the team of can'ts: Can't bat, can't bowl, can't field".

On the eve of the first Test, Botham stood up in the dressing-room and told the team to switch on. Not always the most reliable of role models, he proceeded to walk the walk this time, beefing up England's first innings with a masterly 138. He barely scored another run in the series, but a seven-wicket win in that first Test win gave Gatting's men momentum. Botham then struck again in the fourth Test, matching Small's five-wicket haul with one of his own, and Chris Broad's third ton of the series did the rest. Truly, Botham was Australia's bogeyman.

Given England's pre-series problems, her supporters were far too excited about the retention of the Ashes to worry about a narrow fifth-Test defeat. But Gatting was incensed. By losing at Sydney by 55 runs, England had just done something regarded as a terrible sin within Australian sport: they had given a sucker an even break. Sure enough, the two top-scorers in that Sydney Test – Dean Jones (184 not out) and Steve Waugh (73) – would return in 1989 to administer one of the heaviest spankings in Ashes history.

If 1981 and 1985 were great summers to be an English cricket fan, 1989 was about as depressing as they come. The averages say it all: 29 players were picked, only one short of the 1921 record, and the best bowling return was Neil Foster's 12 wickets at 35. Though England introduced two very fine players of the future in Mike Atherton and Angus Fraser, they also threw in a few duds too. Tim Curtis, anyone?

With one of the weakest bowling hands in history, it is hardly surprising that England conceded massive totals, time after time. Australia's lowest first-innings score was 424, and Waugh scored 393 runs in five

1989

The smiling assasin: Terry Alderman (right) took 41 wickets during the 1989 series and reduced Graham Gooch to such a shambles that he asked to be left out of the Test team

Time to get serious: Australian Prime Minister, Bob Hawke, shares the buoyant mood of the Australian dressing room at a pre-Ashes match in June 1989. Over the summer Australia would regain the Ashes, setting the tone for the years of Australian dominance which were to follow

innings before he was dismissed.

There shouldn't have been too much wrong with England's batting, but Alderman was finally back on English soil, and he put in another huge performance with 41 wickets at 17. One famous piece of toilet-wall graffiti consisted of two lines: Thatcher Out! written in one pen, with lbw Alderman 0 added underneath it.

Alderman's wicket-to-wicket method was too much for Gooch, who stepped down from the team for the fifth Test to get his game straight. Bumping into a group of journalists, he remarked sarcastically: "I'm just off to the nets to practice my falling-over shot." But the manoeuvre didn't help: Gooch was lbw Alderman 0 at the Oval as well. Border, now maintaining a narrow-eyed policy of not fraternising with the opposition, became the first Australian captain since Woodfull to regain the Ashes in England.

Gooch was captain for the next round of humiliation, in 1990-91. England now had Micky Stewart as a sergeant-majorish coach, but what they really needed was a team doctor. Gooch missed the first Test, which Alderman again dominated, after an operation on a poisoned finger. Fraser then disappeared from the tour with a career-threatening hip injury, and vice-captain Lamb ruled himself out of the second Test, straining a calf while jogging back from the ground to the team hotel. The Test itself

was distinguished by an England collapse of six wickets for three runs.

The defining moment came during a tour match in Queensland. Dismissed early on the third morning, Gower and England's spare batsman John Morris promptly hired a Tiger Moth from a neighbouring airfield and buzzed the ground. The England management took a dim view, and would probably have sent Gower home but for the fact that he was one of the few batsmen in form. Instead they fined him £1000. His relationship with Gooch – which was never full of love and understanding – took a further turn for the worse when Gower was dismissed by the last ball before lunch in Adelaide, flicking a lazy leg-side pick-up to a man placed behind square for the purpose. England lost 3-0.

The 1993 series heralded the arrival of the greatest modern cricketer: Shane Warne. He came on the tour as a promising but by no means established youngster, but his first ball in Ashes Tests is generally agreed to be the most famous delivery of all. It drifted in to Gatting's pads, then changed direction abruptly and clipped the top of his off-stump. This was cricket's equivalent of the laser-guided missile that turns left once inside the front door.

England never really recovered from the shock, as Warne took 34 wickets to wrap up a 4-1 win. Gooch resigned after the fourth

Test, as did chairman of selectors Ted Dexter, a man now more famous for such malapropisms as "Who can forget Malcolm Devon?" than his own distinguished playing career. Atherton took over and notched a belated win at the Oval where his great mate Fraser was man of the match.

POMMY-BASHING

Border finally retired in March 1994, having led Australia in a record five Ashes series. England, by contrast, were still trying to wring a few more runs out of Gooch (now 41) and Gatting (37). The gamble failed, despite one last defiant hundred from Gatting at Adelaide, and both men retired at the end of the series.

There were bright spots for England. Darren Gough impressed Australia with his wholehearted bowling and tailend bravado before flying home with a broken foot. Fraser won a late call-up and battled as hard as ever. But the tone set by the first ball of the series – a DeFreitas long-hop that Michael Slater panned to the cover fence – was largely maintained. Warne was magisterial again, claiming a hat-trick on his home ground in Melbourne, though Craig McDermott topped the wickets table with 32.

England were a rather more robust unit in 1997, thanks to the departure of the cranky Illingworth as supremo. They claimed a morale-boosting 3-0 sweep of the one-

1993

Merv Hughes sees eye to eye with a stray dog that stopped play at Trent Bridge in 1993. Once back on two legs, Hughes took five for 92. Allan Border's (above right) tenacity transformed Australian fortunes

It's all over now: England coach Keith Fletcher shows his frustration as England finally slump to a 4-1 series defeat in 1993

players, then won the first Test at Edgbaston – incredibly, the only "live" Test, in the sense of the Ashes still being at stake, that Australia would lose in eight series after 1986-87.

England could have sprung a surprise this time, with Gough and Andrew Caddick working well as a strike pairing. They had their opportunities: Australia were 42 for three at Old Trafford when Waugh escaped an early lbw shout; in the next game at Headingley, the tourists might have been 50 for five had Graham Thorpe not dropped a dolly of Matthew Elliott.

Both men, inevitably, went on to make centuries as Australian certainty buried English hope. Still, a thrilling win at The Oval – set up by matching seven-fors from Caddick and Phil Tufnell – meant that the 3-2 scoreline reflected the closer-than-usual contest.

For England, the absence of Warne until the last Test of 1998-99 meant another juicy opportunity. Again they failed to capitalise, making the inferior Stuart MacGill look every bit as good in a feeble batting display. A fit Atherton might have helped, but he was struggling so badly with his back that he was unable to duck Glenn McGrath's bouncers and averaged just 13.

After the low point of the tour, when they let Australia A score 376 for one to win in Hobart, England rallied with a fine win at Melbourne. Dean Headley staged an ambush as Australia chased one of those low fourth-innings targets that they have often found so difficult. Then Gough claimed a sensational hat-trick at Sydney with late-swinging yorkers and England were suddenly in the hunt for 2-2. That they failed to get it was down to the strange case of Peter Such's backside, which obscured the side-on cameras when Michael Slater appeared to have been run out. Slater went on to make 123 out of 184 and England were 3-1 losers again.

Nasser Hussain and Duncan Fletcher were installed by 2001, and already injecting a new steeliness into England. But this was Australia at the peak of their powers. Already graced by at least three all-time Ashes greats in Warne, McGrath and Waugh, they now found another in Adam Gilchrist, who led the carnage with 152 from 143 balls in the first Test at Edgbaston

Perhaps the overwhelming odds caused England to tense up. Certainly there was a rash of dropped catches and pulled muscles. But Hussain had one magical afternoon to enjoy. Australia were looking good for 5-0 before rain interrupted the fourth Test at Headingley, forcing them to gamble by declaring just 315 runs ahead. Mark Butcher's exquisite 173 not out made them pay.

Still Waugh had one twist up his sleeve. Having torn his own calf muscle badly in the third Test at Trent Bridge, he returned unexpectedly at the Oval to make an unbeaten 157 batting on one leg. It was a damning comment on England's commitment and quality.

In 2002-03, Hussain's Australian escapade seemed to have ended before it had begun. He stuck the opposition in on a belter at Brisbane, and watched as they piled up 492. The horrors of that first day were further compounded by Simon Jones's appalling knee injury, sustained as he attempted an ill-advised slide on the Gabba's sandy outfield.

After escaping the worst of Matthew Hayden in 2001, England watched him make twin hundreds in the first Test and 496 runs in the series. Gratifyingly, though, they had a destroyer of their own in Michael Vaughan, who responded with 633 including three big centuries. Vaughan achieved a rare feat, being named man of the series while his side went down 4-1.

The fifth Test at Sydney was England's high point. Hysteria surrounded Waugh's final match, and there was pandemonium in the stands when he reached a valedictory century from the last ball of the second day. But in the absence of both McGrath and Warne with injury, England declared on a lead of 451 and Caddick shot Australia out on an exploding pitch. Life, perhaps, could be looking up for the Poms. ●SB

2001

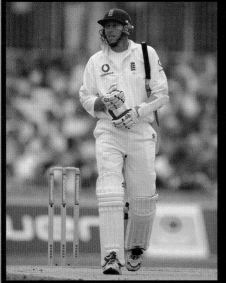

Sledger-proof: Mike Atherton was an opener in the classic English mode. Australia seldom saw the best of him, but for opponents his was a wicket to be prized above all others. Thrust into the captaincy at the age of 25, he proved more enduring than successful and ended his career without an Ashes series win

2003

Captain ruthless: Steve Waugh and his inseparable Baggy Green cap. In all he wore it 167 times

PRE-SERIES
BUILD UP

THE AUSTRALIANS ARRIVE

Before arriving in England in early June, the Australians had not played a Test match for seven weeks, and had only had a short training camp in Brisbane to prepare for the tour. Resurgent England meanwhile had dismissed international fledglings Bangladesh with a more than comfortable 2-0 series win. Arriving as the world's No. 1 side, Australia were universally considered firm favourites to retain the Ashes – after all, no England side had managed to win a series against Australia for 18 years and in eight attempts. Australia themselves were bullishly confident; some members of their party were predicting a 5-0 whitewash.

Yet not all the omens were with the visitors. At the airport Ricky Ponting, the Australian captain, momentarily took his eye off his luggage trolley and when he turned back was horrified to find it gone. Had he been mugged so soon? Well, actually no. His luggage had merely trundled 30 metres down a slope away from the team bus. This was the first example of things getting away from Ponting, though it would not be the last.

Ponting's team faced a full itinerary of one-day internationals, including a triangular tournament against their hosts and Bangladesh, plus three further games, before the Test series was due to get underway at Lord's on July 21. For many it would be an agonising wait. The nation's cricket fans wanted the phoney war of pyjama-clad, limited over stuff out of the way so that the most eagerly awaited sporting contest of the year could begin.

There was considerable criticism levelled at those who had negotiated the touring team's itinerary, arguing that the amount of cricket the Australians would get to play before the opening Test – as well as the choice of Lord's, where England had failed to beat Australia since 1934, as the venue for that opening Test – handed the advantage straight to the visitors.

Ponting thought the timetable would allow his side to adjust and score some psychological points over England before the real business of the summer started. "It could be a bit of an advantage for us the way the summer has panned out with us having a long break and then 10 one-dayers before the first Test," Ponting said. "It could seem like the end of the summer for England and we have got time to get playing."

First stop was Arundel Castle, where the tourists delivered an eight-wicket victory over the PCA Masters XI. Matthew Hayden and Adam Gilchrist were in dominant form scoring 79 and 53 respectively in the Twenty20 curtain-raiser, suggesting that both would be in fine and threatening fettle. For the English team, Kevin Pietersen failed to shine, seen off early by Michael Clarke who claimed a hat-trick to stall the Masters' batting impetus.

Two days later and the Australians faced their first county opponents, Leicestershire,

Young gun: first-time tourist Michael Clarke was soon into the action during Australia's Twenty20 warm-up at Arundel Castle, where his left-arm tweakers claimed a hat-trick

Baggy green bag: a relieved Ponting is reunited with his kit after an early scare at Heathrow airport

Ricky Ponting took his eye off his luggage trolley and turned back to find it gone. Had he been mugged so soon? Well, actually no. His luggage had merely trundled 30 metres down a slope away from the team bus. This was the first example of things getting away from Ponting, though it would not be the last

in a 50-over game, winning by 95 runs. Matthew Hayden was once again in terrific form scoring 107 runs off 96 balls including two sixes and 13 fours.

At this point the plot started to deviate from the script. And so Australia began their 'Week from Hell'.

On June 13 England took on Australia for the first time in the NatWest International Twenty20 match at the Rose Bowl. England cruised to a 100-run victory. Chasing 180 in front of a 15,000 sell-out crowd, Australia slumped from 23 without loss to 31 for seven in the space of 20 balls before being skittled out for just 79 in 14.3 overs – the second lowest total in Twenty20 cricket in England.

Two days later they travelled to Taunton to take on the might of Somerset in a 50-over game, losing by four wickets. It should be pointed out, though, that Somerset fielded two mighty hitters in South African captain Graeme Smith and Sri Lankan Sanath Jayasuriya, who both reached centuries – and two Australian batsmen had retired when well set.

Two bad losses in two matches could be put down to the Australian's easing themselves into the summer and not entirely taking these early proceedings too seriously. However, a five-wicket defeat by Bangladesh in their opening NatWest Series match could not have been more ignominious.

Of 74 completed one-day internationals over

Brains trust:
England's think-tank of Duncan Fletcher and Michael Vaughan

Looking on:
Andrew Flintoff never had a chance to bat in the two-Test series against Bangladesh, such was the dominance of England's batsmen

the years, Bangladesh had won two of them against Test countries other than Zimbabwe. That is won two, lost 72. No wonder Australia were 1-500 with one bookmaker before the start.

Ricky Ponting admitted: "This is probably the biggest upset in the history of the game," particularly as Bangladesh had been thrashed by 10 wickets by England at the Oval a couple of days earlier.

Still, a month to go before the start of the Test series would give the Aussies plenty of time to find their feet and form, surely? But the signs of their mortality were now there for all to see and debates about Warne's decline and the ageing of the squad began to surface.

Australia's problems were only exacerbated by the strange case of Andrew Symonds, who missed their first two matches after breaking team rules with a drinking spree in Cardiff. His absence was a serious handicap, because Symonds had become the star of this one-side, as influential for Austalia as Andrew Flintoff is for England.

To add to the wry amusement with which England supporters were now viewing Australia's faltering progress, both teams faced each other in their second NatWest match at Bristol. Step forward Kevin Pietersen who, with a blistering 91 off 65 balls, presented England's selectors with their most difficult selection conundrum for the Test series to come: long-serving stalwart Graham Thorpe or rising star Pietersen?

Not since Ian Botham had Australia's bowlers been so cowed by someone in England's colours. Pietersen's blitz altered the home camp's outlook from hope to expectation. Like Botham, Pietersen clearly relishes the big stage and, despite the adrenaline that surged through those watching, his nerveless assault proved that his massive well of confidence was a truth rather than a bluff, and the carnage was the result of a cool and calculating mind.

England won the match by three wickets.

The caravan rolled on to Chester-le-Street for a day-night match against England, who would be minus Michael Vaughan. Australia trounced England by 57 runs. Perhaps their awakening was due to two days of warm weather, or maybe it was the ghosts of Lumley Castle, who had spooked the Australians into swapping rooms at midnight. Either way, the real Australia stood up at last. England suffered their first defeat of the summer and Lee's bowling was persuasive, fast and straight. One odd feature of the match was stand-in captain Marcus Trescothick's decision to insert the Australian's after winning the toss.

With the sun beating down, and the prospect of batting second under floodlights, it seemed an odd decision at best. Trescothick's explanation was that he was not sure what the pitch would do and, therefore, what a good score might be had he batted first. It is worthy of note because, arguably, the Test series would in part be decided by Ricky Ponting's equally bizarre decision to insert the opposition after winning the toss at Edgbaston – though that may have had more to do with Australian hubris than strategy.

Bangladesh were unable to mount anything like a challenge when they next met Australia at Old Trafford. After bowling the minnows out for just 139 in the 35th over, Australia required only 19 overs to win, losing no wickets in the process.

Electrical storms and heavy rain during the second half of the match at Edgbaston dampened a fiery encounter to the disappointment of the 21,000 crowd. The Duckworth/Lewis formula decreed that England required 200 from 33 overs, a target Andrew Strauss pursued with glee, hitting Glen McGrath for 17 in his first over after rain interrupted play. But his dismissal and further rain caused the match to be abandoned. Emotions had run high throughout the game and Matthew Hayden had, at one point, faced up to Simon Jones after the fast bowler had struck him on the chest with a wild throw at the stumps. The umpires had to wade in, warning the captains to control their players, before calm was restored.

In the past, England's players would have been ruffled, but there was something steely and confident in Vaughan's team, honed by 18 months of success, and the Australians grew increasingly aware that the reports of an

Exhibitionist streak: Kevin Pietersen loves nothing more than being the centre of attention, a trait that endeared him to his team-mates during a summer of spectacular innings

Morning after: Andrew Symonds waits to hear his punishment after breaking curfew with a big night in Cardiff

English cricketing revival were proving to be accurate.

Watching England standing toe-to-toe with Australia on a cricket pitch is not something England's supporters have grown accustomed to, but the astonishing, thrilling tie at Lord's as the teams shared the NatWest Series Trophy was a foretaste of what was to come.

After dismissing Australia for 196, Michael Vaughan would have fancied his team's chances, though not once they had slumped to 33 for five in the 10th over. However, clever batting from Geraint Jones and Paul Collingwood reduced the target to 53 off the last eight overs, before both were dismissed with 36 needed. In one final twist, Ashley Giles and the tail got 35 of them to share the spoils. Another insight of what was ahead.

England's performance, right down to the two that Giles scrambled off the last ball, revealed the team's development during Vaughan's term as captain. Under him, England have improved to the point – at least in Test cricket – where they are Australia's closest rivals. As Glenn McGrath magnanimously pointed out after the match: "England are playing with a lot more confidence, and to me confidence is a huge thing when it comes to international cricket."

By now it was clear, Ponting had yet to have the dominion over England enjoyed by his predecessor Steve Waugh. Un-Australian chinks, such as the fumble by Lee at third man

that allowed Giles the second run to tie the match, were beginning to appear. Indeed, the small details that Australia were always so good at – basic things like fielding, catching and shot selection – were being flunked more and more often. With hindsight it's possible to see that hitherto unimagined Australian frailties were emerging, blinking into the warm sunlight of the British summer.

And so on to the final three one-day games. Both players and spectators were baffled by new rules introduced by the ICC, which allowed a named 12th player to bat and bowl if required. Two five-over periods of fielding restrictions (only two men outside the 30-yard circle) would also apply, in addition to the opening 10 overs.

Substitutes, as it happens, would become Ricky Ponting's bête noir as the Australian's grip on the Ashes weakened, but for the moment they prospect of a fast bowler being

Tigers, tigers, burning bright: Bangladesh celebrate their first-ever win over Australia at Cardiff

Anxious wait: a pensive young spectator at Bristol as England and Australia prepared to lock horns for the first time in

United colours of Australia: a pair of eye-catching fans enjoy the atmosphere at Bristol

replaced, after he had completed his 10 over spell, by a batsman provided some much needed novelty value.

Both teams headed for Headingley for the NatWest Challenge – a mini series of three extra one-dayers that would, with every ticket for every Test match long since sold, give the hungry public a further chance to see the teams in the flesh.

England won the toss and inserted the Australians who in tough batting conditions scored 219 for seven. Simon Jones became the first player substituted in international cricket after he had completed his 10 overs. In the weeks to come he would earn far greater accolades.

Marcus Trescothick made an unbeaten 104 in England's reply of 221 for one. Trescothick was delighted with this hundred, his first in any form of cricket against Australia and a timely response to the criticism of his bat-dangling habit from John Buchanan, Australia's coach.

England romped home by nine wickets, their largest margin of victory against Australia in one-day cricket.

Afterwards, Ponting said it was the most challenging pitch upon which he had played a one-day international. The pitch certainly helped bowlers more in the morning, an advantage England did not wholly grasp, but the captain added to the impression that by now Australia were seriously rattled.

Talking a good game: Michael Vaughan prepares for one of hundreds of interviews during the busiest summer of his life

Worryingly for England, the decider at the Oval offered considerable evidence of the growing immensity of Australia's cricket. Adam Gilchrist smashed a thrilling, unbeaten 121 from 101 balls to secure the NatWest Challenge

However, there was a disturbing glimpse of past horrors when Australia beat England comprehensively by seven wickets in the second NatWest Challenge match at Lord's.

Ponting made 111 as they chased a below-par total of 223, and Australia dominated throughout after putting England in to bat. Before the match, Ponting's form had become a concern for his team, but the brilliance of his 18th hundred in one-day cricket quietened Australian nerves.

Much had also happened away from the cricket in between the Headingley and Lord's matches. London had suffered an appalling terrorist attack three days before the Lord's game. But few spectators, it seemed, were cowed into staying at home.

And so finally to the Oval for the decider where, worryingly for England, there was considerable evidence of the growing immensity of Australia's cricket. Their comfortable win secured the NatWest Challenge, after England hiccuped their way to a mildly respectable 228. Adam Gilchrist's thrilling, unbeaten 121 from 101 balls, a knock that included two sixes and 17 fours, saw Australia home.

With only a last warm-up match against Leicestershire to play – during which Brett Lee would take a wicket with the first ball of the game and Ponting, Justin Langer and Damien Martyn would all score centuries – an eternity of sideshows was coming to an end. The Ashes were about to start. At last.

Shouting for joy:
Bangladesh's Tapash Baisya (left) trapped Ricky Ponting lbw during Australia's shock defeat.
Right: Kevin Pietersen prepares for a training session at the Rose Bowl, his home ground

NatWest Series Final Scoreboard

ENGLAND V AUSTRALIA
LORD'S, LONDON
2 JULY 2005 (50-over match)

TOSS: ENGLAND

AUSTRALIA INNINGS	R	M	B	4	6
A Gilchrist c Pietersen b Flintoff	27	43	32	5	0
ML Hayden c Giles b Gough	17	29	19	3	0
***RT Ponting** c GO Jones b Harmison	7	26	18	0	1
DR Martyn c GO Jones b Harmison	11	43	24	1	0
A Symonds c Strauss b Collingwood	29	104	71	2	0
MJ Clarke lbw b SP Jones	2	18	19	0	0
MEK Hussey not out	62	95	81	6	0
GB Hogg c GO Jones b Harmison	16	16	22	1	0
B Lee c GO Jones b Flintoff	3	6	5	0	0
JN Gillespie c GO Jones b Flintoff	0	1	1	0	0
GD McGrath c Collingwood b Gough	0	11	4	0	0
Extras (b 4, lb 5, w 7, nb 6)	22				
Total out 48.5 overs, 208 mins)	196				

FOW: 1-50 (Hayden, 6.5 ov), **2-54** (Gilchrist, 9.5 ov), **3-71** (Ponting, 12.1 ov), **4-90** (Martyn, 18.6 ov), **5-93** (Clarke, 23.6 ov), **6-147** (Symonds, 38.5 ov), **7-169** (Hogg, 44.1 ov), **8-179** (Lee, 45.5 ov), **9-179** (Gillespie, 45.6 ov), **10-196** (McGrath, 48.5 ov)
BOWLING: Gough 6.5-1-36-2 (1nb, 2w); **SP Jones** 8-2-45-1 (1w); **Flintoff** 8-2-23-3 (1nb, 1w); **Harmison** 10-2-27-3 (1nb, 3w); **Collingwood** 8-0-6-1 (1nb); **Giles** 8-0-30-0

ENGLAND INNINGS	R	M	B	4	6
ME Trescothick c Ponting b McGrath	6	15	16	0	0
AJ Strauss b Lee	2	21	8	0	0
***MP Vaughan** b McGrath	0	12	7	0	0
KP Pietersen c Gilchrist b Lee	6	10	10	1	0
A Flintoff c Hayden b McGrath	8	14	9	2	0
PD Collingwood ro (Symonds/Gilchrist)	53	154	116	4	0
+GO Jones lbw b Hogg	71	150	100	4	3
AF Giles not out	18	42	21	1	0
SP Jones b Hussey	1	2	2	0	0
D Gough run out (McGrath)	12	26	13	0	0
SJ Harmison not out	0	1	0	0	0
Extras b 2, lb 12, w 3, nb 2)	19				
Total 9 wickets, 50 overs, 232 mins)	196				

FOW: 1-11 (Trescothick, 3.3 ov), **2-13** (Strauss, 4.2 ov), **3-19** (Vaughan, 5.6 ov), **4-19** (Pietersen, 6.4 ov), **5-33** (Flintoff, 9.2 ov), **6-149** (Collingwood, 43.3 ov), **7-161** (GO Jones, 44.5 ov), **8-162** (SP Jones, 45.1 ov), **9-194** (Gough, 49.5 ov).
BOWLING: Lee 10-1-36-2 (1nb, 1w); **McGrath** 10-4-25-3 (1nb); **Gillespie** 10-0-42-0 (1w); **Symonds** 10-2-23-0; **Hogg** 6-0-25-1; **Hussey** 4-0-31-1 (1w)
UMPIRES: BF Bowden (NZ) and **DR Shepherd TV UMPIRE: JW Lloyds** (NZ)
MATCH REFEREE: JJ Crowe (NZ)
MAN OF THE MATCH: GO Jones PLAYER OF THE SERIES: A Symonds

RESULT: MATCH TIED
SERIES: 2005 NATWEST SERIES SHARED

Happy ending: Ricky Ponting enjoys Australia's return to form in the final one-day exchanges

THE ASHES 2005

**1ST TEST MATCH
LORD'S
21 – 25 JULY**

THE ASHES SERIES 2005

Old masters target young England

Lord's
Test preview
Derek Pringle

After an eternity of sideshows, speculation and rant, it is time to release the balls. Not that this Ashes series, which at long last gets under way will be a lottery – anything but. As in any event, slices of fortune will have their say and cause strong men to waver, but over five Tests it will be the side who bat deepest, and whose bowlers sustain pressure for longest, that will prevail.

Recent history, and in particular an Ashes monopoly that stretches back 16 years, suggests the winners will be Australia and not England. Yet having won their last 10 Tests on home soil, Michael Vaughan's side possess a refreshing lack of self-doubt unusual in sporting teams from the northern hemisphere. Whether it will be enough against a team superior in skills but short on youth is what the next five days, as well as the seven weeks of hightension cricket that follow, are all about.

Vaughan says, "I think both sets of players are glad the series is starting, We believe we've played good cricket over the past two years and warrant our No 2 position in the world. But this is the ultimate test of a young England team as to how far we can go."

Unlike Australia, whose more vocal team members have been predicting a 5-0 whitewash of England, Vaughan would not be drawn on predicting a result. Instead he argued that his team would break the series down into more manageable pieces and proceed from there.

"It's dangerous to get too far ahead of yourself in any series. Our intention is to focus on the first game, the first day and the first session, then take it from there. If we do that and take care of the little things, the end result looks after itself."

It is not a novel idea, but the first session of the series, nay the first over even, has infected recent Ashes contests like a running sore, at least for England. Who can forget the dull sensation in the stomach in Brisbane two years ago when, with weather set fair and pitch firm, Nasser Hussain won the toss and decided to field rather than bat, with calamitous result?

The decision, apparently made in haste after Hussain smelt his team's panic in the dressing room, handed the initiative straight to Australia just as cravenly as Phil DeFreitas's opening over had on the 1994-95 tour. On that occasion, the first ball of the match, a rank long hop, was smashed for four by Michael Slater, who proceeded to take 26 off the opening four overs. Unsurprisingly, Australia won both Tests by handsome margins.

Saddled with those memories, Vaughan's team know they must start well, but knowing is not the same as doing, especially when Australia are past masters at seizing the moment by the throat and when you have five players with no experience of Ashes Tests.

"People have frozen against Australia before but I just look at the characters in the side and how they've reacted to situations in the past and it bodes well," Vaughan said. "Obviously, an experienced player like Graham Thorpe will be missed in some ways, but Kevin Pietersen will bring a lot to the England cricket team. Not only with his batting but his attitude, which has been outstanding. Time will tell whether our inexperience is a positive or a negative, but in the last few Ashes series we've gone in with experienced players and we haven't come out with much."

Australia have a bloodhound's nose for weakness and will have noticed the scent trail leading to England's middle order of Ian Bell, Pietersen, Andrew Flintoff and Geraint Jones, none of whom has played a Test against the Aussies before. Yet they form a pool of talent that even the most one-eyed Okker would be foolish to write off, which is perhaps why Ricky Ponting pulled his punches when given the chance to throw them.

"The inexperience of their middle order could have positives and negatives as far as England are concerned," Ponting said. "It can be a bit of weakness, but it can also be where they can change the course of the game. Pietersen and Jones are attacking players like Adam Gilchrist. At the same time those guys can be vulnerable early on in their innings and that's what we're hoping to exploit."

Despite leading the best side in the world, Ponting's rhetoric is more equivocal than that of his predecessor, Steve Waugh. His actions are less certain too and his decision to announce his team on the first morning of the Test contrasts strongly with Waugh's on Australia's last tour, when he announced his team several days before the Test – a move designed to reveal England's dithering.

The pitch is dry and, according to the groundsman Mick Hunt, is a day ahead of time. With all the recent sun, the surface could deteriorate earlier than usual (Sunday afternoon), which means the captain winning the toss will almost certainly bat first.

For England, some runes have already been read. But having acquitted themselves pretty well in the one-day series, they now find themselves up against the masters of the longer game. Broadly, Australia's tactics are simple: attack with the bat and, with the exception of Brett Lee, defend with the ball. This classic one-two attempts to break teams by humiliating them and then wearing them down.

Australia's batting strengths are well known, with Ponting and Damien Martyn looking in ominous form after a sluggish start. Yet most of their batsmen take enormous risks to score at four runs an over and mistakes are often made.

India's Anil Kumble, a man not without his successes against them, reckons bowlers have to be philosophical when bowling to them. Be prepared to have good balls smashed for four, especially by Gilchrist, but do not let that put you off your game plan, seems to be the gist of his advice.

It is their bowling, with its two over-achieving 35-year-olds, Glenn McGrath and Shane Warne, that more often than not, pulls the prize from the hat. Like the Spanish Inquisition, Warne and McGrath, on 583 and 499 Test wickets respectively, skewer batsmen by asking incessant questions of them.

Over the coming days and weeks, Vaughan and his men will have to find answers, and good ones at that. ● **DP**

Down and not out: new boy Kevin Pietersen's alarming inability to hold on to catches became a national talking point as the series wore on

Day 1
Lord's
McGrath sparks England free-fall

Teams

England	*Australia*
M E Trescothick	J L Langer
A J Strauss	M L Hayden
*M P Vaughan	*R T Ponting
I R Bell	D R Martyn
K P Pietersen	M J Clarke
A Flintoff	S M Katich
+G O Jones	+A C Gilchrist
A F Giles	S K Warne
M J Hoggard	B Lee
S J Harmison	J N Gillespie
S P Jones	G D McGrath

Glenn McGrath took his 500th Test wicket and immediately set about adding to his tally as England walked into an Australian ambush in the first Npower Test at Lord's. Pace bowler McGrath took five for 21 as England closed on 92 for seven, a deficit of 98 runs, after they had bowled Australia out for 190 in the first act of a remarkable opening day's cricket on which 17 wickets fell.

But for a stand of 58 between Kevin Pietersen and Geraint Jones, the situation might have been far worse for England, who must have been cock-a-hoop after Steve Harmison's five for 43 had helped to scuttle Australia an hour and a half after lunch. At that point, England must have thought they had got Ned Kelly clapped in irons and just where they wanted him, only for his mates come along and spring him from gaol.

Australia's tenacity and resilience are renowned. You do not become the world's best Test team without having to overcome adversity once in a while and, though the batsmen crumpled, the bowlers, especially McGrath, were never going to bend so easily.

His riposte sent the match into free-fall, as new plots were developed, canned and then rewritten by the hour. England will continue with Pietersen on 28 and just the tail to come, a situation that has often brought the best from him in one-day cricket.

England had not begun an Ashes campaign this well since 1997, when they dismissed Australia for 118 in the first Test at Edgbaston. Then as now, it was Australia who had won the toss and batted. But if Harmison used the pace in the pitch to blast batsmen out, it was McGrath, with his high arm and snappy wrist action, that shaded the bowling prize. A little devilry here and bit of indifferent bounce there were enough for him to conjure mayhem.

It was not as if England's batsmen were as carefree as Australia's in risking their wickets. Instead of preying on flashing edges and miscued hooks, McGrath breached doughty defence. Only Marcus Trescothick played anything like a poor shot, when he edged an attempted clip through midwicket to third slip, though the sight of Ashley Giles trampling on his stumps, trying to avoid a bouncer from Brett Lee on the last ball of the day, probably trumped him.

Although Lee took two wickets late in the day, including the important one of Jones, who made a spirited 30 before spooning up a miscued hook to Adam Gilchrist, it was 35-year-old McGrath who turned the Lord's slope into an escarpment of menace from the Pavilion End.

The sharp movement he found was enhanced by the awkward length he seems to find at will. Some, like Michael Vaughan and

Speed thrills:
Brett Lee fought his way into the Australian side and became one of the pivotal figures of the series. Here he has bowled Ashley Giles for 11 runs

Timber!
Andrew Flintoff later admitted that he had not played his usual uninhibited game at Lord's, where Glenn McGrath ruled the roost

Ian Bell, will claim the ball kept low, but part of McGrath's illusion is that he makes you think the ball is shorter than it is. What is not in doubt – and Flintoff's duck can also be included here in the trio of those clean bowled – is the amount the ball moved, in his case at least eight inches. To negate the movement it was imperative to get forward, something both Pietersen and Jones did.

Bowling unchanged for 13 overs, McGrath rather neutralised Harmison's efforts earlier in the day after England's opening bowler had recorded his best figures against Australia in a Test. Like the West Indies pace quartets of the Eighties, Harmison mixed pace with aggression to brilliant effect as Australia's batsmen, hostages to fortune over their reputation for aggressive cricket, tried to hit their way out of trouble.

England's aggressive intent was there before the first ball was bowled. Over the past 18 months it has been Hoggard who has bowled the opening over, now Vaughan handed the honour to Harmison, determined that Australia should get no easy sighters. Actually, it was not easy however far down you batted – and Harmison later topped the tail by taking four for seven off 14 balls

The aggression worked a treat too, as the lanky fast bowler, steaming in from the Pavilion End and eager for the fray, struck each of Australia's top three in his opening five overs. They were nasty blows too. The first landed when Justin Langer allowed a short ball to strike him just above the right elbow. A black belt at martial art zen do kai, Langer is trained to blot out pain, something he struggled to do at first. But he soldiered on to make a hasty 40 before mis-hooking Flintoff to Harmison at square leg.

It was two attempted hook shots off Harmison that saw both Hayden and Ponting struck on the helmet. Ponting's looked particularly nasty after the impact caused the metal grille to cut his right cheek. He did not make light of his wound and, having already enjoyed one reprieve on nought, when Pietersen dropped him in the gully off Hoggard, it was not long before he edged Harmison to third slip.

A brief rally by Gilchrist, Simon Katich and Shane Warne, that took Australia from 87 for five to 178 for eight gave the visiting bowlers something to work with. As he had done in the one-day series, Flintoff dismissed the ever-dangerous Gilchrist, caught behind after coming around the wicket.

His extravagant victory jig revealed just how ecstatic England were at that stage. Unhappily, the mood did not last and, three hours later, after McGrath had wreaked his havoc, nobody seemed to be dancing. ● DP

Day 1 Scoreboard

AUSTRALIA/FIRST INNINGS		M	B	4	6
J L Langer c Harmison b Flintoff	40	77	44	5	0
M L Hayden b Hoggard	12	38	25	2	0
*R T Ponting c Strauss b Harmison	9	28	18	1	0
D R Martyn c G O Jones b S P Jones	2	11	4	0	0
M J Clarke lbw b S P Jones	11	34	22	2	0
S M Katich c G O Jones b Harmison	27	106	67	5	0
+A C Gilchrist c G O Jones b Flintoff	26	29	19	6	0
S K Warne b Harmison	28	39	29	5	0
B Lee c G O Jones b Harmison	3	13	8	0	0
J N Gillespie lbw b Harmison	1	18	11	0	0
G D McGrath not out	10	7	6	2	0

Extras (b 5, lb 4, w 1, nb 11)	21
Total (40.2 overs, 209 mins)	190

FALL OF WICKETS: 1-35 (Hayden 8.0 overs); 2-55 (Ponting 12.5); 3-66 (Langer 14.4); 4-66 (Martyn 15.1); 5-87 (Clarke 21.5); 6-126 (Gilchrist 28.3); 7-175 (Warne 36.1); 8-178 (Katich 35.3); 9-178 (Lee 38.4) 10-190 (Gillespie 40.2)
BOWLING: Harmison 11.2-0-43-5 (7-0-32-1, 4.2-0-12-4); **Hoggard** 8-0-40-1 (nb 2, 7-0-33-1, 1-0-7-0); **Flintoff** 11-2-50-2 (nb9, 9-1-42-2, 2-1-8-0); **S P Jones** 10-0-48-2 (w 1, one spell)

ENGLAND/FIRST INNINGS		M	B	4	6
M E Trescothick c Langer b McGrath	4	24	17	1	0
A J Strauss c Warne b McGrath	2	28	21	0	0
*M P Vaughan b McGrath	3	28	20	0	0
I R Bell b McGrath	6	33	25	1	0
K P Pietersen not out	28	118	85	5	0
A Flintoff b McGrath	0	7	4	0	0
+G O Jones c Gilchrist b Lee	30	84	56	6	0
A F Giles c Gilchrist b Lee	11	13	13	2	0

Extras (lb 3, nb 5)	8
Total (7 wkts, 37 overs, 173 mins)	92

FALL OF WICKETS: 1-10 (Trescothick 6.1); 2-11 (Strauss 6.5) 3-18 (Vaughan 12.2); 4-19 (Bell 14.3); 5-21 (Flintoff 16.1); 6-79 (G Jones 34.1); 7-92 (Giles 37.0)
TO BAT: S P Jones, M J Hoggard, S J Harmison.
BOWLING: McGrath 13-5-21-5 (One spell); **Lee** 14-5-34-2 (nb 4, 8-3-10-0, 6-2-24-2); **Gillespie** 8-1-30-0 (nb 1, one spell); **Warne** 2-1-2-0 (one spell)
G D McGrath 500th test victim Trescothick

LORD'S AT FEVER PITCH NO MATCH FOR 'SIMPSONS'

Martin Johnson

The home of cricket has witnessed some remarkable sights down the years, but none more than the stampede for seats when the MCC members' gate opened at 8.30 on the first morning of the Lord's Test.

We all suspected that this summer's strain of Ashes fever might turn out to be a particularly virulent one, but hordes of middle-aged men in striped blazers, straw hats and egg-and-bacon ties barging each other out of the way with their cool bags? You'd have got shorter odds on spotting the Archbishop of Canterbury at a lap-dancing club.

There was also a hint of Wimbledon about the most sober theatre in world cricket, with people camping out overnight on the pavement in the hope of getting one of the 150 spare tickets recovered from illegal re-sales. When people start taking primus stoves and sleeping bags to cricket matches, and octogenarian MCC members start behaving as though they're taking part in the Pamplona bull run, it's a sign that something special is afoot.

After 20 years of coming to heel whenever Australia snap their fingers, it would have been more appropriate for England to emerge from a dog kennel than a pavilion, so no wonder that the most competitive-looking series in two decades has given rise to abnormal behaviour. Not least from the people who decided that the official cut-off point for yesterday's play revolved not around the number of overs remaining, darkness, pestilence, or flood, but Channel 4's 6pm screening of The Simpsons.

Officially, Test cricket is run by the International Cricket Council. In practice, however, it is run by television, which is why the players left the field at the end of the first day's play with 10 of the 90-over allocation remaining. Those 10 will never be made up, and if one of these sides ends up a few overs short of claiming victory, it could be the first Test in history to be decided by an American cartoon show.

The way things have gone, however, a result is still favourite even if they decide that the match must end before Sunday's omnibus edition of The Archers. And what's more, everything we suspected about this series is holding up. Australia have found out that this England team represent a scalp rather than the theft of a blind man's toupee, and England have discovered that Glenn McGrath is not quite ready for the pipe and slippers.

The single most important revelation for England is the one that Australia – though a long way from the Dad's Army they've been labelled – may not like it up them. It began as early as the second ball of the series, when Steve Harmison struck Justin Langer on the elbow, and the Australian stared back down the pitch with a kind of "is that all you've got sonny?" expression. About three seconds later, however, Langer's attempt to bluff his way out of it fell apart when the pain forced him to drop his bat and wave, with his good arm, for the restorative spray.

Harmison then hit Matthew Hayden hard enough on the helmet for the protective headgear to require repairs, and then drew blood when he struck Ricky Ponting on the visor. While Ponting was being patched up with swabs and towels, it looked less like Lord's than Madison Square Garden. Australia's batsmen must have known there was always liable to be a bullet with their name on it.

There are various ways of dealing with this, and in the final Blackadder series, Baldrick cunningly deduced that if he wrote his name on a bullet and put it in his pocket, the bullet with his name on couldn't get him. And with a similar kind of perverted logic, Australia's batsmen decided that if they hit every ball for six, they couldn't get out.

So while England's bowlers disappeared to the boundary on a regular basis, so did Australia's batsmen towards the pavilion. Australians are among the most patriotic people on the planet, but yesterday's display of bat flailing suggested that no one felt quite inclined to risk going down the literal route of dying for the cause.

McGrath's riposte was an ominous sign for the rest of the series, and the whole day was a warning to everyone in possession of tickets for the Sunday, in all five Tests, to get them on Ebay as quickly as possible. People may be sleeping on pavements to see this series, but they're not packing too many spare shirts.● MJ

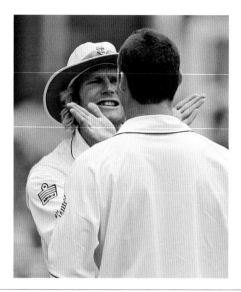

**Slap happy:
Simon Jones benefits
from some friendly
encouragement from
Matthew Hoggard**

Day 2
Lord's
Ruthless Australia turn the screw

A slightly more sedate day of Test cricket for those still catching their breath from Thursday's crazy reel, but a far more dangerous one for England as Australia, through telling innings from Michael Clarke and Damien Martyn, chose calm consolidation over reckless abandon to drive home their advantage.

Australia's change of tack – though they still scored at a rate of four runs an over – meant that England's bowlers had to adopt strategies to take wickets, something they appeared ill-prepared for as Australia ended the day on 279 for seven and a lead of 314 runs.

A mini-strike towards the end of play, when Australia lost four for 24 in 51 balls, would have raised English spirits, but with Ashley Giles barely turning a ball, England's best spin on their grim situation will be that they successfully chased 282 batting last here 12 months ago against New Zealand.

Unhappily for them, Australia possess twice the bowling firepower of Stephen Fleming's side and that before you consider the influence of Shane Warne on a wearing pitch. With three days to go, and John Kettley ominously quiet on the weather front, it looks as if other miracles will be needed if they are to leave Lord's undefeated.

It was never going to be any different once Australia took a first-innings lead of 35 after bowling England out for 155 an hour before lunch. With the old patterns of dominance over the Poms reinforced, Ricky Ponting's side went into business mode, a blinkered world in which winning is the only goal.

The beauty of this side is that any of the top six are equipped to deliver it, though on this occasion it happened to be Clarke and Martyn, their stand of 155 for the fourth wicket essentially scotching any hope of a meaningful England fightback.

Both are superb talents, yet England will be disappointed they allowed Clarke, a man out of form for most of the tour, a second chance to find his touch after Kevin Pietersen dropped him at extra cover off Simon Jones. Clarke was on 21 at the time and Australia 139 for three. When he finally departed for 91 after dragging-on to Matthew Hoggard, his team were 255 for four and controlling the game.

It was a bad miss, the back-foot drive at knee height when Pietersen floored it – the third catch he has fluffed in two days. For a player whose extraordinary eye for a ball makes up for a multitude of technical sins, it is curious he should be so flaky in the field. It is not as if his mind wanders like some, for he was like a harrier when swooping from extra cover to run out Justin Langer with a direct hit earlier in the day.

The miss had the dual effect of re-invigorating Clarke and crushing England, who had been struggling for wickets after Australia's batsmen

**Command performance:
Shane Warne appeals in
vain for an lbw against
Kevin Pietersen. Warne's
anguished pleading
would become one of the
hallmarks of a summer
that brought him 40
wickets from 252.5 overs**

Running away with it: Andrew Flintoff looks disconsolate as Ricky Ponting and Damien Martyn set about building an unbeatable lead

had stopped making the charitable donations of day one. A fine player of spin, Clarke used the opportunity to accelerate Australia's progress against Giles, who for once found his leg-stump attack wanting against batsmen keen to get bat on ball and he leaked five runs an over. That expense forced Vaughan to bowl his quick bowlers before they had been properly rested. It showed too as tired bodies fired too straight, a line that is meat and drink to most decent Test batsmen.

England probably felt that bowling straight was the right thing to do on a pitch with variable bounce and the move does have logic to it. But if the length is wrong, it can prove expensive, which is why you usually see a miser like Glenn McGrath probing a line six inches outside off stump.

A man once troubled by the extravagances of youth, Martyn is now the sensible rock in Australia's gung-ho middle order, a fact borne out when he passed 4,000 Test runs, in this his 91st Test innings.

A stunning catch, to remove Pietersen in front of a packed grandstand, meant Martyn began his day well, a feeling he fed upon as he and Clarke, steadily, then with narrow-eyed intent, dragged the game from England's reach. The catch was as important as it was spectacular. Pietersen, in the kind of role he relishes, was belting Australia's bowlers to distraction.

One six off McGrath, which bounced off the middle tier of the pavilion, was thought to have brought on Graham Thorpe's retirement from international cricket, which was announced indecently soon afterwards.

A textbook four off McGrath, this time through the covers, then brought up his maiden fifty in his first Test innings. Yet just as carnage beckoned, after he had hoisted Warne into the grandstand for another six, a miscued slog cost him his wicket as Martyn made 20 yards before diving to hold the chance.

Despite the 33-run waggle of the tail from Harmison and Simon Jones, which confined Australia's lead to 35, England really needed quick wickets from them to stay in touch with their opponents. In his second over after lunch, Flintoff dismissed Matthew Hayden, but it was hardly planned after the batsman bottom-edged his pull on to his stumps via his leg. Later, Flintoff also got his bunny rabbit, Adam Gilchrist, for 10, but not before Australia had taken heavy toll of his usually parsimonious bowling.

Matthew Hoggard also took two wickets, including Ponting, who passed 7,000 Test runs – the seventh Australian to reach this landmark – when he reached 41. He rode the storm and, though he fell playing a loose shot to Hoggard, he had drawn England's sting, making life easier for all those that followed. ● **DP**

Day 2 Scoreboard

ENGLAND/FIRST INNINGS		M	B	4	6
K P Pietersen c Martyn b Warne	57	147	89	8	2
M J Hoggard c Hayden b Warne	0	18	16	0	0
S J Harmison c Martyn b Lee	11	35	19	1	0
S P Jones not out	20	24	14	3	0
Extras (b 1, lb 5, nb 5)	11				
Total (48.1 overs, 198 mins)	155				

FALL OF WICKETS: 8-101 (Hoggard 41.4); **9-122** (Pietersen 43.4); **10-155** (Harmison 48.1). **BOWLING: McGrath** 18-5-53-5 (13-5-21-5, 5-0-32-0); **Lee** 15.1-5-47-3 (nb 4, 8-3-10-0, 6-2-24-2, 1-0-13-0, 1-0-0-1); **Gillespie** 8-1-30-0 (nb 1, one spell); **Warne** 7-2-19-2 (2-1-2-0, 4-1-10-2, 1-0-7-0)

AUSTRALIA/SECOND INNINGS		M	B	4	6
J L Langer run out (Pietersen)	6	26	15	1	0
M L Hayden b Flintoff	34	67	54	5	0
*R T Ponting c sub (J Hildreth) b Hoggard	42	99	65	3	0
D R Martyn lbw b Harmison	65	214	138	7	1x5
M J Clarke b Hoggard	91	151	106	15	0
S M Katich not out	10	43	28	2	0
+A C Gilchrist b Flintoff	10	25	14	1	0
S K Warne c Giles b Harmison	2	13	7	0	0
Extras (b 9, lb 5, nb 5)	19				
Total (7 wkts 70.2 overs, 324 mins)	279				

FALL OF WICKETS: 1-18 (Langer 5.3); **2-54** (Hayden 14.4); **3-100** (Ponting 27.3); **4-255** (Clarke 62.0); **5-255** (Martyn 62.1); **6-274** (Gilchrist 67.2); **7-279** (Warne 70.2) **BOWLING: Harmison** 18.2-2-35-2 (6-2-10-0, 6-2-10-0, 6.2-0-15-2); **Hoggard** 12-0-46-2 (2, 2-0-12-0, 6-0-20-1, 4-0-14-1, 4-1-10-0); **Flintoff** 19-4-84-2 (nb, 2-0-16-0, 7-2-24-1, 6-1-32-0, 4-1-12-1); **S P Jones** 11-1-46-0 (nb 1, 7-0-29-0, 4-1-17-0); **Giles** 9-1-46-0 (one spell); **Bell** 1-0-8-0 **ENGLAND ALL OUT. 11.25. LUNCH:** Australia 47-1 (12 overs) **Hayden 32, Ponting 7. TEA:** Australia 140-3 (39 overs) **Martyn 24, Clark 22**

Analysis
Simon Hughes

By comparison with day one, yesterday's play was relatively subdued. It was as if Horlicks had replaced Red Bull as the players' pre-match drink.

Only when Kevin Pietersen was lambasting Glenn McGrath and Shane Warne and during the Damien Martyn-Michael Clarke liaison did the run rate creep above four an over. Fielding restrictions will have to be brought in to move the game on again.

In their very different ways, Clarke and Martyn stole the show. Martyn, the gum-chewing outlaw with the low heartbeat and the slightly contemptuous air, caressed the odd boundary but in between was watchful and resistant, absorbing the fast bowlers' sting. Clarke, a Michael Slater clone, was more effervescent, nimbly using his feet and lashing balls through the covers. Clarke is from buzzing, dynamic Sydney, Martyn from slow, laid-back Perth. Their styles, like their backgrounds, are 3,000 miles apart.

It was just after tea when the balance of the game shifted. At that point Australia were 140 for three with a manageable lead, for England, of 175. Making early inroads then could have been decisive. Steve Harmison had just bowled a testing spell from the Pavilion End, but instead of summoning him or Andrew Flintoff immediately after tea, Michael Vaughan preferred Simon Jones. This surface rewards tall bowlers, not whippy skidders, and Ashley Giles was unable to maintain control from the Nursery End.

The damage was done, and Flintoff, trying to make a breakthrough afterwards, was unusually expensive. It is tough on him and Harmison, but at critical moments in these matches one of them has to bowl. England resorted to trying to frustrate Clarke with Matthew Hoggard bowling wide to a packed off-side field. The plan worked as Clarke dragged on a drive in sight of a hundred.

England, down but not out, can cling to the fact that Pietersen has shown better technique and shot selection than practically anyone else in the match, and that the pitches in recent Lord's Tests have actually got better rather than worse. ● **SH**

High fives:
Shane Warne and Ricky
Ponting celebrate the
departure of Ian Bell
as Australia draw
ever closer to victory

Day 3
Lord's
Australia make England suffer

The rain came and then the rain went, but not as quickly as England's last five batsmen. Needing a strictly academic 264 more runs to win after they had lost their first five wickets on Saturday, the home side were dismissed in just 61 balls at Lord's as Australia won the first Npower Test by 239 runs.

With the pre-match hype suggesting an even contest, the margin of victory will be worrying for England, who have only lost more heavily to Australia here once before, to Don Bradman's 1948 side. Now the Australians have their noses in front, Michael Vaughan's side will have to chase victory ever harder, a tactic, like a mug punter chasing his losses with ever-increasing bets, that will surely play yet further to their opponent's strengths.

England's performance here, despite plenty of effort and aggression, was found wanting in all departments. Their batting, with the exception of Kevin Pietersen, who reads the game well and countered its pressure points with tenacity and flair, was a confusion of edgy footwork and suspect judgment.

The bowling, which began in a blaze of wickets and adrenalin on the first day, soon betrayed an over-reliance on Steve Harmison and Andrew Flintoff, whose batting will surely continue to suffer while he bowls the bulk of the overs. Ashley Giles and Matthew Hoggard, the keep-it-tight bankers, leaked at five runs an over, a worrying situation for Vaughan. Yet those faults might not have been so badly exposed had England not dropped seven catches, five of them regulation in Test match cricket.

As they have done in every Ashes series for the past 16 years, Australia have thrown England's plans into disarray after just one Test. 'Bring back Graham Thorpe' seemed to be the general chorus after Glenn McGrath, and then Shane Warne, had bled all resilience out of the batting line-up.

Yesterday's capitulation, while not new for England in an Ashes series, was always likely once Australia got their Baggy Greens out in front. Only Pietersen, who finished unbeaten on 64, looked untroubled by the resumption of play as McGrath mopped up rag, tag and bobtail, with a devastating spell of four for three in 23 balls.

The tall pace bowler finished with match figures of nine for 82, a fine send-off in what is likely to be his last Lord's Test.

With resistance limited to Pietersen, his was merely the completion of a job begun by Warne and Brett Lee on Saturday. Warne has bowled with superb control and flair throughout the match, the dip and fizz of old turning the minds of those facing him to jelly. Back among old mates, and in an Ashes Test match to boot, he plainly had another gear from the one he uses with Hampshire.

Like McGrath, this is Warne's last Lord's Test and you could see he was desperate to end with the five-for that would ensure his name gets on to the famous dressing-room boards that record centuries and five-wicket hauls. He needed two though, with McGrath running through batsmen like a bushfire, he needed to be quick.

A slider promptly removed Harmison lbw to leave him three balls at No 11 Simon Jones. A wild yahoo from the left-hander led to the ball shaving the off stump, but with that near-miss the chance was gone. In the next over, McGrath whipped out Jones, with Warne taking the edge at first slip.

Earlier, the match had looked destined for the final day after steady rain had wiped out the first two sessions of play. Before the new outfield and drainage channels were laid, the outfield would have flooded and the game been called off by mid-afternoon. But once the rain stopped, and the ground was ready for play in 45 minutes, England's fate was sealed.

Geraint Jones pulled the 15th ball of the day, from McGrath, to mid-on, where Jason Gillespie took the catch. It was a poor shot that lacked judgment, and one that many will link to the two catches the wicketkeeper dropped the previous day.

McGrath struck again two balls later when Giles poked a catch to Matthew Hayden in the gully. Like one or two in this match, Giles had a poor game and while players can often bounce back against lesser sides, Australia have a keen memory for those afflicted with doubt.

Although Hoggard also fell for a duck, his second of the match, Pietersen found enough support to reach his second fifty of the match, a feat achieved by only seven England players on debut. He even managed to use the dire situation for a brief exhibition of hitting against Warne, a show of defiance that included a six and a four. ●**DP**

Down at heart: Andrew Flintoff wonders where it all went wrong after a brilliant start
Far right: Warne and the Australians leave Lord's feeling sure that normal service has been resumed

1st Test Scoreboard

CLOSE DAY 1 England 92-7 (37 overs, Pietersen 28)
CLOSE DAY 2 Australia 279-7 (70.2 overs, Katich 10)
CLOSE DAY 3 England 156-5 (48 overs, Pietersen 42, G O Jones 6)

AUSTRALIA/FIRST INNINGS

		M	B	4	6
J L Langer c Harmison b Flintoff	40	77	44	5	0
M L Hayden b Hoggard	12	38	25	2	0
*R T Ponting c Strauss b Harmison	9	28	18	1	0
D R Martyn c GO Jones b S P Jones	2	11	4	0	0
M J Clarke lbw b S P Jones	11	34	22	2	0
S M Katich c G O Jones b Harmison	27	106	67	5	0
+A C Gilchrist c G O Jones b Flintoff	26	29	19	6	0
S K Warne b Harmison	28	39	29	5	0
B Lee c G O Jones b Harmison	3	13	8	0	0
J N Gillespie lbw b Harmison	1	18	11	0	0
G D McGrath not out	10	7	6	2	0
Extras (b 5, lb 4, w 1, nb 11)	21				
Total (40.2 overs, 209 mins)	190				

FALL OF WICKETS: 1-35 (Hayden 8.0 overs); **2-55** (Ponting 12.5); **3-66** (Langer 14.4); **4-66** (Martyn 15.1); **5-87** (Clarke 21.5); **6-126** (Gilchrist 28.3); **7-175** (Warne 36.1); **8-178** (Katich 35.3); **9-178** (Lee 38.4) **10-190** (Gillespie 40.2)
BOWLING: Harmison 11.2-0-43-5 (7-0-32-1, 4.2-0-12-4); **Hoggard** 8-0-40-1 (nb 2, 7-0-33-1, 1-0-7-0); **Flintoff** 11-2-50-2 (nb9, 9-1-42-2, 2-1-8-0): **S P Jones** 10-0-48-2 (w 1, one spell).

ENGLAND/FIRST INNINGS

		M	B	4	6
M E Trescothick c Langer b McGrath	4	24	17	1	0
A J Strauss c Warne b McGrath	2	28	21	0	0
*M P Vaughan b McGrath	3	28	20	0	0
I R Bell b McGrath	6	33	25	1	0
K P Pietersen c Martyn b Warne	57	147	89	8	2
A Flintoff b McGrath	0	7	4	0	0

		M	B	4	6
+G O Jones c Gilchrist b Lee	30	84	56	6	0
A F Giles c Gilchrist b Lee	11	13	13	2	0
M J Hoggard c Hayden b Warne	0	18	16	0	0
S J Harmison c Martyn b Lee	11	35	19	1	0
S P Jones not out	20	24	14	3	0
Extras (b 1, lb 5, nb 5)	11				
Total (48.1 overs, 198 mins)	155				

FALL OF WICKETS: 1-10 (Trescothick 6.1); **2-11** (Strauss 6.5) **3-18** (Vaughan 12.2); **4-19** (Bell 14.3); **5-21** (Flintoff 16.1); **6-79** (G Jones 34.1); **7-92** (Giles 37.0); **8-101** (Hoggard 41.4); **9-122** (Pietersen 43.4); **10-155** (Harmison 48.1).
BOWLING: McGrath 18-5-53-5 (13-5-21-5, 5-0-32-0); **Lee** 15.1-5-47-3 (nb 4, 8-3-10-0, 6-2-24-2, 1-0-13-0, 1-0-0-1); **Gillespie** 8-1-30-0 (nb 1, one spell); **Warne** 7-2-19-2 (2-1-2-0, 4-1-10-2, 1-0-7-0).

AUSTRALIA/SECOND INNINGS

		M	B	4	6
J L Langer run out (Pietersen)	6	26	15	1	0
M L Hayden b Flintoff	34	67	54	5	0
*R T Ponting c sub (J Hildreth) b Hoggard	42	99	65	3	0
D R Martyn lbw b Harmison	65	214	138	7	1x5
M J Clarke b Hoggard	91	151	106	15	0
S M Katich c S P Jones b Harmison	67	178	113	8	0
+A C Gilchrist b Flintoff	10	25	14	1	0
S K Warne c Giles b Harmison	2	13	7	0	0
B Lee run out (Giles)	8	15	16	1	0
J N Gillespie b S P Jones	13	71	52	3	0
G D McGrath not out	20	46	32	3	0
Extras (b 10, lb 8, nb 8)	26				
Total (100.4 overs, 461 mins)	384				

FALL OF WICKETS: 1-18 (Langer 5.3); **2-54** (Hayden 14.4); **3-100** (Ponting 27.3); **4-255** (Clarke 62.0); **5-255** (Martyn 62.1); **6-274** (Gilchrist 67.2); **7-279** (Warne 70.2); **8-289** (Lee 74.1); **9-341** (Gillespie 90.0); **10-384** (Katich 100.4).
BOWLING: Harmison 27.4-6-54-3 (6-2-10-0, 6-2-10-0, 6.2-0-15-2, 7.4-2-16-0, 1.4-0-3-1); **Hoggard 16-1-56-2** (nb 2, 2-0-12-0, 6-0-20-1, 4-0-14-1, 4-1-10-0); **Flintoff 27-4-123-2** (nb 5, 2-0-16-0, 7-2-24-1, 6-1-32-0, 4-1-12-1, 4-0-24-0, 4-0-15-0); **S P Jones** 18-1-69-1 (nb 1, 7-0-29-0, 4-1-17-0, 7-0-23-1); **Giles** 11-1-56-0 (9-1-46-0, 2-0-10-0); **Bell** 1-0-8-0

ENGLAND/SECOND INNINGS

		M	B	4	6
M E Trescothick c Hayden b Warne	44	130	103	8	0
A J Strauss c & b Lee	37	117	67	6	0
*M P Vaughan b Lee	4	46	26	1	0
I R Bell lbw b Warne	8	18	15	0	0
K P Pietersen not out	64	119	79	6	2
A Flintoff c Gilchrist b Warne	3	13	11	0	0
+G O Jones c Gillespie b McGrath	6	48	27	1	0
A F Giles c Hayden b McGrath	0	1	2	0	0
M J Hoggard lbw b McGrath	0	17	15	0	0
S J Harmison lbw b Warne	0	2	1	0	0
S P Jones c Warne b McGrath	0	12	6	0	0
Extras (b 6, lb 5, nb 3)	14				
Total (58.1 overs, 271 mins)	180				

FALL OF WICKETS: 1-80 (Strauss 26.3); **2-96** (Trescothick 29.2) **3-104** (Bell 33.1); **4-112** (Vaughan 36.1); **5-119** (Flintoff 39.3); **6-158** (G Jones 50.3); **7-158** (Giles 50.5); **8-164** (Hoggard 55.0); **9- 167** (Harmison 55.3); **10-180** (S Jones 58.1).
BOWLING: McGrath 17.1-2-29-4 (8-0-19-0, 4-1-6-0, 5.1-1-4-4); **Lee** 15-3-58-2 (nb 1, 5-2-9-0, 6-1-28-1, 4-0-21-1); **Gillespie** 6-0-18-0 (nb 2, 4-0-12-0, 2-0-6-0); **Warne** 20-2-64-4 (15-2-46-3, 5-0-18-1).
UMPIRES: Aleem Dar (Pakistan) **& R E Koertzen** (South Africa)
AUSTRALIA WON BY 239 RUNS, MATCH AWARD: G D McGrath

Analysis
Simon Hughes

John Buchanan, the Australia coach, organised a picnic in Regent's Park for his team on Wednesday afternoon to relax his players on the eve of their big test. It could be said that English cricket has followed suit and offered its own brand of hospitality.

Not only did they organise a one-day schedule guaranteed to give the Australians an ideal acclimatisation for the Ashes series, they also scheduled the first Test at Lord's, where Australia have not lost a Test for 71 years. And when the tourists arrived they found a pitch more typical of NSW than NW8.

It was hard and dry with hairline cracks, the kind you might find at the Sydney Cricket Ground. Which just happens to be the home patch of one Glenn Donald McGrath. Add in the Lord's slope which drags some, but crucially not all, of McGrath's stock deliveries towards the stumps, and you have a 22-yard strip of earth that the latest member of the 500 club would happily roll up and carry round with him forever.

England did throw a few stinging punches that first morning, but thereafter they contributed to the Australian festivities. The batsmen, apart from Kevin Pietersen, seemed mesmerised by the relentlessness of McGrath and dumbfounded by Shane Warne. The bowling, Steve Harmison and Andrew Flintoff excepted, was patchy. And the fielding was fatally flawed.

What is it about the Ashes, and Lord's in particular, that causes England to shell eminently catchable chances?

It's a combination of factors. Tension must be one. Every time England sacrifice the little urn, there's more pressure on them to wrest the initiative next time. At crucial moments you sense their bodies tense up. Tight fingers make for terrible spillages. The crucial miss – Pietersen's of Michael Clarke when he was on 21 and Australia were 139 for three with a lead of 174 – came moments before tea on Friday. It deflated the dressing room at the interval, instead of galvanising it, and when they emerged afterwards the team's spark seemed to have been extinguished. ● SH

Warne sets perfect example

1st Test afterword
Derek Pringle

"Shane Warne is bowling better than ever," reckoned his captain, Ricky Ponting, after Australia 239-run rout of England at Lord's, words guaranteed to give one or two of the home team's batsmen the collywobbles before the second Test.

A fortnight earlier, Ponting's eulogy about his champion spinner would have been unthinkable after Warne failed to prevent Middlesex from beating Hampshire in the championship – a game in which Warne took two for 108 off 29.4 overs in the second innings.

The word was that his legendary accuracy, as well as some of the buzz-saw spin, had deserted him. Yet Warne, who had just returned from a break to sort out his private life, knew before anyone that something was amiss and called in his coach and guru, Terry Jenner.

A wrist-spinner who played nine Tests for Australia between 1970-75, Jenner knows Warne's action well and set about rectifying the flaws with a strenuous two-hour session in the Lord's nets two days before the first Test.

England captain Michael Vaughan plans a similar one-on-one tutorial with coach Duncan Fletcher to correct the sluggish footwork that saw his defences breached by Glenn McGrath and Brett Lee in the Test.

Some coaches do not believe in tinkering with players' techniques before a big match. Most players don't either, especially those with preternatural talent. But while Warne, the world's highest wicket-taker in Tests with 589 wickets, is a virtuoso, he is not a prima donna – at least not when it comes to working on his bowling.

The public rarely see the effort sportsmen put in on the practice ground, only the end results. Warne's hard yakka in the nets mostly concentrated on his follow through. The problem, at least as it appeared from the sidelines, was that Warne had been falling away too sharply after releasing the ball. What Jenner did was to alter the length and direction of Warne's stride pattern so that his momentum, led by his head, would continue on towards the batsmen rather than be pulled sideways.

With the theory clear in his mind, Warne then grooved the changes by bowling to batsmen for the next hour. Like great fast bowlers, there is a psychological side to his bowling that complements the technical brilliance of being able to bowl, and control, his arsenal of leg-breaks, googlies and sliders.

At Test level, one cannot be sustained for long without the other, which is why, with the technical glitch corrected, he could torment England's batsmen, especially Andrew Strauss and Ian Bell, with a display of bowling that brought him six wickets in the match.

If the cause and effect mechanism here seems obvious, working on specific problems is mostly the remit of batsmen. Before the 1987 World Cup semi-final between England and India in Bombay, Graham Gooch took one look at the dry, dusty pitch prepared for India's spinners and decided the sweep was the only shot that was going to bring him runs.

Instead of batting in the nets against England's bowlers, Gooch summoned the locals to bowl at him. For the next 30 minutes he attempted to sweep every ball regardless of length or line. While team-mates looked on perplexed, all became clear a day later when England won with 115 runs from Gooch, most of them swept.

Matthew Hayden worked on something similar on Australia's 2000-01 tour of India. Although he had a reputation for bullying bowlers, he was considered vulnerable against spin. Like Gooch he practised sweep after sweep, including the slog sweep, which during matches often sailed into the stands for six. That Test series is remembered for India's 2-1 win, after one of the great fightbacks of modern times, yet Hayden made 549 runs at an average of 109.

Not all Test batsmen play to get bat on ball as often as Hayden, especially against spinners who turn the ball. Unsure of the degree or direction of spin, many use their pads to nullify the threat. Fed up with being kicked away by batsmen, and with umpires doing little to prevent it, Sri Lanka's Muttiah Muralitharan dedicated hours to perfecting the 'doosra', a ball that spins like a leg-break with an off-spinner's action.

The illusion quickly brought him a spate of wickets as batsmen, used to negating his off-spin with their front pad, found they were being given out lbw. He even overtook Warne as the world's greatest wicket-taker, though a moratorium on his 'doosra', while the International Cricket Council sorted out tolerance levels on elbow flexion for bowlers, meant he is behind again.

England's cricketers are also trailing the Aussies, a not unfamiliar position in Ashes series. Like all diligent teams they will prepare well before the next Test, no doubt redoubling their efforts in areas such as catching in response to the costly drops at Lord's.

Yet, as the great players above have shown, practice works best when you foresee problems in advance rather than react to them once they have happened, something Vaughan's team may struggle to do now that they are 1-0 down in the series. ● **DP**

185

DCXXVI

PIETERSEN'S ONLY REALISTIC CLAIM TO BE RECOGNISED AS ENGLISH IS BY THE CATCHES HE DROPS

Martin Johnson

Would you believe it? A paltry 264 runs to win, five wickets in hand, a full six sessions in which to get them, and down comes the rain. Granted, they're a half-decent team, but if there has been one common factor in Australia's domination over the last eight Ashes series, it's that they've had all the luck.

How else can you explain Geraint Jones hoiking one straight to mid-on when the rain finally relented yesterday? So much time had been lost that an England pea-shelling operation of 1.5 per over had crept dangerously close to two, and Jones really had no option but to start slogging from the word go.

Alternatively, Jones was merely reinforcing the belief that England still manage to play like complete wallies when faced with a side as accomplished and attritional as Australia, and if anyone really believed that England had any chance of saving this Test match, it would rest with Kevin Pietersen. The trouble with that is Pietersen is still adjusting to his newly-acquired nationality, and people will refuse to accept his right to call himself a genuine member of an England dressing room until he realises that the sight of a baggy green cap brings with it the immediate requirement for the bulldog to turn into a poodle.

After only one Test match, Pietersen is already being talked about as good enough to get into the Australia team, and who knows? He might yet apply. He's a bright lad, and is doubtless already instructing his agent to get up to Somerset House and start scouring the archives for a third cousin who eloped with a jolly swagman, or a great-grandmother who played the didgeridoo.

Thus far, Pietersen's only realistic claim to be recognised as English is by the catches he drops, and there is something about him that you don't often see in players making their England debuts. If you dropped Pietersen in the middle of a desert with one canteen of water and two bits of twig to rub together to make a fire, you'd expect him to walk into an oasis several weeks later, and, having gorged himself on a diet of roast coyote, several pounds heavier.

In terms of confidence, he almost makes Ian Botham look shy and retiring, and it may even be that his chat with Jones before they resumed batting yesterday involved – with more rain forecast for the fifth day – getting the match won as quickly as possible. Whatever, Jones's stroke, if such it can be called, was all the proof Australia needed that they were up against the same old Poms.

Jones, though, does have the potential to launch an England fightback in the next Test at Edgbaston. He has a pair of wicketkeeping gloves that appear to have been hewn from a trampoline, and his attempt to catch Jason Gillespie by sticking out an arm was less like watching a professional athlete than one of those old Morris Minors with a semaphore trafficator. So the plan now must be to have him stand up to all the English bowlers and hope that he fells a couple of the Australian batsmen with vicious rebounds. Preferably either Glenn McGrath or Shane Warne.

It was a good effort for the Lord's grounds-man to prepare a juicy first-day surface for a bloke homing in on 500 Test wickets, which changed into a drying turner later on for a chap with his eye on 600. It's the equivalent of Colin Montgomerie walking on to the tee and offering to give Tiger Woods a few strokes.

Warne, to the relief not only of neutral cricket watchers but a fair few English ones too, may not be quite the bowler he was, but he is still bewitchingly good. If reports of all his extra-curricular activities are to be believed, he should scarcely have the strength to run up to the wicket, but only Pietersen appears able to remove himself from the hypnotist's chair when the ball is on the way down. And so, with the series only one match old, it already looks like another Australian Ashes, but at times like this it is good to know that there is one area in which they come a hopeless second. No sooner had the last English wicket fallen than the sponsors handed out a press release informing us, under the title "Red Hot Facts About The End Of Test Presentation Ceremony", that the podium takes "approximately 3 minutes 42 seconds to erect", and that the record for this is "3 minutes 14 seconds".

Good old Npower. We can gloss over the fact that this is roughly as long as an English batting partnership, do away with the cricket altogether, and take on the Australians in the podium equivalent of a Kwik-Fit Fitter operation. You can see the headlines now. "Super England Romp Home As Aussie Podium Collapses". Bring it on! ● MJ

Warne's two-card trick proves a winning hand

1st Test review
Simon Hughes

A dozen years since he first came here, the man whose deliveries only marginally exceed the speed of a milk float is still confounding us all. At Lord's, Shane Warne confounded predictions, he confounded expectations, occasionally he confounded the laws of trigonometry. Most significantly he confounded the England batsmen. They will be spending a disproportionate amount of time over the next week debating how best to combat him in the second Test at Edgbaston.

There is some good news and some bad news. In most previous Ashes series he has arrived with a bag full of different deliveries: leg-breaks, toppies, googlies, flippers, zooters and sliders, one that was called the 'pickpocket' and another that nicked the off bail, whistled Waltzing Matilda and bobbled off to light the barbecue. The good news is that now he has basically just two: the leg-break and the slider. The bad news is that none of the England batsmen, apart from his Hampshire mate Kevin Pietersen, appeared to be able to distinguish between them.

The glorious simplicity of his bowling philosophy is what makes him such compulsive viewing. Adhering to the basic advice drummed into him by his coach, Terry Jenner, and reaffirmed by Richie Benaud, his main priority is consistently to propel a hard-spun leg-break. The vagaries of the pitch, the hardness of the ball and the wonders of natural variation ensure that some of these turn more than others.

Mixed into that stock is one bit of spice: the slider. This is bowled with the same action and from a distance it looks quite similar to the leg-break. There is a subtle difference. It is pushed out of the front of the hand rather than spun out of the side. On pitching it goes straight on and is liable to skate through low. If he gets this ball on line, he is often breaking into a "Howzat?" before it has even reached the batsman's pad, and then regarding the umpire with open-mouthed astonishment when he has said not out.

The slider is not a new delivery. Benaud himself bowled it in the 50s – he called it the "skidder" – and says he was taught it by an Australian leg-spinning predecessor, Doug Ring (wrist spinners communicate like members of the magic circle). Warne used it on the last tour here. Now he is fiendishly accurate with it. So, in essence, he has one ball that spins, and one ball that goes straight. That's it. A two-card trick.

It is knowing when to produce each card that defines his art, as his second-innings wickets at Lord's proved. He had already ripped several big, turning leggies into the left-handed Marcus Trescothick's pads and the batsman was looking out for turn. Thus when the slider arrived, he was playing down slightly the wrong line and glided the ball to slip. The right-handed Ian Bell left several leg-breaks pitched outside off stump and spinning wider. He riskily did the same to a leg-break that was straighter. It didn't turn and he was plumb lbw. In that sense he was unlucky, he had read the delivery well but it was dangerously straight to leave and Warne may have influenced the outcome by varying his grip.

Andrew Flintoff defended his first ball, a leg-break, adequately. But Warne had already noted that he was playing for spin. So he gave him the slider second ball. Flintoff, attempting an ambitious cut, was defeated by its skiddiness and edged to the wicketkeeper. As with many tail-enders, Warne didn't bother toying with Steve Harmison. He gave him the slider first ball. He was lbw for nought.

Why can't English batsmen play leg spin? Kent's Titch Freeman took 304 first-class wickets with it in 1928, so perhaps they never could. By the mid-60s every county had a leggie. But with the advent of the one-day league in 1969, containment became a captain's priority, and the fragile art of wrist spin was regarded as an expensive luxury. By the mid-80s there were none. In recent years, only Ian Salisbury, among home-grown leggies, has survived for any length of time on the circuit. As a result, batsmen lack prolonged exposure to leg spin, as the success of Mushtaq Ahmed and Danish Kaneria in county cricket underlines.

That said, Warne is by no means unplayable. Pietersen illustrated that, scoring 47 runs off the 63 balls he faced from his Hampshire colleague at Lord's. He obviously benefited from time in the nets against him, picked his variations, and his shot selection was appropriate. Pietersen was not afraid to slog-sweep balls pitching outside the leg-stump, which forced Warne to alter his approach. What the other England batsmen need to do is stay in against him for a while, to get used to his rhythms and wiles and evaluate their options. Sure, this is not as simple as it sounds and it's not suddenly going to nullify his effect. But it might at least wipe that satisfied smile off his face. ●SH

WE CAN PUSH FOR 5-0 GOAL

Matthew Hayden

With victory at Lord's we have put ourselves in a position of real strength and can push on to fulfil our goal of winning this series 5-0.

In the run-up to the game, there had been a lot written about England, and I'm not trying to be arrogant when I say this, but I don't really care about what's being said about them. We know that if we are playing to the best of our ability then England will not come close to us.

Just because we are 1-0 up in the series does not matter so much – it is the fact that we are playing well, but can still improve. That is really ominous for England.

There had been a lot of talk about how our side are ageing and past their best. That is absolute rubbish and we proved that in the first Test. We have never been in better shape and if you look at the past 12 months we have achieved things that no other side in history has managed.

Our destiny is in our own hands and we are in a position to make a really assertive statement in the next Test at Edgbaston.

The Test at Lord's was a great start for us and great start to the series. For England the performance of Kevin Pietersen on his debut was a plus. I love his aggression and I thought it was a fantastic performance. I simply love the way he plays his cricket. He plays like a true South African.

For Australia, we know there are areas we can work on. Our batting could be more authoritative and wear the opposition down more.

Seventeen wickets on the first day was certainly too many. It was not an easy batting wicket, and the way it played on the first day shows that, with plenty of sideways movement and up and down bounce. But that really puts into context the first innings performance of Justin Langer. On the first morning he made 40 which gave us a platform. It was a crucial innings played in trying circumstances.

In the second innings, even though Michael Clarke made 91, the player of the innings was Damien Martyn. He counter-attacked England's short bowling strategy really well and played exactly the kind of mature knock we needed at that time. It shows the strength we have coursing through the middle-order.

And then came the bowling. The legends of Glenn McGrath and Shane Warne continue to grow. I would hate to be facing them at the moment. The performance of McGrath on the first day was incredible. He is like a bowling machine. He just runs in and puts the ball on the spot every time. He bowls in the areas that put people under real pressure. I am always in awe of him. He is a fantastic athlete and I can't see any way of stopping him.

He is ruthless and has been bowling really well for the last six months. Then there was Brett Lee. He made an incredible impact with his extra pace. His sheer aggression and speed made a huge difference. He is the destroyer and he really shot England's tail down.

Just having Shane Warne bowling the way he is at the moment adds a fantastic string to our attack. No matter what pitch England prepare for him – a seaming wicket or good batting strip that deteriorates – he will definitely hold us together. We have power in all departments. Our bowlers are merciless in their lines and length, and once the quicks have finished Warney is there. He is a handful for anyone.

It is now up to us to carry on putting in great performances day in, day out. The last two months have been fabulous. We love being here and we are starting to play some great cricket.

If we play to our best then who knows what we can do. We are ready for any challenge that England can throw down at us and that is something we have been in a position to accept for a very long time.

As for my personal form, I feel really good. I was happier with my second innings performance when I made 34. It is vital for the top three to do the majority of the batting and that was not always the case in this match. It is down to the guys at the top of the order to still be batting when the ball is 60 overs old. I feel I'm ready to achieve that. I'm very excited about the way I've been playing and it is just a matter of putting all the aspects of my game together.

This tour is only one Test old yet we are loving the pressure of being here. It is a great challenge fighting for the Ashes and we can't wait for the next Test to start. ● MH

**2ND TEST MATCH
EDGBASTON
4–8 AUGUST**

THE ASHES SERIES 2005

England bank on Edgbaston factor

Edgbaston
Test preview
Derek Pringle

Michael Vaughan, now that the elbow he injured in the England nets has been steadied by pain-killing injections, needs Edgbaston to be his Agincourt, El Alamein and Rorke's Drift all rolled into one as the second Test gets under way. If not, and Ricky Ponting's side leave for Manchester 2-0 up, the Ashes will not be a trophy so much as a monument to Australian supremacy.

As Edgbaston is England's most successful Test match venue, the chances of a reversal against Australia are higher here. Since the ground staged its first Test in 1902, England have won exactly half of the 40 Tests they have played in Birmingham, though 12 of those victories have come when it has been the opening Test of the series, a time when opponents tend to be acclimatising.

"There's a lot of good memories at Edgbaston for us," Vaughan said in advance of the game, perhaps recalling his side's victory against Australia there last September in the ICC Trophy. "The crowd are always good here and there is just a general feel-good factor about the place."

Many of those currently pinned down under Australian microscopes also have fine records at the venue. Marcus Trescothick averages 45 in Tests overall, but at Edgbaston that climbs to an incredible 89, a mere 10 runs below Sir Donald Bradman's untouchable career average of 99.94.

Andrew Flintoff, too, has good cause to feel comfortable at Edgbaston after making his highest Test score of 167 against the West Indies last year. His batting has gone AWOL for England of late, though a return to that kind of form would certainly boost his team's chances. After all, it was lack of runs that scuppered England at Lord's, not lack of firepower with the ball.

The release of Paul Collingwood to play for Durham in their championship match against Essex suggests that both Vaughan and England coach Duncan Fletcher are agreed that the pitch does not hold enough demons to warrant an extra batsman.

Two days of sun have baked a crust Fanny Craddock would have been proud of and Ashley Giles might yet get some decent conditions on which to answer his critics and end the summer whine he has served up since Lord's. With Ian Bell also set for a Test on his home ground, it will be the first time that two Warwickshire players have played there for England since Bob Willis and Andy Lloyd took on the West Indies in 1984, a Test that was to be Lloyd's last after being felled by a Malcolm Marshall bouncer.

Opinion is divided over how the pitch will play. Steve Rouse, the groundsman, reckons the ball could dent the surface early on in the game, something that tends to cause uneven bounce – conditions tall pace bowlers tend to feast on – as the game progresses. Yet, some of Australia's players reckon that the moisture left by last week's rain will rise as the match goes on, providing ideal conditions for seam bowlers who pitch the ball up, like Matthew Hoggard and Simon Jones, Glenn McGrath and Jason Gillespie. The correct reading could prove crucial.

Presuming Chris Tremlett does not get the nod this morning, England will field an unchanged side for the second Test in a row. Though not unusual, given the successes of the last 18 months, it has never happened before in a home series, at least not after England have lost the first Test.

Tremlett came closest to upsetting the status quo when he struck Vaughan on the elbow in Tuesday's net practice. Apart from the pain, it was an uncomfortable moment for England's captain, who initially presumed the worst.

"When I couldn't feel my arm I thought that it was a break," Vaughan said. "I felt a lot of emotions at that point. But once the scan showed there was no break, only a trapped nerve, I knew I'd be fine because you can ease nerve pain with an injection."

Before yesterday's confirmation of his fitness, Vaughan had batted in the nets without problems, though there was an uncomfortable moment when Steve Harmison struck him a nasty blow on his right index finger. It was a brute of a ball, climbing abruptly from short of a length, and one that would have consigned Nasser Hussain, a man with fragile fingers, to six weeks in plaster.

You cannot relax for long against Australia and no sooner had Vaughan announced his good news than Ponting revealed Australia's plans for England's captain on the hop. "It's up to the bowlers to put pressure on him, while he's not scoring as freely as he likes," Ponting said, clearly disregarding Vaughan's century for Yorkshire last Sunday. This aggressive stance was somewhat diluted by the sight of Matthew Hayden and Justin Langer meditating on the pitch later on. Visualisation can be a powerful tool in sports psychology, though the sight of Hayden, sitting with shoes off and bat in mouth gazing off into the middle distance, should encourage England's bowlers come the hour.

You cannot imagine Kevin Pietersen opting for such a Zen-like approach, which may be why Australia spent most of their team meeting discussing him. Pietersen's bold batting and armour-plated belief in self have won him much admiration as well as a summer contract, the latter just announced by the England and Wales Cricket Board.

Now he is being taken seriously by Australia, the proper challenge begins, though there has been nothing to suggest he cannot cope. The heightened attention should stimulate him even more, a situation that can only benefit England as they try to level the series. ●DP

**Cometh the hour:
Andrew Flintoff reaches
50 on his way to 68 during
England's first innings.
The signs are there for the
future man of the series**

Day 1
Edgbaston
Whirlwind England rekindle Ashes

Teams

England	*Australia*
M E Trescothick	J L Langer
A J Strauss	M L Hayden
*M P Vaughan	*R T Ponting
I R Bell	D R Martyn
K P Pietersen	M J Clarke
A Flintoff	S M Katich
+G O Jones	+A C Gilchrist
A F Giles	S K Warne
M J Hoggard	B Lee
S J Harmison	J N Gillespie
S P Jones	M S Kasprowicz

After the carnage at Lord's a fortnight ago, the sight of Australia's bowling attack being smashed around Edgbaston by a rejuvenated England team took on the thrill of an outrageous illusion as Shane Warne and Brett Lee were treated as if they were playing in a Twenty20 match rather than a five-day Test.

Dismissed for 407 in 79.2 overs, England's highest first day score since the Second World War, it was arguably the greatest domination of Australia's bowlers in a "live" Ashes Test since Ian Botham's pomp. It was certainly the most muscular as Marcus Trescothick, whose 90 was his highest Test score against Australia, Kevin Pietersen and Andrew Flintoff exploited a bowling attack shorn of Glenn McGrath after the pace bowler tore ligaments in his right ankle before the start of play.

On a day when an amazing 10 sixes and 54 fours were struck, all three batted with breathtaking verve, Flintoff overcoming sketchy recent form by smiting five sixes in a whirlwind 68 off 62 balls. With Pietersen swatting Lee for six as if carting a medium pacer over midwicket, rarely can a cricket ball have been hit harder or more often than it was today. India's batsmen have given the Aussie bowlers the run-around on more than one occasion, but this was carnage, something England's run-rate of 5.13 confirmed.

Yet, despite the domination that saw Warne and Lee run up the only centuries of the day, there remains a suspicion that Michael Vaughan's team should have converted such dominance unto an unassailable, rather than a merely promising, position.

Still, England's captain would have taken a 400-run total had it been offered when Ricky Ponting won the toss and decided to field. Before the game, Australia's captain revealed that just one of the last 13 Tests at Edgbaston, had been won by the team batting first.

It is a persuasive statistic to those open to number-crunching as a tool for decision-making, though a closer look at the figures reveal that the first innings of the last two Tests here, against West Indies and South Africa, both yielded over 500 runs. For Ponting to ignore that, as well as the fact that his best bowler had been hobbled, made his decision to put England in first curious to say the least.

Even more bizarre is that their opening gambit to England's left-handed openers, Trescothick and Andrew Strauss, was to bowl well wide of off-stump. On true pitches with bounce and pace, as most in Australia are, it can be a productive tactic when two batsmen are set. On a slow flattie in England, it gives batsmen room to hit the ball.

After their capitulation in the opening Test at Lord's, England's batsmen have clearly decided to be positive. While Trescothick

**Not-so-funny bone:
physio Kirk Russell
inspects Michael Vaughan's
elbow after he is hit in
the nets by England's 12th
man Chris Tremlett the
day before the second Test**

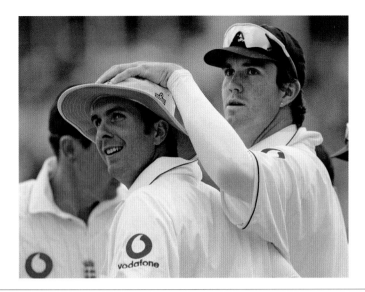

Running the show: Michael Vaughan's intelligent and protean captaincy would have a major influence on the outcome of the series

merrily blazed away through the covers, Strauss confirmed the new mindset by hitting Warne over the top in the spinner's first over. The pair added 112 before Strauss was bowled cutting at Warne, their sixth hundred opening stand since their partnership began last May. With Warne bowling around the wicket at the time, it was the first of several bad shot selections made by England's batsmen, mistakes that will become more quantifiable after the bowlers have had their say.

The wicket did not slow Trescothick, who took 18 off the pre-prandial over bowled by Lee. Joined by Vaughan, the pair continued the dominant mood, the captain looking unhindered by his bruised elbow.

For once, England appeared to enjoy some fortune with the bat. Apart from McGrath ricking his ankle tripping over a cricket ball while chasing a rugby ball during Australia's warm-up, Trescothick was caught off a no-ball and there were two dropped catches, albeit difficult ones.

Trescothick's demise, caught wafting at one from McGrath's replacement, Michael Kasprowicz, brought a minor collapse as Ian Bell and then Vaughan fell in quick succession, bringing up Jason Gillespie's 250th Test wicket.

By making six, Bell joined a long list of Warwickshire failures against Australia at Edgbaston. Before Ashley Giles weighed in with 19 yesterday, only one Warwickshire player involved in Ashes Tests here had made double figures – Bob Willis in 1981.

The wobble brought together Pietersen and Flintoff, the big batting guns, who until then had enjoyed no more than passing acquaintance at the crease for England. It looked as if that trend might continue as Flintoff scratched around against Warne. A few speculative swipes saw him ride his luck until the middle was located and boundaries flowed like cheap lager in the packed stands.

Flintoff is a confidence player who needs time in the middle, yet the facile wins over Bangladesh ensured that he reached the beginning of August with only a handful of first-class innings under his belt. Perhaps his knock during the Twenty20 finals day – of all things – helped steel his nerve.

Flintoff's innings was an adrenalin rush and perceptively Pietersen did not try to compete, keeping his own counsel until the bad ball arrived. Only when Flintoff departed, edging a leaden-footed poke to the wicketkeeper, did he assume the alpha male role.

By making 71, he became the sixth England batsman in history to pass fifty in his first three innings. But while his impatience over farming the tail probably cost him a maiden hundred, it is an impressive feat when made against the world's No 1 side. ●DP

Day 1 Scoreboard

ENGLAND/FIRST INNINGS		M	B	4	6
M E Trescothick c Gilchrist b Kasprowicz	90	143	102	15	2
A J Strauss b Warne	48	113	76	10	0
*M P Vaughan c Lee b Gillespie	24	53	41	3	0
I R Bell c Gilchrist b Kasprowicz	6	2	3	1	0
K P Pietersen c Katich b Lee	71	152	76	10	1
A Flintoff c Gilchrist b Gillespie	68	72	62	6	5
+G O Jones c Gilchrist b Kasprowicz	1	14	15	0	0
A F Giles lbw b Warne	23	33	31	4	0
M J Hoggard lbw b Warne	16	62	49	2	0
S J Harmison b Warne	17	14	12	2	1
S P Jones not out	19	39	24	1	1

Extras (lb 9, w 1, nb 14)	24
Total (79.2 overs, 356 mins)	407

FALL OF WICKETS: 1-112 (Strauss 25.3 overs); **2-164** (Trescothick 32.3) **3-170** (Bell 33.0); **4-187** (Vaughan 37.0); **5-290** (Flintoff 54.3); **6-293** (G Jones 57.4); **7-342** (Giles 65.1); **8-348** (Pietersen 66.3); **9-375** (Harmison 69.4); **10-407** (Hoggard 79.2)
BOWLING: Lee 17-1-111-1 (nb 3, w 1, 5-1-24-0, 2-0-19-0, 4-0-29-0, 6-0-39-1); **Gillespie** 22-3-91-2 (nb 3, 6-1-24-0, 4-1-13-0, 5-0-27-1, 4-1-10-1, 3-0-17-0); **Kasprowicz** 15-3-80-3 (nb 8, 7-3-25-0, 4-0-38-2, 4-0-17-1); **Warne** 25.2-4-116-4 (7-1-40-1, 10-0-49-0, 8.2-3-27-3)
J N Gillespie reaches 250 Test wickets

Analysis
Simon Hughes

With their main tormentor Glenn McGrath crocked and an unblemished pitch to frollick on, the England batsman had a party in the middle. Jason Gillespie and Michael Kasprowicz passed round the pizza slices, Brett Lee handed out some juicy sausages. Shane Warne's fare was a little more indigestible, but the batsmen tucked into it anyway.

They gorged themselves to such an extent that many of them were obliged to leave the festivities early with a touch of indigestion.

England, so meek with the bat at Lord's, exuded vitality here from the moment Marcus Trescothick brought his bat down into the path of a Lee delivery in the third over and saw the ball whistle through the covers. The absence of McGrath's inquisition freed the spirit. Trescothick was reacquainted with that rare species when playing against Australia - a half volley - and unleashed two more identical shots in the same over. It helps to be on your favourite patch where the pitch is submissive, the boundaries are short and the outfield is like glass. At Edgbaston, when an innings gets some momentum, it's pretty hard to arrest.

In a sense England arrested themselves. Andrew Strauss, having declared his intent by depositing Warne twice over the top - shots he'd rehearsed the day before against Merlyn, the spin-bowling machine - perished through over ambition. Michael Vaughan, driving the ball gorgeously, was a little careless to get out pulling for 24, a figure which, incidentally, represents his batting average in the past 12 months, if you discount his two innings against Bangladesh. After an uncomplicated innings that he will have derived great benefit from, Andrew Flintoff couldn't resist an early dart at a wide one from Gillespie. Another pulsating Kevin Pietersen innings ended only when he attempted to hit the ball into the Birmingham Bull ring.

If you live by the sword you have to accept that you will sometimes die by it. Still, it's infinitely preferable to subsiding in a welter of pokes and prods. ●SH

FIREWORKS PARTY PUTS A NEW SPIN ON TEST CRICKET

Martin Johnson

Just when we were beginning to think there was no known cure for modern-day Test cricket, in which a chap can no longer take the traditional after-lunch doze for fear of having a cricket ball land on his cranium, long forgotten conversations were being nostalgically revived at Edgbaston. "Langer still batting, Bert?" "Fraid so, Harry." "Okay, wake me up again at tea."

Justin Langer (no relation to Bernhard, the world's slowest golfer) brought a bit of sanity back to the old game with an innings more in keeping with Australian left-handers of yesteryear, like Bill Lawry and Ken 'Slasher' McKay. The nickname was an ironic one, in much the same way as a bald man is called Curly.

Australia would have been in an even deeper mess without Langer's contribution, but 4½ hours to score 82 runs nowadays is enough to earn you at least a parking ticket, and more likely a wheel clamp.

A far cry from Thursday's pyrotechnics, when the pointy-eared equivalent of Geoffrey Boycott arriving in a spaceship from a parallel universe might have said: "It's Test cricket, Jim. But not as we know it."

It was dear old Boycs who docked England marks for being in too much of a hurry on the opening day, declaring that 500 should have been their minimum target on such a benign surface. He did have a point, although if the great man himself had been in charge of the race to 500, Australia would have been starting their first innings around lunchtime tomorrow.

There were others pointing out that England's performance in smiting 10 sixes on Thursday was slightly exaggerated by the boundary ropes being brought in from the advertising boards, a sentiment that would have been endorsed by at least one former England captain.

When Raymond Illingworth was bowling for Leicestershire at Grace Road, he constantly complained that the spinner's art was being compromised by the presence of a sponsored tent on the outfield, and when one of his deliveries was retrieved from the corporate marquee, he strode over to the committee balcony, waved a cricket ball dripping with strawberry mousse, and yelled: "That should have been a ruddy catch!"

However, the proximity of the boundary rope these days is less of a factor than modern bats and attitudes, both of which were again in evidence when Australia began their own first innings. Matthew Hayden hit his first ball to short extra-cover and after Ricky Ponting had bludgeoned 61 runs off 67 balls, he fretted and fidgeted so much about failing to score off his next eight that he obligingly lobbed up a catch off Ashley Giles.

You'd have thought he'd been stuck on nought for an hour, but it was the start of a very good day for Giles on his own ground, not least because of the knock-on effect on sales of his special tea mug in the Warwickshire shop. Inscribed 'Ashley Giles – The King of Spain' after a misprint on the initial order form, they proved such a success that the original 'King of Spin' order has now been discontinued. Either that, or they were removed after a visit from a trades description officer.

Giles himself is a modest bloke, and wouldn't claim to be an outrageous spinner of the ball, but he's a much underrated cricketer, and passionate enough about England to have spouted off in his newspaper column after Lord's about former Test players being over-critical of the team. It certainly re-inforced Australian beliefs in the Pommy capacity for whingeing, but at least it was the first known instance of one of these columns not sending the reader into a deep coma. Given the way Test cricket is going, it's quite possible Langer was batting yesterday as much for his Sunday newspaper editors as much as Australia, and trying to become the first player this summer to make his column more interesting than his innings.

So how many runs do England need to be sure of victory? Well, as we keep seeing, Test cricket is now exhibit A for Henry Ford's view of history. Bunk. There is no total beyond the reach of anyone any more, and there's really no point trawling back through old Wisdens to check the history. For about 130 years, teams going into bat for a second time in England's position were traditionally 0-0 after one ball. Yesterday, they were 4-0 after one ball. ●MJ

**Polka dotty:
Fancy dress and cricket
go together like Mickey
and Minnie Mouse**

Day 2
Edgbaston
Giles does
England
a good turn

Ashley Giles left his war of words with the media to turn both his attentions and the ball on Australia with three crucial wickets. After an anonymous Test at Lord's, the left-arm spinner used the dusting pitch to send a retort not only to his critics but to the Australian batsmen who will have to bat last in this effervescing match.

Giles was well supported by Andrew Flintoff, who is on a hat-trick after taking Australia's last two wickets in successive balls, and Simon Jones, who finished with two wickets as England dismissed their opponents to take a 99-run lead. By the close that had been increased to 124 runs with the loss of Andrew Strauss, bowled by a fizzing leg-break from Shane Warne that turned at least two feet out of the rough.

It was a beauty that made Warne the first bowler in history to take 100 Test wickets in a foreign country. It also signalled where England's main problem lies today, as they try to extend their lead beyond 350. Warne has the stamina and guile to block up one end for most of the day, which means most of the run-scoring, and therefore risk-taking, must come at the other. After the excesses of the first two days, this one promises to be cat and mouse of a high calibre on a deteriorating pitch.

In a match where much of the cricket has been frenetic, the sight of Giles wheeling away from the City End and Justin Langer nudging his way to 82, gave a rare glimpse of how Test match cricket used to be played. It proved the overriding theme of the day as England slowed the game down following their feverish batting the day before.

Edgbaston has proved fecund for Giles of late, his nine wickets here against the West Indies last year being matched by some purple form for Warwickshire earlier this season when he took a record 24 first-class wickets in April, a feat unheard of for a spinner.

Opponents claim the pitch ends were specially roughed up for him. But while the dusting foot holes left by the faster bowlers certainly increased his threat, especially to left-handers, this pitch is deteriorating because it is under-prepared not specially prepared.

This last week has brought the gripes of wrath for Giles, who was determined to prolong his spat with a media he felt had been unfairly critical of him after England's defeat in the first Test. Some felt it would not affect him in the slightest, though judging from the fuss team-mates made of him when Ricky Ponting became his first scalp of the day, there must have been some vulnerability.

Caught at fine leg after top-edging a paddled sweep, Ponting was second man out, following Matthew Hayden's dismissal for a duck to the first ball he faced. It was Matthew Hoggard's

**The thinking man's
fast bowler: Steve
Harmison would not
scale the heights of his
Lord's performance again,
but he left his mark on
both the series and a
number of Australians**

Holding the line: Michael Clarke beats a fielding return during his dangerous Edgbaston rearguard. His innings was cut short by a magnificent Steve Harmison slower ball in the final act of the third day's play

first ball too, which meant Hayden had sprung the trap set for him – Michael Vaughan deliberately posting a fielder at short extra-cover – at the earliest opportunity.

Hayden's departure followed an aggressive opening over from Stephen Harmison in which Langer was struck on the head by the third ball of the day. After England's lack of concern over Ponting following the cut cheek he sustained hooking Harmison at Lord's, there were inquiries from Ian Bell and Kevin Pietersen.

Langer has been crusted so many times that he has been banned from fielding at short leg, just in case he takes a blow there too. He looked groggy too, which may have accounted for the near run out of Ponting when they went to pinch a quick single.

Pietersen's throw to the bowler's end missed, as did another later in the day. However, a brilliant one-handed pick-up, swivel and throw by Vaughan from mid-on did strike the jackpot, though Damien Martyn was guilty of dawdling as he set off for the single.

Left-handers have supplied some of cricket's most elegant batsmen, but there is a breed that looks crabbed and ugly. Langer is in the latter group, but Australia will be grateful for the squirts and dabs that formed the basis for his 82. Indeed, a century looked likely until Simon Jones had him lbw with one that reverse-swung late into his pads.

It proved the start of a telling spell with the old ball from Jones, who might have finished with more wickets had his out-swingers found the edge rather than the air just outside it. He did get Brett Lee, swallowed at second slip by Flintoff, but on another day he might have landed better batsmen.

All the while Giles was wheeling away into the rough, timing his strikes just when England most needed them. Even when Michael Clarke looked as if he had got the measure of the spin and rough, Giles managed to dart one in that the batsman feathered to Geraint Jones. As he made his way down to third man the entire Wyatt and Raglan stand rose to give him a standing ovation.

There was a similar response when he bowled Warne after the leg-spinner was having a wild yahoo. It was poor piece of cricket by the maestro as it left the tail exposed to Flintoff. With a huff and a puff, big Freddie blew them away, leaving Adam Gilchrist stranded on 49.

For once, Australia's saviour was unable to get his team up with the opposition, who must now fancy their chances of levelling this series. ●DP

Day 2 Scoreboard

AUSTRALIA/FIRST INNINGS		M	B	4	6
J L Langer lbw b S P Jones	82	275	154	7	0
M L Hayden c Strauss b Hoggard	0	5	1	0	0
***R T Ponting** c Vaughan b Giles	61	87	76	12	1x5
D R Martyn run out (Vaughan)	20	21	18	4	0
M J Clarke c G O Jones b	4	20	18	1	0
+A C Gilchrist not out	49	120	69	4	1x5
S K Warne b Giles	8	14	14	2	0
B Lee c Flintoff b S P Jones	6	11	10	1	0
J N Gillespie lbw b Flintoff	7	36	37	1	0
M S Kasprowicz lbw b Flintoff	0	1	1	0	0

Extras (b 13, lb 7, w 1, nb 10)	31
Total (76 overs, 346 mins)	308

FALL OF WICKETS: 1-0 (Hayden 1.1); **2-88** (Ponting 19.5); **3-118** (Martyn 24.5); **4-194** (Clarke 44.2); **5-208** (Katich 49.4); **6-262** (Langer 61.3); **7-273** (Warne 64.5); **8-282** (Lee 67.1); **9-308** (Gillespie 75.4) **10-308** (Kasprowicz 76.0)
BOWLING: Harmison 11-1-48-0 (nb 2, 7-1-35-0, 4-0-13-0); **Hoggard 8-0-41-1** (nb 4, 4-0-26-1, 4-0-15-0); **S P Jones** 16-2-69-2 (nb 1, w 1, 3-2-13-0, 6-0-29-0, 7-0-27-2); **Flintoff 15-1-52-3** (nb 3, 6-1-20-0, 7-0-29-1, 2-0-3-2); **Giles 26-2-78-3** (5-0-20-1, 21-2-58-2)

ENGLAND/SECOND INNINGS		M	B	4	6
M E Trescothick not out	19	33	26	4	0
A J Strauss b Warne	6	29	12	1	0
M J Hoggard not out	0	3	4	0	0
Extras	0				
Total (1 wkt, 7 overs, 33 mins)	25				

FALL OF WICKETS: 1-25 (Strauss 6.2)
Bowling: Lee 3-0-13-0, Gillespie 2-0-7-0, Kasprowicz 1-0-5-0, Warne 1-1-0-1

Analysis
Simon Hughes

The motto of today's play was, "when the party's going a bit flat, trust in Welsh swing". Tom Jones, or in Michael Vaughan's case, Simon Jones. The Australian innings was threatening to recover from its patchy performance in the first two sessions, but it was Jones'

exhibition of old ball swing that turned the match back in England's favour. The strength of this England attack is that it has a man for every situation.

Half an hour after tea Jones was handed the 60-overs-old ball. The score was 250 for five, Justin Langer was in solid residence at one end and Adam Gilchrist had won an important little battle and seen off his current nemesis, Andrew Flintoff, at the other. England supporters would have been bracing themselves for Gilchrist's offensive, doubtless remembering his demoralising assault on England's bowlers here four years ago.

Jones, however, has shown steady improvement this year, with an action that is more grooved. He bowled well without luck at Lord's – the victim of several dropped catches – and he was the outstanding England paceman in practice this week. He seemed undaunted by the prospect of a confrontation with the man generally reckoned to be the most intimidating batsman on the planet. Employing the reverse-swinging skills he first acquired from that honorary Welshman Waqar Younis when he played for Glamorgan in the late 1990s, he curved the ball away from the left-handers from round the wicket,

giving the batsmen no respite.

He went back over the wicket to Langer and set him up beautifully. First he slanted one across him towards the slips which Langer, getting well across, countered with a typical nudged single on the leg side. Yes, we know all about reverse swing; it only ever goes one way, the shot seemed to say. Jones' next ball to him defied that argument. Flipping the shiny side, he made it curve back into Langer, pinning him on the crease and ending the nuggety left-hander's 4½ hours of doughty resistance. It was the decisive wicket of the innings. The way he got it would have made Waqar proud. ●SH

Punch drunk:
Justin Langer's pre-series
preparation included
boxing training to improve
his footwork . A regular
target for Harmison,
he was hit often during
the series but finished as
Australia's top batsman

Edgbaston

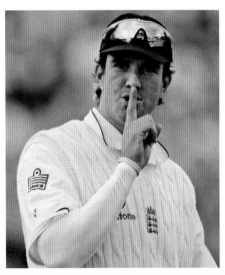

Fist of fury:
Steve Harmison celebrates
after his brilliantly
conceived slower ball
accounts for Michael
Clarke on the third evening

The old firm: Shane Warne and Adam Gilchrist celebrate the wicket of Kevin Pietersen. Yet Gilchrist underperformed over the series, losing his personal battle with Andrew Flintoff

Days 3 & 4
Edgbaston
England triumph goes to the wire

Levelling this series should have been a formality for England, but it was typical of this extraordinary Test match that the interested parties were kept on tenterhooks until the last possible moment. Well, almost the last possible moment because when Geraint Jones took a tumbling catch off Steve Harmison to dismiss Michael Kasprowicz, England still had two runs in hand, albeit a sweaty one.

The two-run margin is the narrowest yet in an Ashes Test. But while that surely elevates this one to being the greatest between these two old foes, the fact that England have come from behind to level with Australia for the first time since 1981 is far more pertinent.

It was a big moment, at least for England. As umpire Billy Bowden raised his finger, Michael Vaughan and his team became airborne as one, a collective leap of joy counterbalanced by Kasprowicz and his batting partner, Brett Lee, who sank heavily to their haunches in disbelief that their last-wicket heroics should count for nought. Lee cannot have played a better or braver innings – he took a nasty blow to his left hand off Andrew Flintoff – and he was plainly distraught.

The differing reactions of the combatants revealed the draining amounts of emotion and effort invested in this ding-dong Test match. While his team-mates went to mob Harmison, Geraint Jones went what used to be described as ape-jumping, snarling and punching his right glove at a group of Australia fans who had been sledging him from the Wyatt stand.

As at Lord's, Jones has not enjoyed the best of matches with bat or gloves (he let through four byes at a crucial moment), though to be involved in the dramatic last act of levelling the series will have raised his spirits as the team head for Manchester and the third (and back-to-back) Npower Test.

Although Kasprowicz would not have known it at the time, he was not out. While there is no doubt the bouncer from Harmison brushed his right glove as he took evasive action, television replays revealed his hand to be about three inches off the handle at the time (it has to be in contact), but it would take a brave and eagle-eyed umpire to spot and call it in a match so finely poised.

Certainly, Australia did not appear to feel cheated by the decision, something they had every right to be the previous day when Lee had a plumb lbw against Simon Jones turned down by the same umpire. Jones and Flintoff, whose last-wicket partnership of 51 was the clinching act of this match, added only two more runs before Shane Warne ended the spree – the same margin as England's victory.

By chiselling the 62 runs they needed down to just three – before Harmison found the ball with an Aussie name on it – Lee and Kasprowicz proved that death by a thousand cuts can floor you more effectively than any Mike Tyson uppercut. Had the ball gone for four, or even three, and England lost the match to go 2-0 down in the series, they would have needed something a lot stronger than smelling salts to revive them.

"I don't think we would have come back from 2-0 down against a team like Australia, the number one side in the rankings. It's fantastic to get back to 1-1," Vaughan said. "To get over the line is a real good boost. It sets the series up fantastically well. The most important thing now is to take this momentum into the third Test and start well again on Thursday at Old Trafford."

Australia's captain, Ricky Ponting, tried to be upbeat about his team's defeat. "It was probably the most nervewracking end to a match that I've ever played in, right up there with the World Cup semi-final against South Africa in 1999 [also at Edgbaston]. But we can take as much away from this as England can after the way we fought it out."

After an amazing Saturday in which 17 wickets fell (not to mention the frenetic cricket on the first two days), yesterday promised to be something of an anti-climax with England expected to wrap up victory quickly, their thunderous fast bowlers knocking over Australia's last two wickets.

Yet, led by Warne, Australia's tail was not about to be bobbed as 24 runs were taken off the opening four overs. Needing 107 to win did not turn them into statues, though that came later once the target got below 10 and the pressure of expectation took hold.

Warne has made two first-class hundreds for Hampshire this season and would have fancied his chances. Ironic then that a batsman's flourish, a flick of the right heel when attempting a clip to leg off Flintoff, should prove his undoing as he trod on his stumps.

Heavy hitter: Andrew Flintoff's batting is a thing of punishing beauty, invested with new maturity and raw menace

Having been England's enforcer with bat and ball in this match, Flintoff was expected to crown an immense personal performance – that saw him score 68 and 73, as well as take seven wickets – by delivering the coup de grace.

It did not come and with Lee carving to off and Kasprowicz shovelling to leg, the sell-out crowd began to get fidgety as the runs kept coming. England began to look anxious, too, though Vaughan kept his cool, at least outwardly. Inundated with offers of advice from his team throughout the match, he revealed that none was forthcoming as the terrible prospect of a monumental choke drew nearer and nearer.

With five runs needed, Lee and Kasprowicz changed their approach, which went from attack to the belief that they could get the runs in singles. Lucky, then, that a juicy full toss from Harmison, which Lee struck hard, was cut off by Ian Bell, hovering on the boundary at deep point. Not only did Bell save the four, but the resulting single brought Kasprowicz on strike.

Sensing that this was the last chance saloon, Harmison, who had bowled Michael Clarke the previous evening with an outrageous slower ball, banged one last bouncer in short. The rest, as Kasprowicz parried to Jones, has kept the Ashes and the summer from football's greedy grasp.

The hard bare expanses of Old Trafford beckon next, but while Australia are sure to be without Glenn McGrath, following his ankle injury here, they are talking up Warne's prospects of going well beyond his 600th Test wicket (he is presently on 599).

But while Warne can turn it on most surfaces, England should take heart from Old Trafford's reputation as a place for reverse-swing. In this Test, Flintoff and Simon Jones used the skill far better than Australia did and should retain their edge in Manchester.

England's pace bowlers were also more aggressive, though Jones was deemed by the match referee, Ranjan Madugalle, to have overdone the aggro when he showed Matthew Hayden the way back to the pavilion after dismissing him on Saturday. Jones was fined 20 per cent of his match fee (roughly £1,000), but after yesterday's win he will recoup that, and more, the next time he does a photo shoot with his clothes off. ●DP

2nd Test Scoreboard

CLOSE DAY 1 England 407ao
CLOSE DAY 2 England 2nd innings 25-1
(7 overs, Trescothick 19, Hoggard 0)
CLOSE DAY 3 Australia 175-8 (43.4 overs, Warne 20)

ENGLAND/FIRST INNINGS		M	B	4	6
M E Trescothick c Gilchrist b Kasprowicz	90	143	102	15	2
A J Strauss b Warne	48	113	76	10	0
*M P Vaughan c Lee b Gillespie	24	53	41	3	0
I R Bell c Gilchrist b Kasprowicz	6	2	3	1	0
K P Pietersen c Katich b Lee	71	152	76	10	1
A Flintoff c Gilchrist b Gillespie	68	72	62	6	5
+G O Jones c Gilchrist b Kasprowicz	1	14	15	0	0
A F Giles lbw b Warne	23	33	31	4	0
M J Hoggard lbw b Warne	16	62	49	2	0
S J Harmison b Warne	17	14	12	2	1
S P Jones not out	19	39	24	1	1
Extras (lb 9, w 1, nb 14)	**24**				
Total (79.2 overs, 356 mins)	**407**				

FALL OF WICKETS: 1-112 (Strauss 25.3 overs); **2-164** (Trescothick 32.3) **3-170** (Bell 33.0); **4-187** (Vaughan 37.0); **5-290** (Flintoff 54.3); **6-293** (G Jones 57.4); **7-342** (Giles 65.1); **8-348** (Pietersen 66.3); **9- 375** (Harmison 69.4); **10-407** (Hoggard 79.2).
BOWLING: Lee 17-1-111-1 (nb 3, w 1, 5-1-24-0, 2-0-19-0, 4-0-29-0, 6-0-39-1); **Gillespie** 22-3-91-2 (nb 3, 6-1-24-0, 4-1-13-0, 5-0-27-1, 4-1-10-1, 3-0-17-0); **Kasprowicz** 15-3-80-3 (nb 8, 7-3-25-0, 4-0-38-2, 4-0-17-1); **Warne** 25.2-4-116-4 (7-1-40-1, 10-0-49-0, 8.2-3-27-3)

AUSTRALIA/FIRST INNINGS		M	B	4	6
J L Langer lbw b S P Jones	82	275	154	7	0
M L Hayden c Strauss b Hoggard	0	5	1	0	0
*R T Ponting c Vaughan b Giles	61	87	76	12	1x5
D R Martyn run out (Vaughan)	20	21	18	4	0
M J Clarke c G O Jones b Giles	40	85	68	7	0
S M Katich c G O Jones b Flintoff	4	20	18	1	0
+A C Gilchrist not out	49	120	69	4	1x5
S K Warne b Giles	8	14	14	2	0
B Lee c Flintoff b S P Jones	6	11	10	1	0
J N Gillespie lbw b Flintoff	7	36	37	1	0
M S Kasprowicz lbw b Flintoff	0	1	1	0	0
Extras (b 13, lb 7, w 1, nb 10)	**31**				
Total (76 overs, 346 mins)	**308**				

FALL OF WICKETS: 1-0 (Hayden 1.1); **2-88** (Ponting 19.5); **3-118** (Martyn 24.5); **4-194** (Clarke 44.2); **5-208** (Katich 49.4); **6-262** (Langer 61.3); **7-273** (Warne 64.5); **8-282** (Lee 67.1); **9-308** (Gillespie 75.4) **10-308** (Kasprowicz 76.0).
BOWLING: Harmison 11-1-48-0 (nb 2, 7-1-35-0, 4-0-13-0); **Hoggard** 8-0-41-1 (nb 4, 4-0-26-1, 4-0-15-0); **S P Jones** 16-2-69-2 (nb 1, w 1, 3-2-13-0, 6-0-29-0, 7-0-27-2); **Flintoff** 15-1-52-3 (nb 3, 6-1-20-0, 7-0-29-1, 2-0-3-2); **Giles** 26-2-78-3 (5-0-20-1, 21-2-58-2)

ENGLAND/SECOND INNINGS		M	B	4	6
M E Trescothick c Gilchrist b Lee	21	51	38	4	0
A J Strauss b Warne	6	29	12	1	0
M J Hoggard c Hayden b Lee	1	34	27	0	0
*M P Vaughan b Lee	1	2	2	0	0
I R Bell c Gilchrist b Warne	21	68	43	2	0
K P Pietersen c Gilchrist b Warne	20	49	35	0	2
A Flintoff b Warne	73	113	86	6	4
+G O Jones c Ponting b Lee	9	34	19	1	0
A F Giles c Hayden b Warne	8	43	36	0	0
S J Harmison c Ponting b Warne	0	1	1	0	0
S P Jones not out	12	40	23	3	0
Extras (lb 1 nb 9)	**10**				
Total (52.1 overs, 250 mins)	**182**				

FALL OF WICKETS: 1-25 (Strauss 6.2); **2-27** (Trescothick 11.2) **3-29** (Vaughan 11.5); **4-31** (Hoggard 13.5); **5-72** (Pietersen 25.0); **6-75** (Bell 26.5); **7-101** (G Jones 34.0); **8-131** (Giles 44.3); **9- 131** (Harmison 44.4); **10-182** (Flintoff 52.1).
BOWLING: Lee 18-1-82-4 (nb 5, 3-0-13-0, 7-1-19-3, 5-0-26-1, 3-0-24-0); **Gillespie** 8-0-24-0 (nb 1, 2-0-7-0, 6-0-17-0); **Kasprowicz** 3-0-29-0 (1-0-5-0, 2-0-24-0); **Warne** 23.1-7-46-6 (1-1-0-1, 22.1-6-46-5)

AUSTRALIA/SECOND INNINGS		M	B	4	6
J L Langer b Flintoff	28	54	47	4	0
M L Hayden c Trescothick b S P Jones	31	107	64	4	0
*R T Ponting c G O Jones b Flintoff	0	3	5	0	0
D R Martyn c Bell b Hoggard	28	62	36	5	0
M J Clarke b Harmison	30	106	57	4	0
S M Katich c Trescothick b Giles	16	27	21	3	0
+A C Gilchrist c Flintoff b Giles	1	7	4	0	0
J N Gillespie lbw b Flintoff	0	2	2	0	0
S K Warne hit wkt b Flintoff	42	86	59	4	2
B Lee not out	44	100	75	5	0
M S Kasprowicz c G O Jones b Harmison	20	61	31	3	0
Extras (b 13, lb 8, w 1, nb 18)	**40**				
Total (64.3 overs, 309 mins)	**279**				

FALL OF WICKETS: 1-47 (Langer 12.2); **2-48** (Ponting 13.0); **3-82** (Hayden 22.5); **4-107** (Martyn 26.1); **5-134** (Katich 32.0); **6-136** (Gilchrist 33.5); **7-137** (Gillespie 34.2); **8-175** (Clarke 43.4); **9-220** (Warne 52.1) **10-279** (Kasprowicz 64.3).
BOWLING: Harmison 17.3-3-62-2 (nb 1, w 1, 6-2-13-0, 3-0-12-0, 1.4-1-1-1, 3.2-0-27-0, 3-0-9-1); **Hoggard** 5-0-26-1 (3-0-16-0, 2-0-10-1); **Giles** 15-3-68-2 (3-0-18-0, 8-1-34-2, 4-2-26-0); **Flintoff** 22-3-79-4 (5-1-15-2, 7-1-19-1, 7-0-35-1, 3-1-10-0); **S P Jones** 5-1-23-1 (3-1-7-0, 2-0-16-1)
UMPIRES: B F Bowden (New Zealand) & **R E Koertzen** (South Africa)
ENGLAND WON BY 2 RUNS
MATCH AWARD: A Flintoff

Beware the pie in the sky syndrome

2nd Test afterword
Derek Pringle

Test matches don't come much closer than England's thrilling two-run victory over Australia at Edgbaston. The condensed nature of the action and the bewildering twists and turns to the plot invested every ball with meaning. Eventually, the excruciating tension had to give, which it did England's way, a result that has set up the Ashes for the rest of the summer.

Contests like that come along once in a career, though Justin Langer can claim experience of an even tighter finish when West Indies beat Australia by one run in Adelaide 12 years ago. Australia have also been involved in two ties, against the West Indies in 1960/61 and India in 1986/87, so they have some experience of games that go down to the wire.

With those three firmly entrenched in the game's folklore, the astounding match at Edgbaston will have to settle for greatest Ashes encounter, exceeding as it has the three-run margins of 1903 and 1982/83, the last a match I played in. Time dulls the memory, but I don't recall feeling as frazzled then as when Brett Lee and Michael Kasprowicz closed on their target last Sunday.

The Boxing Day Test in Melbourne is a massive event and in 1982 England arrived there 2-0 down in the series. Crowds of 75,000 are the norm, which makes the atmosphere more gladiatorial than festive, especially when the Ashes are at stake.

With neither team able to reach 300 in the first three innings, Australia's target of 290 in the fourth made them clear second favourites. It looked warranted, too, when with one wicket left they still needed 74 runs to win.

After England's win, Vaughan paid tribute to the Edgbaston crowd, saying they were like having a 12th man permanently on the field. At the MCG, the effect is multiplied several times, as one or two England players found out after having meat pies dumped on their heads by spectators in Bay 13, an infamous place even the police feared to tread.

One victim was Ian Gould, whose brilliant catch had helped dismiss Greg Chappell off Norman Cowans. Gould was on as sub but copped a pie, resplendent with dollops of tomato sauce, when he later went to patrol the boundary. Not given to histrionics, Gould turned to the wall of guffawing oiks and through a fringe of minced beef and gravy said: "Steady on son, I've just had me barnet done."

His good humour did not spread among the rest of us, at least not once Allan Border and No11 Jeff Thomson began to chip away at the target with ones and twos.

Before Melbourne, Border had been out of sorts but, having borrowed a bat off Ian Botham, was rebuilding his confidence as England captain Bob Willis spread the field to try to get Thomson on strike.

Having looked vulnerable the previous evening, Thomson was chivvied along by Border. Their plight caught the mood and as the final day began, with Australia still needing 37 to win, 20,000 spectators turned up for a finale that could conceivably have lasted one ball and, according to reports, the entire country virtually ground to a standstill as people tuned in.

With only four more runs needed, it certainly didn't look as if Australia would lose. I was fielding at third man when Willis threw the ball to Ian Botham, the miracle worker, for one final toss of the dice. As Beefy marked out his run, I recall feeling angry and that having taken so much abuse from the Melbourne crowd, our sweetest riposte could be denied us.

Though not exactly warmed-up, Botham got enough on his first ball to produce a false stroke from Thomson who, perhaps sensing the hot breath of destiny, edged it to Chris Tavare at second slip. But the drama still had some legs as Tavare parried the chance over his head only for first slip Geoff Miller to stoop and conquer by catching the rebound.

I saw the whole sequence from behind and it unfurled in slow motion, certainly slow enough for impending doom to be replaced by bouncing joy as Beefy, with one of the stumps as booty, charged off like a demented rhino.

In the dressing room afterwards, I began snapping away with my camera. The one of Botham, happy but relaxed with cheroot in mouth and beer in hand, could sum up Andrew Flintoff's mood yesterday. The photo of Willis, drinking lemonade with a thousand-yard stare, revealed a captain physically and emotionally drained by the crushing tension of the moment, an impression Vaughan also gave glimpses of in his press conference on Sunday.

Having got back to 2-1, the team headed to Sydney for the final match of the series. Then, as with Thursday's third Test at Old Trafford, the games were scheduled back-to-back, though England performed as if the Melbourne win had clinched the series and the game was drawn. In the end, that famous victory counted for little and the 2-1 scoreline handed the Ashes to Australia.

With not everyone's batteries likely to be recharged, it is an attitude Vaughan's team must guard against this week. Without Glenn McGrath, Australia are vulnerable and England must take advantage while the fault line is there. ●DP

Back to his best:
Andrew Flintoff traps
Jason Gillespie. After an
indifferent first Ashes
Test, 'Freddie' came alive
at Edbaston, hitting 68
and 73 and taking seven
wickets in the match

Edgbaston

It's Test cricket, Jim, but not as we know it: another Pietersen six is deposited into the crowd

The great escape: Michael Kasprowicz (below) falls and Andrew Flintoff grabs a celebratory stump

Intuitive Vaughan
wins battle of skippers

2nd Test review
Simon Hughes

If it is possible to take stock so soon after such an exhilarating spectacle, the second Test indicated two things. That there are only a couple of wood shavings between the teams. But there is an oak tree between the captains.

In motivational and tactical terms, Michael Vaughan is vastly superior to his opposite number, Ricky Ponting. Vaughan has a broader imagination and greater personnel skills, and he used both to decisive effect. The victory was engineered by him as much as by his bowlers. Ponting is not a bad captain, but he lacks an extra sense, an intuition, which is invaluable in a series of encounters that are bound to seesaw dramatically because of the intense competition between the sides. Ponting's decision to field first was a major error, and he nobly

admitted as much. It was born out of muddled and inflexible thinking. Arriving on Tuesday to find the pitch damp, he had probably already decided to bowl first, and stuck to that despite the surface looking flat and friendly on Thursday morning and his premier bowler, Glenn McGrath, having suddenly been incapacitated. Perhaps he was reluctant to admit the situation had changed or that his team were over-reliant on one great fast bowler. Or maybe he was apprehensive of the England fast bowlers' early threat after their first-day demolition job at Lord's.

Either way, it was no justification for putting England in when the blindingly obvious option was to bat first, grind out a big score and invest faith in Shane Warne to conjure his magic on a wearing pitch. That he took the opposite course clearly irked Warne, contributing to his first-innings dismissal, a wild slog against Ashley Giles that said, 'I should be bowling into this rough, not batting on it,' and created a stir in the dressing room.

Generally Ponting, a likeable man, was unable to stamp his authority on the field when matters were getting out of hand. Partly this is because things have rarely got out of hand before. When he has needed control he has always been able to apply the McGrath-Warne squeeze. Denied that at Edgbaston, he stood at slip chewing his gum, and early in England's second innings it was Warne rather than Ponting who gave Brett Lee a long pep talk and got him back on target. Then, of

course, Warne himself unleashed his latest ball of the century to send jitters round the England dressing room.

Vaughan, less effective at Lord's, excelled himself here from the moment, on Friday morning, that he posted an unusual off-side spread to Matthew Hayden and watched him scoop his first ball to short extra cover. He set inventive fields where Ponting's tend to be stereotyped, and made good use of his bowlers' different capabilities. He will whip an ineffective one out of the attack after two overs, rather than giving him the regulation six.

During yesterday's nailbiting climax Vaughan was a tower of strength. It wasn't a time for imagination or tub thumping. It was a time for calm and rationale. He remained unflappable in the jaws of adversity. "One more," he kept reassuring everybody with Australia nine down. His composure and sense ultimately prevailed. He did, of course, have the considerable advantage of a man-mountain called Flintoff.

Long after the Ashes urn has been presented and the shadows have lengthened and Roy Keane has had his latest spat with a referee, it will remain one of the sporting year's most enduring images: Andrew Flintoff stooping to console Brett Lee moments after England had won at Edgbaston. Two prize heavyweights, at each other's throats for 3½ days, in a tactile embrace. Flintoff had narrowly avoided being maimed by some of Lee's 93 mph bouncers, one of which he somehow fended off into the stand →

without looking. Lee had withstood harrowing blows to his arms and body from the furious pace of Flintoff, remaining battered but unbowed at the end. Flintoff's England had won, just, Lee's Australia had lost. But victor and vanquished were united as one at the end, Flintoff misty-eyed, Lee distraught, in a classic vision of sporting solidarity.

It was not done for show. Flintoff recognised in Lee a kindred spirit, who has strived long and hard for success. Someone who can run in and bowl until he can barely walk, someone who can smile in adversity and not let the brickbats knock him off his stride. And someone whose quest for victory does not override his respect for his fellow man.

Flintoff's compassion is extra-ordinary in a sportsman of such explosive qualities. Yet he is a gentle soul at heart. Friendly Fred. He will play his 50th Test on his home ground, and will behave bashfully during his hero's welcome. A switch trips when he has the ball in his hand; he turns into a fire-breathing demon. Fearsome Fred. Oddly, a bat does not have the same effect on his personality, and that is what he attended to after the debacle at Lord's, where he had come out to bat as Friendly Fred, looking diffident, a little daunted by the impending inquisition. His movements were hesitant, and his results barely registered. After some soul-searching with trusted companions, and a vigorous net on Tuesday, he strode out at Edgbaston more assertively. He still resembled a foal on roller skates at first against Shane

Warne, but the boundaries were small and the gods were smiling on him. One lofted drive skewed off his bat just out of reach of mid-off, an inside edge went through his legs, and, crucially, there was no Glenn McGrath. He settled in to play some outlandish shots, all brute strength and renewed conviction, including that amazing duck-hook, defying the notion to always keep your eye on the ball. Warne was twice planted in the direction of New Street. His first innings dismissal (to Gillespie) might, however, have reminded him that it isn't a criminal offence to leave the odd wide ball.

Flintoff's second innings was helped not hindered by his bizarre shoulder injury. It meant he reigned in his ambition until the pain had worn off. Simply, he played himself in, something he is often strangely averse to. He is no technician. He must play to his strengths, a fantastic eye and withering power. He realised that at Edgbaston.

His bowling has, for the last 18 months, been his more reliable suit. The intimidating presence and muscular perseverance have compensated for a lack of real bowling nous. He has never done a great deal with the ball apart from hammer it into the pitch on a precise line at considerable velocity. At Edgbaston he moved it prodigiously both ways. The abrasive nature of the pitch had brought reverse swing into the equation earlier than usual. You don't need an action with a perfect coil to bowl reverse swing. Just a decent release and, as

they say in the trade, 'good wheels'. Flintoff has both and used them to telling effect, in the first innings to polish off the tail and in the second to make crucial early inroads. His opening six balls on Saturday afternoon, beating Justin Langer with the sheer intensity of the second delivery, then dismissing Ricky Ponting with a classic outswinger to follow a series of sharp induckers, was the defining over of the match.

Such are the mental and physical demands of Test cricket, star all-rounders rarely excel in both departments in the same game (though it is often forgotten that Ian Botham took six for 83 at Headingley in 1981 to go with his 199 runs). Yet, late on Saturday evening, Flintoff, who had been in the thick of things from mid-day, still had the wherewithall to dive and intercept Warne's solid push from the last ball of the penultimate over. It ensured Michael Clarke was kept on strike for Harmison's final six balls, the fourth of which, that delicious slow swinger, bowled him, giving England a bolt of confidence for Sunday morning. Overconfidence, as it turned out.

There is an essence of England's 2003 rugby team about Michael Vaughan's side. A sense of togetherness and a belief that this is their destiny. Edgbaston was their World Cup final and Harmison's clinching wicket was a true Jonny Wilkinson drop-goal moment. And in the course of an epic match, one man – for Andrew Flintoff read Martin Johnson – metamorphosed from proud warrior to true champion. ●SH

"Flintoff consoling Brett Lee at Edgbaston will remain in the memory like Bobby Moore and Pele's embrace at the Mexico World Cup and Ali's quote when asked if he meant all those terrible things he said about Frazier. He looked wearily at his inquisitor and said: 'Man, you understand nothing. Fact is we are two brothers trying to earn a living.'"
Michael Parkinson

This game with everything will stand the test of time

2nd Test review
Martin Johnson

It is not so long ago that one-day cricket was threatening to take over the universe, and the year 2077 was being earmarked for a special match to commemorate the 200th birthday of Test cricket, a format heading for the same graveyard as the dinosaur and the local Roxy. And as the game progressed at a leisurely pace, strange conversations would be overheard. "What's that over there, Grandad?"

"That, my boy, used to be known as three slips and a gully."

Well not any more. There is no more vibrant form of the game than Test cricket, and neither does it need ridiculous gimmicks to fool you into thinking you're getting something you're not. If it did, the match just ended in Birmingham – quite possibly the best in history – would doubtless have been marketed as the Autralian Aardvarks versus the English Electrics.

The survival kit for the Test-match spectator has undergone a sweeping change in recent years, from sandwich tin and coffee flask, to incontinence pants and blood pressure pills. You leave your seat for a call of nature at your peril, for fear of coming back to find someone's stumps splattered, a search party attempting to locate the ball from the pavilion roof, or two players standing eyeball to eyeball proffering what is euphemistically known as a frank exchange of views.

If watching it at the ground is accompanied by the danger of a burst bladder, there is even the risk of death by dehydration watching from the lounge sofa. From Thursday morning right through to lunchtime on the final day, it was hard to recall a single delivery in this entire match that was not attached to the kind of tension which precluded any excursion to pop out to the kitchen and put on the kettle.

If you were to wring out a modern Test cricketer's shirt at the end of a day's play there'd be enough adrenalin to fill an Olympic swimming pool. We've almost arrived at the point where a bowler taking a wicket will make a Premiership footballer's goal celebration look a model of self-restraint. The hugging and high-fiving at Edgbaston was all so different from the Ashes series of 1956, when Jim Laker greeted all 19 Australian wickets he took in the match with a hitch of his trousers and a polite handshake.

When play began yesterday morning, you'd have put your house on an England victory, but by the mid-session drinks interval, you'd scarcely have risked what the Australians refer to as an outside dunny. The only plus point was the fact that the Barmy Army had fallen almost totally silent. Anyone who still believes these charmless oiks actually enhance a day at the cricket have either never sat anywhere near them, or share their belief that chanting "where's your missus gone?" at Shane Warne on Saturday was a bit of harmless fun.

Whether or not this prompted Warne to bat like Bradman we can only guess at, but the morning's remarkable events made you suspect that the Australians, tired of knocking over the Poms without breaking sweat, were amusing themselves by imposing some kind of handicap system.

You could almost imagine the dressing-room conversations. "Two hundred and thirty isn't much of a target, let's give 'em another fifty for the last wicket." "Six down overnight? Nah, that'll make Sunday far too easy. Let's make it eight." "We're getting a bit close now, Warney. Why not do something daft, like treading on your own stumps, then leave it to Brett and Kaspar? That'll really p*** 'em off."

A deranged thought process maybe, but there are too many scars from too many Ashes series to entirely rule it out. Australian cricketers returning from a victorious tour of England used to qualify for a ticker-tape reception, but nowadays it's more like, "We don't want a load of waste paper blowing across the harbour. They've only beaten the Poms after all."

However, if Australia's oft-stated desire for a close series is in any way genuine, they've finally got it, albeit after a contest in which they were freakishly deprived of their finest pace bowler, and England's long search for a post-Botham Superman (after a series of auditions from people who turned out to have a chunk of Kryptonite stuck in their tights) finally ended.

In the end, the only possible challenger to Andrew Flintoff for the man of the match award was the unsung hero who left a cricket ball lying around the outfield on Thursday morning for Glenn McGrath to trip over. (Loose balls and McGrath have never gone together all that well.)

Without such heavenly intervention, who knows how many fewer runs Australia might have required. The irony of yesterday was that with McGrath not coming in at No 11, the game still had, so to speak, a sting in the tail.

Brett Lee and Michael Kasprowicz came uncomfortably close to breaking English hearts, and with a slightly wider deflection off Kasprowicz's glove, they would have done. We may all live to be a lot older before we see anything like this again, but given the way this series is going, and the fact that Manchester is almost upon us, we may only have to live for another week. And the betting? Evens England, evens Australia, and 10-11 Warne or Flintoff taking the last six wickets with a double hat-trick to secure the tie. ●MJ

**3RD TEST MATCH
OLD TRAFFORD
11–15 AUGUST**

THE ASHES SERIES 2005

Australian Test players have a habit of biting on the bullet when it comes to Ashes matches

Old Trafford
Test preview
Derek Pringle

The sight that England's batsmen would least like to see during the third Npower Test match may yet materialise at Old Trafford this morning should Glenn McGrath pass a late fitness test on his injured right ankle. With Brett Lee fit to play, following his recovery from a knee infection, Australia could be back to full bowling strength, at least on paper.

After the carnage at Edgbaston, where only Shane Warne retained some control, Australia are clearly desperate for McGrath's depend-ability and accuracy. But while that is a potent weapon when he is fully fit, it could just as readily benefit England if he were not able to operate at full pace.

His return has surprised many, not least England whose batsmen spent yesterday morning running Merlyn, their Warne-buster bowling machine, ragged in the nets. By the time Lee and McGrath were put through their own paces, they had decamped to their hotel dreaming of the strokes they might play against the blond wrist-spinner. After all, it is 12 years since Warne announced himself here with the ball of the last century to Mike Gatting, and his legend still moves mountains.

In a session that lasted 40 minutes, only Lee looked to have the freedom of movement demanded in a Test, especially one that promises to be as frenetic as its predecessors in this series. The antibiotic drip attached to the fast bowler for two nights in a Birmingham hospital has obviously cleared up the infection in his left knee, though a long-distance call from renowned hard man, Steve Waugh, might just as easily have done the trick.

McGrath, on the other hand, looked fairly ginger, bowling at little more than medium pace following the sprain to his ankle after stepping on a ball at Edgbaston during practice. Medical sources say he is still carrying two detached ligaments in the joint, but that some heavy strapping could possibly stabilise it.

Australian Test players have a habit of biting on the bullet when it comes to Ashes matches, though the selectors will wait to see if there is a reaction this morning before picking him. If he is left out, they will disregard the temptation to play spinner Stuart MacGill, and opt for the side who played at Edgbaston.

If the 35-year old McGrath does play, it will be a remarkable recovery for someone still hobbling about on Monday, but then Australia's physio Errol Alcott has a proven track record of getting players back on the park quickly. McGrath is used to bowling with pain, after suffering a heel spur for many years, yet playing him represents a huge risk, especially with two Tests remaining after this one. It shows just how much England's thrilling counterblast at Edgbaston has jolted Ricky Ponting's team.

"We're preparing for Australia to play their best team, and Brett Lee and Glenn McGrath are in that," said the England captain, Michael Vaughan, yesterday. "But whatever side they put out against you, you know it will be competitive and that you will have to play well to win."

So far, England's tactics have been to play high-octane cricket with bat and ball. The rapid tempo has contributed to an equally high turnover of thrills and spills. It is a high risk approach, especially when half the batting line-up is not firing, but one that looks set to continue here if only because the Old Trafford pitch looks hard, fast and full of runs. "The way both teams play their cricket, it's got every chance of staying a fast game," said Vaughan.

"Both sets of players naturally play in a positive manner. It was a very instinctive way of playing at Edgbaston; now we must play in an instinctive way here and see where it takes us."

None were more natural or instinctive in the last Test than Andrew Flintoff, who can expect a rousing welcome from the Lancashire faithful when he strides out for his 50th Test here. Out of sorts with the bat since last summer, if not the ball, Big Freddie returned to the method that has brought him success: namely to stop it or hit it. If it seems simple, it is, but it remains a thrilling sight.

While he looks more refined, Vaughan plays in a similar way, though at present he keeps getting bowled when trying to defend. Despite his confidence that sequences of poor form come to an end as surely as ones where runs flow, the fact that he keeps getting bowled may suggest a technical hitch where his front leg, possibly because of an injury to his left knee, is not flexed enough when playing forward.

England have not won two Tests in succession against Australia for 20 years, so history is against them. It is even longer since they beat them at Old Trafford, the last victory coming when Ian Botham scored a century in 1981. But England have a potent bowling attack now, one that has taken 40 Australian wickets in two Tests. With sunshine forecast until Saturday, Vaughan needs to win the toss, bat, watch his team rack up a big score and then unleash the furies.

The bowling might even be enhanced if they get reverse-swing, something the bare pitch here normally encourages by abrading the ball. It might also be improved by picking the beanpole Chris Tremlett in place of Matthew Hoggard, whose right knee looks to be causing discomfort. Unless it swings conventionally, Hoggard might be as under-utilised as he was in Birmingham, where he bowled just 13 overs in two innings. At that rate you might as well risk the inexperienced Tremlett, whose steepling bounce might discomfort even Aussies used to the wilder excesses of the WACA, like Justin Langer and Damien Martyn.

There are few finer thrills in English sport than an Ashes series that is level and each side jostling for an advantage. Even Stevens then, unless McGrath should appear and upset the balance. ●DP

Fast healers:
Glenn McGrath and Brett
Lee prove their fitness for
the third Test. McGrath
returned to action despite
two detached ligaments
in his right ankle, while
Lee had spent two days
in hospital being treated
for a poisoned knee

Day 1
Old Trafford
Vaughan leads from the front

Teams

England	*Australia*
M E Trescothick	J L Langer
A J Strauss	M L Hayden
*M P Vaughan	*R T Ponting
I R Bell	D R Martyn
K P Pietersen	S M Katich
A Flintoff	+A C Gilchrist
+G O Jones	S K Warne
A F Giles	M J Clarke
M J Hoggard	B Lee
S J Harmison	J N Gilllespie
S P Jones	G D McGrath

Michael Vaughan's day at Old Trafford began with him being awarded an honorary doctorate from Sheffield Hallam University. Five hours and 166 runs later, a period in which Shane Warne took his 600th Test wicket, Dr Vaughan had handed out enough prescriptions to Australia's suffering bowlers to launch an NHS inquiry.

It was a leader's innings more than a captain's one, giving as it did some early direction and purpose to England's cricket as they finished on 341 for five. Just a pity then that Vaughan got himself out with 14 overs of the day remaining, caught at long-on trying to force the pace against part-time spinner Simon Katich.

A late dismissal involving Vaughan has cost England dear before against Australia. Fortunately for England, Ian Bell, unbeaten on 59, did not look as if he was about to squander the captain's good work despite losing Kevin Pietersen and night-watchman Matthew Hoggard to Brett Lee just before the close. Beginning adhesively (he failed to score off 120 of his 146 balls), Bell eventually revealed an impressive range of shots, a double dose of which on day two would suit his team very nicely.

Vaughan's hundred, his fourth against Australia and the 15th Test century of his career, was as timely as it was important.

With just 32 runs from four innings in the series, he was in danger of being carried by his team, never an ideal situation for a modern, proactive captain. This score, the highest here for England against Australia in 41 years, will have settled him and his players, an important factor with all still to play for in the Ashes.

He needed some good fortune and was twice dropped, once on 41 and again a hundred runs later, as Australia began to succumb to the pressure and mistakes they are used to forcing upon others. Over the course of the day, Ricky Ponting's side floored four catches.

Vaughan's first reprieve came when Adam Gilchrist dived across Warne at first slip, only to parry the chance, his second such indiscretion off Glenn McGrath after dropping Marcus Trescothick. Clearly miffed, McGrath immediately responded by clean bowling Vaughan with a no-ball. To add insult to injury, England ran two byes as the ball trickled out towards point.

Try as he might on his comeback following a sprained ankle, McGrath ended the day wicketless, something that cannot often have happened against England.

Vaughan will probably feel he was owed some fortune after having his technique dissected by a forensic media after his four dismissals in the series, three of which had been clean bowled. Despite the various

Early breakthrough:
Andrew Strauss is bowled
by Brett Lee for six. The
Australians thought they
had their man, but Strauss
would go on to get 106 in
the second innings, despite
a bloodied ear – courtesy
of Lee again

The agony and the ectasy: Michael Vaughan is 'bowled' off a Glen McGrath no-ball. Australia would suffer a plague of no-balls throughout the series, but few more painful than this

diagnoses – bad footwork, playing across the line, too slow coming forward – England's captain has remained phlegmatic, confident that his bad trot, as he put it, would come to an end. And how right he was, though he might consider sending a case of ale to Peter Marron, the groundsman here, for producing a pitch close to batting Nirvana.

The surface was so true in pace and bounce, at least once the new ball had been tamed, that even Warne was made to work hard for his lone wicket. When Fred Trueman took his 300th Test wicket in 1964, 600 would have appeared beyond the reach of normal humans. "If they beat it, they'll be bloody tired," was Fred's prosaic assessment. But Warne, in the best possible sense, is a freak of nature. But for two separate operations to his shoulder and spinning finger, he might have been celebrating his 700th wicket.

As a performer, Warne has almost single-handedly raised the arcane art of leg-spin and turned it into a beautiful and deadly weapon. With his short run-up and its theatrical pause, he is like a gymnast before the bars. Only, in his case, it is the ball that does a triple salchow and not the man.

Although he had jokingly earmarked his Hampshire team-mate Pietersen as his 600th victim, it was Trescothick who will be forever marked, his sweep shot setting off a bit of

pinball that involved glove, arm, the back of the bat and Gilchrist's knee before the wicketkeeper finally clasped it. Once his team mates had offered their congratulations, and Warne had kissed the white wristband on his right hand (a present from his daughter), Old Trafford rose to its feet to salute a talent the like of which is unlikely to appear again in their lifetime.

Before that unlucky dismissal, Trescothick looked in fine form for his 63. Although the pyrotechnics of Edgbaston might have been absent, England still scored at four runs an over, despite the early loss of Andrew Strauss, bowled by Lee for six.

It was a brilliant piece of bowling by Lee, who softened Strauss up with the short ball, before slipping him the slower ball, a combination used by Steve Harmison in the last Test when he castled Michael Clarke, missing here for most of yesterday after hurting his back.

Lee bowled with pace and aggression and fully deserved his three wickets, though Pietersen, sporting a blue rinse, will probably feel unlucky that his pull shot picked out substitute fielder Brad Hodge on the square-leg boundary.

If that wicket arose from a speculative bouncer from Lee, there was nothing un-planned about Lee's next wicket. He uprooted Hoggard's off-peg to get Australia, unobtrusive for much of the day, back into this match. ●DP

Day 1 Scoreboard

ENGLAND/FIRST INNINGS			M	B	4	6
M E Trescothick	c Gilchrist b Warne	63	196	117	9	0
A J Strauss	b Lee	6	42	28	0	0
*M P Vaughan	c McGrath b Katich	166	282	216	20	1
I R Bell	not out	59	192	146	8	0
K P Pietersen	c sub (B D Hodge) b Lee	21	49	28	1	0
M J Hoggard	b Lee	4	11	10	1	0

Extras	(b 4, lb 3, w 2, nb 13)	22
Total	(5 wkts, 89 overs, 390 mins)	341

FALL OF WICKETS: 1-26 (Strauss 9.2 overs); **2-163** (Trescothick 41.5) **3-290** (Vaughan 74.3); **4-333** (Pietersen 86.2); **5-341** (Hoggard 89.0)
BOWLING: McGrath 19-3-76-0 (nb 4, 8-0-29-0, 5-1-32-0, 5-2-11-0, 1-0-4-0); **Lee 19-6-58-3** (nb 3, w 1, 5-2-6-1, 5-1-19-0, 5-2-13-0, 2-0-14-0, 2-1-6-2); **Gillespie 15-2-89-0** (nb 2, w 1, 11-2-47-0, 4-0-42-0); **Warne 27-5-75-1** (nb 2, one spell); **Katich 9-1-36-1** (4-0-13-0, 3-0-16-1, 2-1-7-0)

Analysis
Simon Hughes

Australian cricketers are like cockroaches. You can damage their legs, cuff them on the head and poison their knees, but you can't crush them. Their spirit is unbreakable. Left for dead overnight, they have regenerated themselves and are back hunting their prey.

To have seen Glenn McGrath four days ago in the team hotel was to see an invalid who surely couldn't contemplate jogging, never mind bowling, for several weeks. Then there he was yesterday, without crutches or hospital footwear, standing at the end of his mark with the new ball. Was this desperation by Australia, risking their half-fit main man because their pace attack was impotent without him?

Well yes and no. They were clearly worried at Edgbaston by their lack of control in the field, and keen to rush their premier fast bowler back into the team. Yet, at the same time, his injury cannot have been as bad as it looked if his opening over was anything to go by. Three balls passed Trescothick's edge, a fourth flew up and flicked the bat handle on the way to a fortuitous boundary. Every delivery asked a question.

It was Brett Lee, himself hospitalised in previous days, who made the first breakthrough after a succession of the fastest deliveries of the series, upwards of 94mph, with a slower ball that deceived Andrew Strauss. Clearly there is something to be said for Birmingham nurses.

What diminished the Australian bowlers' resolve more than their injuries was the benign nature of the pitch and the shoddiness of the fielders. McGrath's opening burst was every bit as good as his performance at Lord's, but his figures after two spells stood in stark contrast: 0-61 from 13 overs. This situation made it all the more extraordinary that Shane Warne wasn't introduced until the score was 130 for one.

Michael Vaughan, meanwhile, was in his element on a pitch with good, predictable bounce. It was a masterclass of balance and timing; and Ian Bell's contribution shouldn't be underestimated either. ●SH

Parting is such sweet sorrow ... Shane Warne has tormented England like no other bowler since his first Ashes ball castled Mike Gatting in 1993. Only now, as he exits stage left, do we quite appreciate what we are losing. The best spinner of this and any other generation, Warne is captured here dismissing Marcus Trescothick at Old Trafford to notch up his 600th wicket. His record will take some beating

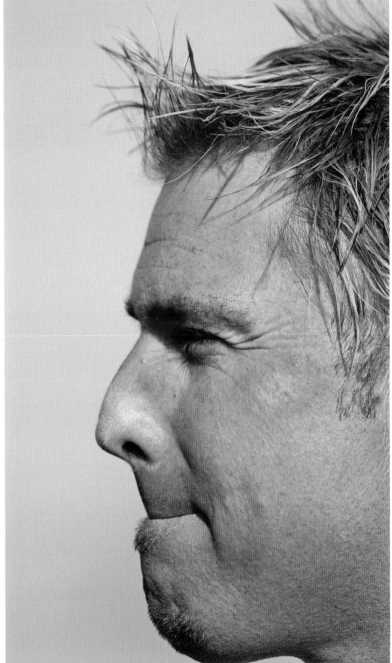

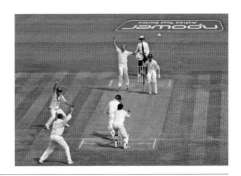

VAUGHAN'S SWING IN FORTUNES JUST WHAT THE DOCTOR ORDERED

Martin Johnson

Wise old judges (G Boycott) have been warning us all summer about the consequences of binge batting, with the inherent danger of spectators lying comatose in the gutter after being skulled by one of Andrew Flintoff's sixes, and yesterday we were back to Test cricket's old licensing laws. Take your time gentlemen, please.

Twenty-four-hour drinking is not half as novel a concept as a five-day Test match, which is what we may possibly have here after England opted to dig a few trenches first before whistling up the cavalry. Mind you, even in the give-it-a-lash-and-hang-the-consequences culture of this series, Michael Vaughan has been a near teetotaller, and rarely can a man have been happier in coming off the wagon.

The England captain had some idea that this was going to be his day when he won his first, but most important, toss of the series so far. Graham Gooch, who once described himself as a "hopeless tosser", like Vaughan had a technical fault during the 1989 Ashes series, when he kept falling over in the crease and getting out lbw to Terry Alderman. On bumping into a group of journalists as he headed to the nets one day, Gooch remarked – in that laconic way of his – that he was "just off to practise my falling over shot", and every time Vaughan has picked up a newspaper lately he's been reading that he's contracted paralysis of the left leg.

Whether or not Vaughan took this to be a medical condition, it may have been no coincidence that, on the same day he was awarded an honorary doctorate by the university of his home town, Sheffield, it was a case of the physician healing himself.

His second stroke of luck, after winning the toss, was the fact that he arrived at the crease at the same time as Jason Gillespie was coming on to bowl. England have a new bowling robot called Merlyn, which appears to have as many settings as a washing machine. Appropriately enough, for Warne, they've been operating on the setting marked "full spin", while for Gillespie they've presumably had to set the dial for something more innocuous.

Gillespie's first over to Vaughan got him off and running with 10 runs to third man, a position which has gone as badly out of vogue as a wing-half on a football field. By far the biggest reason for the high scoring rates in this series has been the players' gung-ho approach, but the only difference nowadays between a run-saving third man and the Loch Ness Monster is that there are far more sightings of the latter.

Getting Gillespie first up, however, was by no means Vaughan's biggest slice of luck. All summer long people have been picking up their morning newspaper to see a photograph of Vaughan, head over the bat in classic defensive pose, while all the time scratching their heads in the suspicion that something's missing. And then they realise what it is. Vaughan's off stump.

This was very nearly the case again yesterday when he was in the forties and facing Glenn McGrath. It made an interesting cameo, with the batsman stuck in his crease wondering how he'd managed to get himself bowled again, the wicketkeeper charging towards the two remaining stumps to congratulate McGrath, Marcus Trescothick charging down the pitch to tell his captain to run for byes and umpire Steve Bucknor standing with his arm extended to signal a no-ball.

On top of this, McGrath had just seen Vaughan dropped by Adam Gilchrist, trying to poach what would have been a comfortable catch to Shane Warne at first slip. Australia dropped four catches in all, and if we hadn't had to sit through some raucous Australian guffawing at England's fielding down the years, complete with mocking crowd banners like, 'Phil Tufnell's Fielding Academy', we might almost have felt sorry for them.

When captains don't pull their weight as players, it can often have a decisive effect on a series, so Vaughan's innings yesterday was as crucial for England as for himself. Now, of course, thanks to Sheffield's honorary degree, he can look his players in the eye and say: "trust me. I'm a doctor." ●MJ

**Return of the King:
Ashley Giles, known to the
Barmy Army as the King
of Spain, removed both
Australian openers in the
first innings. His on-field
performances would
roundly answer his early-
series detractors**

Day 2
Old Trafford
Giles leaves Australia in tatters

For the second Test in a row, England's
bowlers produced a stunning performance
to leave Australia's first innings in tatters,
after England made 444 earlier in the day.
Led by Simon Jones and Ashley Giles, who
produced a wonder ball of his own to dismiss
Damien Martyn, England left the visitors on
210 for seven, still 35 runs short of making
them bat again.

Australia have not followed on in a Test
match for 17 years, having last done so against
Pakistan in Karachi. In Ashes cricket, you have
to go back even further to Brisbane in 1986-87,
the last time they lost a series to England, to
find the moment. Yet, with Australia beaten
comfortably in both those matches, the
portents for regime change after 18 years of
Australian monopoly are beginning to look
promising.

The main impediment to that possible chain
of events is Shane Warne, unbeaten on 45 and
eyeing the growing areas of rough with itchy
fingers. To most it will seem fanciful, but he
will reason that if Australia can avoid following
on and limit England's lead to under 150, the
endgame might not be dissimilar to the one
in the last Test, where the visitors chased 282
and lost by two runs.

Vaughan might not enforce the follow-on
anyway, which would consign England to
batting last should Ricky Ponting's side make

a better fist of things second time around. Four
years ago Steve Waugh made India follow on
in Calcutta and lost. The victory rejuvenated
India who, after losing the first Test, went on
to win the series 2-1 in one of the greatest
comebacks ever.

As at Edgbaston, spin out of the rough and
reverse-swing did for Australia as Giles and
Jones took three wickets apiece on a pitch still
good for batting. The pair form the unsung part
of England's attack, after kingpins Stephen
Harmison and Andrew Flintoff. Yesterday they
became the main attraction, but only after the
other two had softened up the visitors, already
in disarray after Michael Clarke's back spasm
had disrupted their batting order.

With England once again squandering a
chance to nail Australia with a big score, it was
Giles, wheeling away into the rough who began
the bowlers' retort after Matthew Hayden and
Justin Langer had added 58, their highest
partnership of the series. With four left-
handers in their top seven, widespread rough
brings Giles into play as much as Warne,
though it needed a brilliant catch by Ian Bell
at short leg as Langer clipped firmly off his
legs, to start the rot.

Next to go was Ponting, out poking the first
ball after tea from Jones to gully; then Hayden,
lbw playing back to one that turned from Giles.
Neither looked killer balls, though nor did the

Analysis
Simon Hughes

Australia have not been made
to follow on for 17 years. That is
partly a measure of their skill and
exceptional resilience. It is also
a reflection of the lack of really
well-balanced opposing bowling
attacks these last few years. The
West Indies had their fearsome
four-pronged pace combos, South
Africa were also seam-heavy in the
Nineties, but only Pakistan, for
a short time, had a combination
to match England's searing pace,
seam, swing and spin. This five-
man unit really is an attack for
all seasons.

Steve Harmison was the bowler
for the springy surface at Lord's,
backed up by Simon Jones – if only

the fielders could have held their
catches. Andrew Flintoff
overcame the sluggishness of
Edgbaston's crusty pitch to break
the back of the Australian batting
with muscular reverse swing.
He was well supported by Ashley
Giles. Here on Old Trafford's
shinier track it was the skiddy
pace of Jones backed up by Flintoff
and Giles. Only Matthew Hoggard
hasn't significantly contributed.
A more traditional type of bowler,
he is better suited to lusher early-
season pitches.

Michael Vaughan almost has an
embarrassment of riches to chose
from, compared to Ricky Ponting
whose paucity of options was

Running on empty: Matthew Hayden on his way to 34 in the Australian's first innings. Hayden endured a miserable tour until the Oval, where his ponderous century raised as many questions as it answered

one that got Simon Katich, who shouldered arms to Flintoff and lost his off stump.

Soon after, Giles bowled Martyn with a corker that turned from the rough outside leg to clip the top of off. If it possessed the romance of Warne's ball to Mike Gatting here 12 years ago, it also got rid of the opposition's best batsman. England then had a mad half hour where they twice dropped Adam Gilchrist. But Gilchrist is out of nick and though he and Warne added 53 for the sixth wicket, he soon swished at a swinger from Jones and was caught behind.

Summoned from his hotel bed after tea, Clarke batted with a runner, a generous gesture by Vaughan given Clarke's history of back problems. A runner cannot make the important decisions though and when Clarke misread a slower ball from Jones, he was caught at mid-off to leave Australia reeling.

The direction the game has taken will have surprised many, given the fairly placid nature of the pitch. Indeed, after Vaughan's marvellous innings on the first day, England would have pinned their hopes on a big total being built on a partnership between Bell, resuming on 59, and Flintoff. It didn't happen after Bell was out to the 19th ball of the day, though replays suggested the ball did not make contact with his bat. That left matters with Flintoff and Geraint Jones. After the explosive Freddie of

the previous Test, we had responsible Freddie here, his ambition sheathed as he tried to take England beyond 500.

At least that looked to be the plan until Jason Gillespie was brought on, at which point the tempo and tempers were raised as Warne expressed disappointment with umpire Billy Bowden, after he turned down an lbw against Geraint Jones. Warne managed to compose himself quickly enough to lure Flintoff into miscuing a big hit to Langer at long-on.

The leg-spinner whipped out two more to finish with four for 99, while Gillespie finally made a contribution by clean bowling Jones G with one that nipped back. Unless Australia can somehow wriggle out of this one, it might be the last Test wicket he takes. ●DP

Day 2 Scoreboard

ENGLAND/FIRST INNINGS		M	B	4	6
I R Bell c Gilchrist b Lee	59	204	155	8	0
A Flintoff c Langer b Warne	46	93	67	7	0
+G O Jones b Gillespie	42	87	51	6	0
A F Giles c Hayden b Warne	0	11	6	0	0
S J Harmison not out	10	14	11	1	0
S P Jones b Warne	0	7	4	0	0
Extras (b 4, lb 5, w 3, nb 15)	27				
Total (113.2 overs, 505 mins)	444				

FALL OF WICKETS: **6-346** (Bell 92.1); **7-433** (Flintoff 109.2); **8-434** (G Jones 110.2); **9- 438** (Giles 111.4); **10-444** (S Jones 113.2) **BOWLING:** McGrath 25-6-86-0 (6-3-10-0); Lee 27-6-100-4 (nb 2, w 1, 8-0-42-1); Gillespie 19-2-114-1 (4-0-25-1); Warne 33.2-5-99-4 (6.2-0-24-3

AUSTRALIA/FIRST INNINGS		M	B	4	6
J L Langer c Bell b Giles	31	76	40	4	0
M L Hayden lbw b Giles	34	112	71	5	0
*R T Ponting c Bell b S P Jones	7	18	12	1	0
D R Martyn b Giles	20	71	41	2	0
S M Katich b Flintoff	17	39	28	1	0
+A C Gilchrist c G O Jones b S P Jones	30	74	49	4	0
S K Warne not out	45	95	61	6	1
M J Clarke c Flintoff b S P Jones	7	18	18	0	0
J N Gillespie not out	4	15	10	0	0
Extras (b 4, lb 5, w 2, nb 8)	19				
Total (7 wkts, 58 overs, 266 mins)	214				

FALL OF WICKETS: **1-58** (Langer 15.5); **2-73** (Ponting 20.1); **3-82** (Hayden 23.2); **4-115** (Katich 32.1); **5-129** (Martyyn 35.3); **6-182** (Gilchrist 48.1); **7-197** (Clarke 52.3) **BOWLING: Harmison 6-0-37-0** (w 1, 3-0-15-0, 3-0-22-0); **Hoggard 6-2-22-0** (one spell); **Flintoff 12-0-46-1** (nb 3, 5-0-20-0, 6-0-23-1, 1-0-3-0); **S P Jones 11-3-30-3** (nb 1, w 3, 1-1-0-0, 7-2-18-1, 3-0-16-2,); Giles 21-3-66-3 (one spell)

emphasised by him leaving Shane Warne on unchanged for virtually the entire afternoon on Thursday. With only a four-pronged attack, one member of whom (Glenn McGrath) was half-fit, and another (Jason Gillespie) ineffective, he was ultimately obliged to turn to the occasional chinamen of Simon Katich, in the way Nasser Hussain often found himself in desperation whistling up Mark Butcher. The Australians are rapidly discovering what it has been like to be English these last dozen years.

It is Flintoff who has made the crucial difference. He is like having a Courtney Walsh – a physiological phenomenon who

bowled faster for longer than anybody else – who can bat. His transformation from stock to shock bowler has given England a cutting edge in all conditions, as well as a measure of control when necessary. His hold over Australia's counter-puncher, Adam Gilchrist, has been crucial to the shifting equilibrium of the series. It has imbued England with confidence, and upset Australia's balance.

Yesterday he could have dismissed Gilchrist several times, first via a strangely non-existent second slip, then if the men in the covers had clung on to their chances. Instead he had to settle

for a wonderful five-card trick on Katich, Australia's most obdurate batsman after Justin Langer. He gave the left-hander four outswingers from round the wicket, angling in towards him then curving away towards the slips. Katich read these deliveries well, leaving two of them and riding the movement of the others.

There followed a Giles over and a drinks break. Flintoff's first ball on the resumption set off on the same line to Katich, just outside off-stump. He shouldered arms again, but Flintoff had craftily switched the shiny side of the ball and it bent in and spectacularly removed Katich's off-stump. There

are fewer more humiliating ways to go.

It was one of several wickets England seized after an interval or a change in the bowling. Vaughan's great luxury is that as soon as he senses a bowler is a little off-colour, he whips him out of the attack. Harmison, unusually expensive, bowled only two three over spells all day. Ponting, on the other hand, was so bereft of options he was obliged to leave Gillespie on despite him haemorrhaging six runs an over.

Australia aren't dead yet. But if they hope to challenge England's bowling supremacy, their quartet needs a serious rethink. ●SH

Australia lack freshness of youth

3rd Test comment
Simon Briggs

There is a point, roughly halfway through the seven ages of man, where the average human being loses touch with the latest gadgets and gizmos. For those struck down by chronic technophobia, Blackberry is still a flavour of yoghurt and 3G is the last horse to place.

A similar syndrome operates in the arena of team sport. Success is built on repetition, on picking the same players and pressing the same buttons until they can win games in their sleep. But without the odd new installation, even the best hardware can be rendered obsolete.

Clive Woodward's Lions should have provided an object lesson in the perishable nature of greatness. Reputations, as the likes of Jonny Wilkinson and Jason Robinson discovered, count for nothing on the score-board. The same gameplans that won England the 2003 World Cup were blatantly out of date.

Age is not necessarily a problem. The two oldest men in Australia's side, Shane Warne and Glenn McGrath, have already proved themselves enduring champions on this tour. But other senior players look well short of the focus and freshness that top-level sport demands.

Ian Healy suggested last year that Matthew Hayden had become bored with bashing a small piece of leather and cork around a grassy field. His ennui may be understandable, but it is not likely to produce many more innings to match his record-breaking 380 against Zimbabwe. The way Hayden is playing at the moment, he is lucky to reach 38.

It is no coincidence that the two best players on the tour – besides Marvellous McGrath and Wonder-Warne – have been the two most recent additions to the side: Brett Lee and Michael Clarke. Which makes one wonder how other young thrusters like Shaun Tait must feel about being stuck in the dressing-room.

Tait is the raw but rapid 22-year-old who led the wicket-takers' list in last year's Pura Cup. His action is reminiscent of Jeff Thomson's description of his own technique: "I just shuffle up and go wang". Which would be a major improvement on Jason Gillespie. He lopes in and goes "pfffft", producing powder-puff long-hops which fly to the boundary.

Still uncapped at international level, Tait was presumably considered too risky an option for this pivotal Test. Yet he could hardly have served up more four-balls than Gillespie. When a first-change seamer is regularly conceding six runs an over, one wonders what he has to do to get dropped.

In the lead-up to this tour, the aura surrounding Australia's attack was so forbidding that one writer dubbed them "The Four Horsemen". It was mooted, admiringly, that the tourists could go into the first Test with exactly the same bowling line-up – McGrath, Gillespie, Warne and Michael Kasprowicz – that played in the first Test of the 1997 Ashes series.

As it turns out, a couple of those horsemen have cut back on the horsepower at some point over the last eight years. The selectors half acknowledged this when, after some harsh lessons in the one-day series they opted for Lee instead of Kasprowicz at Lord's.

Perhaps now that Gillespie has been marmalised, they will be tempted to go back to Kasprowicz, who does at least represent the devil they know. But this would be to underestimate the value of fearless youth. If Australia want to fight their way back into this series, they have to take some risks.

Hayden has a little more job security than either Gillespie or Kasprowicz, if only because the Australians' faith in his partnership with Justin Langer is so unshakeable that they came away without a spare opener. Brad Hodge, the only batting reserve, is a middle-order strokeplayer.

But if the current run-drought continues, Australia may consider looking outside the squad. There are four left-handers in this top seven, and none of them has produced anything on the whole tour to match Michael Hussey's strokeplay during the NatWest one-day series.

Hussey looked a batsman in the classic Australian mould. He had certainty in his shot-selection, an obvious appetite for runs, and gave the vital impression of steadiness under fire. If he had played in this Test series, even in the unfamiliar position of opener, you suspect he would have given the batting line-up an extra dollop of stickability.

John Buchanan, the Australian coach, tried to blame the team's underperformance on their eagerness to put last week's defeat right. The flesh has been willing – surprisingly so in the case of McGrath and Lee. But the spirit is strangely absent.

It is quite uncanny to see an Australian team running on empty after the intensity of the Waugh years. Some of the problem may lie in Ricky Ponting's strategy, which has been more defensive than anything seen from Australia since the Allan Border era.

Back in the mid-1980s, Border rebuilt Australian cricket, brick by brick, after successive rebel tours of South Africa had all but dried up the talent pool. Like Nasser Hussain some 15 years later, Border had the requisite bloody-mindedness to stick with the same tactics and players until they started winning a few games.

This year's situation, however, is completely different. We have a declining Australian side (average age 31) taking on a resurgent England (average age 27). Ponting needs to recognise that this is no time for stubbornness. Australia's best chance is to send for youth. ●SB

BULLY BOYS BEGINNING TO SEE THE LESS JOLLY SIDE OF LIFE

Martin Johnson

Shortly before this Test match began, the Australian cricket coach paid a visit to the other Old Trafford in an attempt to extract some tactical tips from the Manchester United manager, and if he plans to implement any of them, the flying boot across the dressing room must rank fairly high on the list.

For a team who arrived here as the swaggering bullies of world cricket, they were yesterday reduced to desperate time-wasting tactics, which earned them a wigging from both umpires, a fielding display straight out of Madame Tussauds, and a captain who wears the increasingly desperate look of a man attempting to repair a burst water main with a stick of chewing gum.

There have even been reports of an altercation between Ricky Ponting and Shane Warne, though this may be nothing more than the kind of dressing-room mickey-taking that's always been part of the game. Ergo "great decision to put the Poms into bat at Edgbaston, skipper" might well have been accompanied by gales of laughter, from Ponting included, all round.

No captain, for example, commanded more respect from his players than Raymond Illingworth; neither did anyone attract more hoots of derision for his hilarious attempts to avoid the blame for anything. Illy was never more adept at this than when he returned to the pavilion after being bowled, after which his list of excuses included "would you believe it, t'oompire gave me the wrong guard" and "that flipping bowler grunting, I thought it were t'oompire shoutin' no ball."

However, there is an increasing amount of evidence that the Australian dressing room may no longer be a repository of good-natured badinage. In the previous eight Ashes series, the sound of an England captain uttering the words "I declare" would normally have been in conjunction with the words "that this side is terminally hopeless, and I'm resigning", but yesterday's play was mostly an exercise in seeing how much damage England could do to Australian morale before inviting them to bat again.

If there has been a close contest in this Test, it's been one to see which side have the worse wicketkeeper. If it were part of the official presentation there would certainly be an expectant hush as the sponsor's representative opened the sealed envelope. "And the winner is . . . Geraint Jones."

This could be followed by the customary platitudes ("so hard to pick a winner . . . let's have a big hand for Adam Gilchrist . . .") but Jones would probably take it in a photo finish purely for his ability to drop a ball deviating not one iota on its journey from outside edge to gloves.

It is fair to say that Gilchrist is a better stumper than the one than we've seen in this game, but Jones is so ordinary that his fan club appear to consist of a few close relatives and Duncan Fletcher. The batsmen on both sides have opted to keep wearing a helmet while facing spinners, presumably in case they get clocked on the back of the head from a rebound.

Jones would not be the first wicketkeeper to be picked by England because he can bat, a point he proved when the declaration followed his successive smites for six, four and six off Glenn McGrath. If Jones could keep wicket he would be a genuine all-rounder, as would Jason Gillespie if he could bowl.

England's chances of winning this match would have been that much greater had Jones taken two opportunities to remove Warne on Saturday, while Australia might have bowled with a bit more belief had Andrew Strauss (on one) been caught off an edge which bisected Warne and Ponting at first and second slips. Neither fielder moved, and neither fielder spoke, so maybe they really have fallen out.

The exasperated bowler, McGrath, never said a word either, which was a further sign that something's not quite right with this team. The only Australian pace bowler of recent vintage with a greater range of expletive than McGrath was Merv Hughes, whose observations were all the more fearsome for being snarled through the large koala bear covering his top lip. If the Australians have lost their gift for sledging, they really are on the slide. ●MJ

Days 3 & 4
Old Trafford
Strauss sets up last-day thriller

The thought of taking a precious 2-1 lead in the Ashes will hopefully inspire England's bowlers to superhuman efforts at Old Trafford on the fifth day, as they attempt to dismiss Australia after setting them 423 runs to win. Pressure can do strange things to the sporting mind and Michael Vaughan must make sure his bowlers do not become overwrought in the search for those 10 Australia wickets.

The highest winning fourth-innings Test run chase is 418, scored by the West Indies against Australia two years ago. England owe much of their position to Andrew Strauss, whose sixth Test century allowed Vaughan to declare the second innings on 280 for six.

With such a large target, the old orthodoxy would have only two results possible – an England win or the draw – but we live in a restless age and while the total should be entirely academic, you can never discount Australia while the pitch is still playing true.

For their part England will have a minimum of 98 overs to dismiss their opponents, who, after surviving a tricky 30 minutes in the Manchester murk last night, need another 399. Normally clues to Australia's intentions would already be apparent, but the body language of Ricky Ponting's team has become muted of late.

They played simply to survive, which against the spin of Ashley Giles and Michael Vaughan – on early to prevent Matthew Hayden

and Justin Langer from being offered the chance to go off for bad light – looked to be a battle in itself, as the ball gripped in the rough created by the bowlers' footfalls. There will be more of that tomorrow, as well as sustained hostility and reverse-swing from the quick men.

In setting up the endgame, Strauss battled a cut ear (courtesy of a Brett Lee bouncer) and indifferent form to make 106. As he swished his bat and removed his helmet in delight at reaching the milestone, the field dressing on his left ear recalled Van Gogh's harrowing self-portraits, though Strauss did have a smile on his face.

It was an important innings, though against an Australian side with less on their mind, he might have been out on one, after his edge off Glenn McGrath bisected Shane Warne and Ponting at first and second slip. Neither moved, but even when fielders did, there were plenty of fumbles and misfields, unbecoming of the best team in the world.

As one of those targeted by Aussie propaganda, or more accurately Warne's newspaper column, Strauss will have been pleased with his efforts. After a brisk start with Marcus Trescothick, he oversaw a 127-run partnership with Ian Bell. Although both perished when ordered to raise the tempo, they had steered England through the tricky times with skill

Possessed of a fine classical technique, Bell's pair of 50s at Old Trafford flattered to deceive. A poor series with the bat was partially rescued by his sprightly presence at short leg and a useful haul of eight catches. His time will surely come

Friends and foes: Shane Warne and Kevin Pietersen are best of mates at Hampshire – but fought each other tooth and nail throughout the summer

Taking the strain: Brett Lee, one of the younger men in an ageing side, was asked to carry a ferocious workload. Overlooked by Ponting for two years, Lee will remember his summer in England with pride

and patience, not least when Australia were time-wasting.

If Strauss and Bell were the unsung batsmen of the hour, Simon Jones played the same role with the ball, as England set about bringing a swift conclusion to Australia's first innings in the morning.

Jones took six for 53, his best Test figures. They were also the best figures for an England bowler against Australia at Old Trafford since Jim Laker took all 10 here in 1956.

As a player, Jones possesses the happy knack of making things happen and just as England's attempts to get Warne out had fallen flat, he came on and bounced him out with his second ball.

If that dismissal had an element of good fortune (Warne could not have struck the shot more sweetly or found the man at deep square leg more unerringly) his next wicket was a classic piece of fast bowling – bouncer followed by pitched-up outswinger – that would have brought grudging admiration from its victim, Lee.

Although Warne's bowling was unable to stop England increasing their lead yesterday, his batting in Australia's first innings had certainly helped to limit it. Crucially, his 90, and a stonewalling knock from Jason Gillespie, ensured his team were able to avoid the follow-on – thus using up valuable time as England

batted again – though he did enjoy two lives courtesy of Geraint Jones.

It was his highest Test score against England, who must have been disappointed he had got so many given the bowling firepower at their disposal. More chastening though is how Warne showed Australia's top order batsmen what could be achieved with application and judicious shot selection.

The misses by Jones, a stumping off Giles and a dropped catch off Flintoff, were fairly straightforward though Adam Gilchrist also fluffed two stumping chances and a pad-bat catch off Warne.

A keeper as homemade as Jones (as opposed to a natural, such as Chris Read) can be something of a luxury but his batting skills, as two sixes off McGrath showed yesterday, allow England to play five bowlers as well as bat Flintoff at No 6.

It is that balance that has allowed them to play the aggressive cricket that has brought victories in their last five series. If the Ashes make it six, then those failings, if not quite forgotten, will surely be forgiven. ●DP

Day 3 Scoreboard

AUSTRALIA 264-7 at close of play
Rain all morning, early lunch taken. Rain until after tea, Warne & Gillespie score 31 runs to avoid the follow on. Rained again, then 6 overs possible before close G O Jones dropped Warne

Day 4 Scoreboard

AUSTRALIA 302 all out
S P Jones takes three more wickets for 20 runs

ENGLAND 2ND INNINGS 280-6 declared
A J Strauss 106, I R Bell 65 scored a 127 run partnership. M E Trescothick passes 5,000 runs

AUSTRALIA 2ND INNINGS 24-0 at close of play
(J L Langer 14no, M L Hayden 5no

McGrath gets real

Simon Briggs

England must have been in a strong position last night for Australia's chief cheerleader, Glenn McGrath, to admit the possibility of defeat. "If something happens and we do lose the Test, I feel we play our best cricket

when we're under pressure," McGrath said. "And we would certainly be under pressure then."

After McGrath's repeated predictions of a 5-0 whitewash, English fans would love to see him and his team embarrassed on the last day. But it is not going to be easy. On a pitch that is slowing all the time, every wicket will have to be chiselled out.

"It's reasonably tough to bat out there," said McGrath. "It's turning a bit out of the rough and the ball is reverse-swinging after the 15-over mark. Then there's another 15 or 20 overs when the ball's still hard, but once it goes soft batting gets easier.

"If we can get through that initial period, it's nearly 100 overs to go at four runs per over, so we can get the runs if we don't lose wicket," he added. While this may sound more like the cocky so-and-so we know and love, the truth is that McGrath was talking with his tongue firmly embedded in his cheek.

He confirmed that he is playing with two ligaments detached from the bone in his right ankle, which he damaged at Edgbaston. Errol Alcott, the Australian physio, has been taping up the foot for extra support. But yesterday's five-wicket haul, his 28th in Tests, helped to back up McGrath's

claims that "there are a couple of ligaments in the ankle surplus to requirements".

"With two Tests to go, I'm better for having this run-out. When I started that last spell I felt the rhythm was coming back, and if I can maintain that over the next week I'll be going into the fourth Test a lot better than I went into the third."

Andrew Strauss, England's centurion, predicted that there would "definitely be 10 wickets out there for us if we keep our discipline. We proved last week that we can compete with Australia, which was a big mental hurdle to overcome. ●SB

**Masterclass:
Andrew Strauss shows Ian
Bell (far right) how to play
your way into form. While
Strauss notches 106, Bell
begins to look like the
player who ended Graham
Thorpe's Test career**

One-man stand: Ricky Ponting has endured humiliation before – admitting publicly to a drink problem is never going to be easy – but nobody doubts he has matured into a world-class leader. All the stranger then that he should be so comprehensively out-thought by his opposite number, Michael Vaughan. Nevertheless, Derek Pringle described his match-saving 156 as the captain's innings of the 21st century

Day 5
Old Trafford
Australia stage great escape

There are some forces in the universe so immutable that it takes something extraordinary to change them. Chief among these is the one that impels Australian captains not to lose the Ashes, something that had begun to look increasingly likely until Ricky Ponting arguably played the captain's innings of the 21st century at Old Trafford to save his team from defeat.

In another extraordinary Test match, Ponting was not at the crease to see the game drawn. As ninth man out for 156 he had to watch from a nervous dressing-room balcony as the last pair of Brett Lee and Glenn McGrath batted out the last 24 balls of the day from Andrew Flintoff and Steve Harmison. With Harmison unable to reproduce the last gasp ball of the previous Test, Australia survived to keep the series level, a result that saw their captain mobbed by a grateful team.

As at Edgbaston, the tension among the players and a capacity crowd of 23,000 was acute. Perhaps fitting then that Lee, denied last week in Birmingham where England won another thriller by two runs, should be out in the middle to frustrate England this time.

Those 24 balls became a mini-drama of their own, as the crowd urged England on to a second successive victory. With just one over to go, Australia sent out Stuart MacGill with a towel and a message for McGrath. If it was important, he didn't convey it to Lee at the non-striker's end, though judging from the way he tried to run a bye off the first ball from Harmison, the order must have been to give Lee, the cooler head, the strike.

Apart from a close lbw shout from Flintoff against Lee only one chance presented itself, a run-out as Lee went to keep the strike with a quick single to the substitute fielder, Worcestershire's Stephen Peters.

A direct hit would have made Peters a hero, though his near namesake, Kevin Pietersen, would have increased England's chances of winning had he not dropped Shane Warne at midwicket with 16 overs left. Had Steve Waugh been in the vicinity he might have suggested to Pietersen that he'd just dropped the Ashes. But if that is conjecture, the miss, especially as Warne survived for another seven overs, cost England a better chance of winning this match.

Until yesterday, Ponting had not enjoyed a great series, but this immense innings will have gone some way to assuaging the cock-up in the previous Test at Edgbaston, where his decision to field first allowed England the opportunity to control the match. With scarcely a ball not coming off the middle of his bat, this was a match-saving innings up there with Michael Atherton's Highveld vigil in Johannesburg a decade ago.

To score that many runs in such pressurised circumstances without giving a chance, was a triumph of mental as much as technical robustness. Curious then, unless the fatigue of spending almost seven hours at the crease suddenly got to him, that he should eventually perish to a hook shot off Harmison with 25 balls remaining and Australia a largely irrelevant 69 runs off victory.

Although outplayed from dawn to dusk in this match, Australia will see this as a big escape. Their spin department may even claim it as an England choke, with a polite inquiry as to the whereabouts of Ashley Giles' wickets on a last day pitch. What could not be doubted was the immense effort made by Flintoff, Simon Jones and Harmison.

With expectation that he might be the danger man, Giles palpably tensed up and his control, so crucial when exploiting the rough around leg-stump, was affected. He might blame himself, but bowling sides to victory in the second innings is not something English spinners get a lot of practice at, something reflected in the amount of wickets he has taken for England in the first innings (78), as compared to those taken in the second (57).

His lack of bite meant Vaughan had to use his pace bowlers from both ends rather than rotating them from the Brian Statham End, which had a following wind. As ever, Flintoff was superb, his combination of quality and reliability bringing him four for 71 and deserving of the British Kite mark.

Jones was also excellent and his one wicket was in no way indicative of the danger he posed especially when reverse-swinging the old ball. He will bowl worse for better return and he, like Harmison, must put this one down to experience. They have to come back stronger at Trent Bridge in nine days' time when the fourth Test will reveal if the balance of power, already shifted once from Australia to England since the opening Test, has moved again.

The result here will have disappointed

Tower of strength: Andrew Flintoff led England's drive on the final day, dismissing Adam Gilchrist (left) and Shane Warne (right) in a heroic display of bowling

England, especially after starting the final day with immediate success – Hoggard dismissing Justin Langer with the seventh ball of the day. Before the start, BBC's weatherman, John Kettley, had predicted that Old Trafford would see no rain and it would be Hoggard's day. If was right about the first, he was only partially right about the second as Hoggard took just one more wicket.

Matthew Hayden was the next to go with the score on 96, but only after he and Ponting had steadied the early jitters with a partnership of 71 runs. He had lived dangerously against Flintoff, edging several balls from around the wicket through the gaps in the slip cordon. Instead of persevering with that line of inquiry, Flintoff shifted to over the wicket and promptly bowled Hayden behind his legs.

Two wickets in the morning session represented a decent return given Giles' lack of bite, especially when Damien Martyn followed soon after lunch for 19. Martyn was a victim of a poor umpiring decision from Steve Bucknor – as opposed to the merely marginal lbw he later gave against Jason Gillespie – with the ball coming off a thick inside edge. Such things happen all the time but with a partisan sell-out crowd boosting every appeal by many decibels, the pressure on umpires is huge.

Some of them had camped out overnight to be sure of getting in. But if they were disappointed with the result, they cannot say the same about the entertainment, which for the second Test in a row was riveting. ●DP

3rd Test Scoreboard

CLOSE DAY 1 England 341-5 (89 overs, Bell 59)
CLOSE DAY 2 Australia 214-7 (56 overs, Warne 45, Gillespie 4)
CLOSE DAY 3 Australia 264-7 (70 overs, Warne 78, Gillespie 7)
CLOSE DAY 4 Australia (2nd, 10 overs, Langer 14, Hayden 5)

ENGLAND/FIRST INNINGS		M	B	4	6
M E Trescothick c Gilchrist b Warne	63	196	117	9	0
A J Strauss b Lee	6	42	28	0	0
*M P Vaughan c McGrath b Katich	166	282	216	20	1
I R Bell c Gilchrist b Lee	59	204	155	8	0
K P Pietersen c sub (B D Hodge) b Lee	21	49	28	1	0
M J Hoggard b Lee	4	11	10	1	0
A Flintoff c Langer b Warne	46	93	67	7	0
+G O Jones b Gillespie	42	87	51	6	0
A F Giles c Hayden b Warne	0	11	6	0	0
S J Harmison not out	10	14	11	1	0
S P Jones b Warne	0	7	4	0	0
Extras (b 4, lb 5, w 3, nb 15)	27				
Total (113.2 overs, 505 mins)	444				

FALL OF WICKETS: 1-26 (Strauss 9.2 overs); **2-163** (Trescothick 41.5) **3-290** (Vaughan 74.3); **4-333** (Pietersen 86.2); **5-341** (Hoggard 89.0); **6-346** (Bell 92.1); **7-433** (Flintoff 109.2); **8-434** (G Jones 110.2); **9- 438** (Giles 111.4); **10-444** (S Jones 113.2).
BOWLING: McGrath 25-6-86-0 (nb 4, 8-0-29-0, 5-1-32-0, 5-2-11-0, 1-0-4-0, 6-3-10-0); **Lee 27-6-100-4** (nb 5, w 2, 5-2-6-1, 5-1-19-0, 5-2-13-0, 2-0-14-0, 2-1-6-2, 8-0-42-1); **Gillespie 19-2-114-1** (nb 2, w 1, 11-2-47-0, 4-0-42-0, 4-0-25-1); **Warne 33.2-5-99-4** (nb 2, 27-5-75-1, 6.2-0-24-3); **Katich 9-1-36-1** (4-0-13-0, 3-0-16-1, 2-1-7-0).

AUSTRALIA/FIRST INNINGS		M	B	4	6
J L Langer c Bell b Giles	31	76	40	4	0
M L Hayden lbw b Giles	34	112	71	5	0
*R T Ponting c Bell b S P Jones	7	18	12	1	0
D R Martyn b Giles	20	71	41	2	0
S M Katich b Flintoff	17	39	28	1	0
+A C Gilchrist c G O Jones b S P Jones	30	74	49	4	0
S K Warne c Giles b S P Jones	90	181	122	11	1
M J Clarke c Flintoff b S P Jones	7	18	18	0	0
J N Gillespie lbw b S P Jones	26	143	111	1	1
B Lee c Trescothick b S P Jones	1	18	16	0	0
G D McGrath not out	1	20	4	0	0
Extras (b 8, lb 7, w 8, nb 15)	38				
Total (84.5 overs, 394 mins)	302				

FALL OF WICKETS: 1-58 (Langer 15.5); **2-73** (Ponting 20.1); **3-82** (Hayden 23.2); **4-115** (Katich 32.1); **5-129** (Martyyn 35.3); 6-182 (Gilchrist 48.1); **7-197** (Clarke 52.3); **8-287** (Warne 76.2); **9-293** (Lee 80.4) **10-302** (Gillespie 84.5).
BOWLING: Harmison 10-0-47-0 (nb 3, w 1, 3-0-15-0, 3-0-22-0, 3-0-8-0, 1-0-2-0); **Hoggard 6-2-22-0** (one spell); **Flintoff 20-1-65-1** (nb 8, 5-0-20-0, 6-0-23-1, 1-0-3-0, 5-1-8-0, 3-0-11-0); **S P Jones 17.5-6-53-6** (nb 1, w 1, 1-1-0-0, 7-2-18-1, 3-0-16-2, 2-0-9-0, 4.5-3-10-3); **Giles 31-4-100-3** (w 1, 21-3-66-3, 7-1-27-0, 3-0-7-0).

ENGLAND/SECOND INNINGS		M	B	4	6
M E Trescothick b McGrath	41	71	56	6	0
A J Strauss c Martyn b McGrath	106	245	158	9	2
*M P Vaughan c sub (B D Hodge) b Lee	14	43	37	2	0
I R Bell c Katich b McGrath	65	163	103	5	1
K P Pietersen lbw b McGrath	0	1	1	0	0
A Flintoff b McGrath	4	20	18	0	0
+G O Jones not out	27	14	12	2	2
A F Giles not out	0	3	0	0	0
Extras (b 5, lb 3, w 1, nb 14)	23				
Total (6 wkts dec, 61.5 overs, 287 mins)	280				

FALL OF WICKETS: 1-64 (Trescothick 15.3); **2-97** (Vaughan 25.4) **3-224** (Strauss 53.3); **4-225** (Pietersen 53.5); **5-248** (Flintoff 59.1); **6-264** (Bell 61.5).
BOWLING: McGrath 20.5-1-115-5 (nb 6, w 1, 3-1-4-0, 3-0-13-0, 5-0-20-1, 9.5-0-78-4); **Lee 12-0-60-1** (nb 4, 7-0-39-1, 5-0-21-0); **Warne 25-3-74-0** (1-0-2-0, 24-3-72-0); **Gillespie 4-0-23-0** (nb 4, one spell).

AUSTRALIA/SECOND INNINGS		M	B	4	6
J L Langer c G O Jones b Hoggard	14	44	41	3	0
M L Hayden b Flintoff	36	126	91	5	1
*R T Ponting c G O Jones b Harmison	156	411	275	16	1
D R Martyn lbw b Harmison	19	61	36	3	0
S M Katich c Giles b Flintoff	12	29	23	2	0
+A C Gilchrist c Bell b Flintoff	4	37	30	0	0
M J Clarke b S P Jones	39	72	63	7	0
J N Gillespie lbw b Hoggard	0	7	5	0	0
S K Warne c G O Jones b Flintoff	34	98	69	5	0
B Lee not out	18	44	25	4	0
G D McGrath not out	5	15	9	1	0
Extras (b 5, lb 8, w 2, nb 19)	34				
Total (9 wkts, 108 overs, 474 mins)	371				

FALL OF WICKETS: 1-25 (Langer 11.1); **2-96** (Hayden 29.4); **3-129** (Martyn 42.5); **4-165** (Katich 49.3); **5-182** (Gilchrist 57.4); **6-263** (Clarke 75.2); **7-264** (Gillespie 76.5); **8-340** (Warne 98.2); **9-354** (Ponting 104.0).
BOWLING: Harmison 22-4-67-2 (nb 4, w 1, 2-1-1-0, 3-0-9-0, 5-2-12-1, 5-0-17-0, 3-1-8-0, 4-0-20-1); **Hoggard 13-0-49-2** (nb 6, 1-0-6-0, 4-0-15-1, 1-0-5-0, 5-0-15-1, 2-0-8-0); **Giles 26-4-93-0** (4-1-7-0, 10-1-34-0, 6-1-27-0, 4-0-18-0, 2-1-7-0); **Vaughan 5-0-21-0** (3-0-6-0, 2-0-15-0); **Flintoff 25-6-71-4** (nb 9, 7-1-30-1, 8-2-20-2, 4-0-12-0, 6-3-9-1; **S P Jones 17-3-57-1** (7-2-20-0, 5-1-15-1, 5-0-22-0).
UMPIRES: S A Bucknor (West Indies) & B F Bowden (New Zealand)
MATCH DRAWN, MATCH AWARD: R T Ponting

**The X-factor:
Andrew Flintoff is
delighted by the wicket of
Shane Warne as England
pushed for victory on the
final evening**

Surely now:
Steve Harmison and
company celebrate the
departure of Ricky Ponting.
With four overs still to
bowl at Brett Lee and
Glenn McGrath, a win
seemed assured. But
Australia had other ideas ...

English swingers
keep the tourists guessing

3rd Test afterword
Derek Pringle

Australia may have escaped further damage to their Ashes prospects with their last-gasp draw at Old Trafford, but they remain deeply worried over the threat posed by the reverse swing of England bowlers like Andrew Flintoff and Simon Jones.

After the high-octane cricket of two of the best Ashes Tests ever played, in which both sides battled each other to a standstill, the players have just over a week to prepare for the fourth Test at Trent Bridge. With the series level at 1-1 and everything left to play for, preparations over the next week will be crucial. But while England's players have a note from their coach Duncan Fletcher to excuse even those six belonging to counties in Saturday's C & G Trophy semi-finals, Australia are set to move heaven and earth to nullify the reverse swing that has caused their batsmen, especially the middle-order, so much anxiety in the Test matches since Lord's.

"It's an area we've got to look at, and not only from the batting point of view," Ricky Ponting, Australia's captain, said. "We've also got to work out how we can do it better when we're bowling. There's no doubt it's played a key role in the last couple of games."

At the moment, the middle-order is the most difficult place in the game to bat. I would rather face a new ball that's swinging than a 10-over old ball that's reversing the way it did at Old Trafford. Flintoff does it very well. He uses his angles well, he goes around the wicket a lot to the left-handers and swings it both ways as much as anyone in the game. And he does it at 90 mph."

Ponting's side do not have much time – just a one-day game against Scotland in Edinburgh tomorrow and a two-day match against Northamptonshire over the weekend – to either convert the bowlers or for batsmen to find counter-measures.

Suggestions so far are for batsmen to bat out of their crease, as Glenn McGrath did when facing the last over from Steve Harmison on Monday, a move that would lessen the likelihood of lbw. Yet that has to be balanced against a reduction in the reaction time against the 90 mph-plus balls being sent down by Harmison, Flintoff and Jones.

With England using a bowling machine called Merlyn to help them tame the spin of Shane Warne, with decent success, perhaps Australia should make enquiries to see if there is one for swingers.

Reverse swing is not a new phenomenon, having been around in Test cricket since the Seventies when Sarfraz Nawaz, the Pakistan pace bowler, used it. It has since been handed down and refined by the likes of Wasim Akram and Waqar Younis, two of its greatest exponents, though not all bowlers fully understand how it works. Broadly speaking, one side of the cricket ball needs to be smooth and slightly damp, while the other is dry and abraded. Unlike conventional swing, which requires precise technique and an optimum pace to keep the seam upright long enough to trip the boundary layer of air around the ball, reverse swing seems to work better the quicker it is bowled.

England's bowlers, especially the fiery Welshman Jones, seem to have taken it further still. What used to take 30 overs of wear and tear before it worked, now takes about 10 to 15 overs. What is more, Jones can get it to move both ways at will, something Waqar and Wasim only managed on rare occasions.

Jones's improvements since the winter tour of South Africa have enabled England to keep Australia's batsmen under pressure when the big two, Harmison and Flintoff, take a breather. "Simon has definitely come of age," Fletcher said. "His improvement has been tremendous and when he gets that old ball in his hand he's as good as anyone with reverse swing. He can control it both ways and his next step up is now maybe to use the new ball a little bit more effectively."

Fletcher admitted that England's plans against Australia's batsmen had been working well. Of course the Aussies claim to be experiencing a dip in form, pointing out that despite England's dominance over the last two Tests they have just one win to show for it. The truth is less palatable, with most errors being forced by England's bowlers. "I'm sure there must be some doubts in their minds," Fletcher said. "We've got our plans against all of the Australian batters and the nice part about it is we've got bowlers now who bowl to those plans, which have seemed to work. We're getting 19, 20 wickets a match so somewhere along the line it's got to sow some sort of doubt in their minds." ●DP

THREAT OF FALSE BEARD AND GLASSES INSPIRES PONTING

Martin Johnson

When Ricky Ponting inherited the Australian captaincy from Steve Waugh, the New Zealand all-rounder Chris Cairns proffered the opinion that it may not have been the toughest job in world cricket. "My mother could captain that lot" said Cairns, and the longer this Ashes series has gone on, the more people have begun to suspect that Cairns' mum could have made a slightly better job of it.

No one knows the precise details of Ponting's pre-series motivational talk, but from all the available evidence it may well have involved chalking a three-point masterplan on a blackboard in the team room. "1. Arrive in England. 2. Stuff the Poms. 3. Go Home." If it was anything more cerebral than that, he's kept it carefully hidden.

However, the bloke can't half bat, and it may have been the thought of becoming the first Australian captain for some time to return home wearing a false beard and dark glasses which inspired yesterday's potentially Ashes-saving innings. He still had to endure some gut-wrenching tension on the players' balcony when he was ninth man out, but as heroic rearguard actions go – he batted for just a few minutes short of seven hours – there won't have been many better in the 128 years of conflict between cricket's most ancient enemies.

Australians have known about Ponting's fighting qualities for some time, not least during the England tour of 1998/99 when he emerged from an altercation with a bouncer in a Sydney hostelry sporting a black eye. It earned him a two-match suspension, but as this kind of thing is more or less an Olympic sport in Australia, it wasn't held against him when subsequently he was put forward as officer material.

It was perhaps just as well for Australia that yesterday's predicament required nothing too taxing in the cranial department, just a stout heart and broad bat. But for Ponting's heroics, the crowd scenes at the end would have been almost as frenzied as they were outside the ground before play got under way.

People had slept all night on the pavements to make sure of a seat, huge queues snaked all around the ground, there were small children crying, adults shoving and jostling, angry voices at the 10am announcement that no one else could get in, and a general air of pandemonium. If you'd seen it on a television news bulletin with the sound turned down, you'd have assumed it was the British Airways check-in desk at Heathrow.

This series has not so much captured the public imagination as sent it into orbit. The Monday of a Test match is traditionally the day on which the crowd turns up in the back of the same taxi, and here at Old Trafford you end up with the atmospheric equivalent of Lancashire versus Derbyshire. A handful of members with their sandwich tins, an isolated shout of "get on with it!", and nothing but empty spaces where the hot dog vans used to be.

Yesterday, though, there were almost as many people turned away from the turnstiles as got through them, and the cricket was so compelling – yet again – that you felt sorry for all those who came along and didn't get in. You felt sorrier still for those who came along dressed as nuns and vicars, as they'd have looked pretty daft getting on a tram back into town in the middle of the day.

You wondered if Australia's minds – still traumatised from the events at Edgbaston – would be up to the job, not least for all the distractions taking place at their team hotel. When Allan Border was captain, wives and families were banished to separate accommodation, but here in Manchester the only thing missing from the Australian section of the breakfast room was a creche and a bouncy castle.

However, the atmosphere inside the ground would have concentrated the minds even of those of them who'd been dribbled on by an offspring over the boiled egg soldiers.

It was like the Colosseum inside Old Trafford, with the crowd roaring for leg before wicket every time the ball hit a pad, and the umpires getting booed – like the old Roman emperors – if they gave the thumbs down.

There was even a standing ovation to the England fielders when they emerged in tracksuits for fielding practice, but everyone was impeccably behaved, and the only danger of an arrest as Australia's last two batsmen groped their way through the final 24 balls was a cardiac one. ●MJ

WE KNOW WE HAVE BEEN OUTPLAYED

Matthew Hayden

I'm not sure just who has been appointed script-writer for this Ashes battle, but whoever it is, they've just earned a reputation as the next Alfred Hitchcock, so thrilling and unpredictable has the plot been so far in this series.

For the second time in a week players and fans have been left biting their fingernails as yet another Test went down to the wire. No doubt there was an increase in blood pressure and anxiety levels among those at Old Trafford on Monday, including everyone in the Australian dressing room.

Drawing a match is a strange feeling and not really something that we're accustomed to. We have been brought up in a cricketing environment where we push as hard as possible for a result, and as such we either win or lose matches. But while playing for a draw is not really in our make-up, fighting all the way to the very end is.

Good teams are able to adapt to the situations they're faced with in order to achieve the best possible outcome. That's what we were able to accomplish in the third Test. We found ourselves in a position where it became obvious to most that we could no longer win the match. We had let ourselves down in most areas of the game, but despite not being able to win, we were determined not to lose the match.

Our captain, Ricky Ponting, showed everyone just why he is the stand-out leader in our side. In our hour of need, he played quite possibly his greatest innings. His effort didn't just save the Test, it set the foundations for our assault on the remainder of this series.

We know that we have been outplayed in the last two matches, but given things haven't clicked and we've come so close on both occasions, this suggests to me that when we do inevitably find the form that we know we can produce, we will be ready to take the contest by the scruff of its neck. The time to do that is now.

It's as clear as day to everyone involved in this series that we're playing a role in something very special – special for a variety of reasons.

Firstly, it is without doubt the greatest challenge we have had as a team since I've been playing Test cricket. For years, the cricket world has been asking to see us tested by a quality opponent, and at times that has happened, such as our memorable tour of India in 2001.

But this time, we find ourselves in such a see-saw affair that no one can predict with confidence just what is going to happen next.

That has led to the other special element of the series, which has been the widespread public interest it has generated in the game we love. In England, cricket fever has swept the nation, knocking football off the back pages, and enticing thousands of people through the gates, while in Australia, people are heading to work bleary-eyed, having been glued to their television sets throughout the night.

Until now only in black-and-white newsreel footage of pre- and post-war society have we been able to comprehend packed houses for Test cricket, where the result of the game did so much for national pride.

So for a generation of players who grew up when one-day cricket was seen as the apple of the sport's eye, attracting big crowds and big money, the hysteria surrounding the time-honoured game of Test cricket has taken us back in time to another period in the game's rich history.

Seeing Old Trafford completely full on day five of a Test, with thousands of people turned away at the gate, gave me some idea of what cricket must have been like throughout that famous era when Sir Donald Bradman's 'Invincibles' were packing English grounds.

The on-field contest has also reflected those old-fashioned values. The cricket has been played hard, but fair. There is an incredible spirit out there, due to the healthy respect between both sides, which no one can deny. It might be aggressive cricket, but the sportsmanship has been first-class. ●MH

**4TH TEST MATCH
TRENT BRIDGE
25–29 AUGUST**

THE ASHES SERIES 2005

Pressure point as England go for the jugular

Trent Bridge
Test preview
Derek Pringle

It is the most important match in either captain's career, though you would not have guessed it after Michael Vaughan and Ricky Ponting played down today's fourth Test at Trent Bridge as "just another game of cricket".

Who are they trying to kid? With the series level and two to play, the stakes are massive. Any calm is only skin deep with England captain Vaughan exercised as never before, not least by the expectations of a success-starved nation awaiting the retrieval of its oldest sporting prize – or not, should defeat befall them and Australia retain the urn.

For all the benefits of leading a confident and unchanged side, the situation is as much uncharted territory for Vaughan's team as it was for England sides over the previous eight Ashes series. What a tectonic shift in the cricket mindset awaits then, should their collective nerve hold long enough here to deliver them to the edge of the promised land.

Though Australia only need to draw the series to retain the Ashes, Ponting will be shuddering at the thought of defeat here – more likely should Glenn McGrath's sore right elbow rule him out of the match. For the past 18 years, Australia's captains have slept easy knowing the Poms were safely underfoot. Suddenly the monopoly looks vulnerable,

something that would confer instant pariah status on the man in charge.

The pressure on captains and players over the next few days will be immense, which is presumably why they take sanctuary in routine. Yet not everyone is likely to be comforted. Australia will unleash brawny fast bowler Shaun Tait, a debutant yet to have a routine let alone one to cope with matches as big as this.

Tait replaces the out-of-form Jason Gillespie, though England's batsmen, once they have assessed his unusual slingy action, will be hoping to expose his inexperience as ruthlessly as they dealt with Gillespie's shortcomings over the first three Tests.

"We don't know a great deal about him but we've watched him on video and had a word with a few people at Durham, where he played last year," Vaughan said yesterday. "We'll need to be wary of him early on but he's bound to be nervous on his debut. We hear he's quick, but the boys have played Brett Lee pretty well. He's probably the quickest in the world at the moment, so we're not worried about the pace factor."

Tait's action, a kind of crouching hybrid of Aussie fast bowlers Jeff Thomson and Lennie Pascoe, could prove awkward, simply because of the sudden extra pace generated when his action really clicks. Dennis Amiss used to refer to his type as trapdoor bowlers, because suddenly the ball is on you as if shot from a trapdoor halfway down the pitch.

Tricky or not, Tait is likely to be far more effective in a four-man attack containing McGrath than one that does not. As a card-carrying member of the Steve Waugh hard man club, McGrath, who will have his right elbow assessed this morning, will have to be in excruciating pain to prevent him from playing in this match. If it does, Mike Kasprowicz will take his place.

Unlike tennis elbow, which affects the tendon, the inflammation giving McGrath gyp is inside the joint. A scan in London on

Tuesday evening revealed some swelling as well as "artefacts", something Australia's physio Errol Alcott said were "typical in a veteran fast bowler like Glenn". Sounds like a touch of gout, if you ask me, brought on by a glass too many of Barossa Shiraz.

In Ashes contests, Trent Bridge has been the place where Australia have clinched the last four series held in England. Indeed, you have to go back to 1977 to find a win for the home side, one of only three against Australia in 19 Tests here.

England are playing enough vibrant, thrilling cricket, to debunk history. The plan is simple enough, with England seizing the initiative on the opening day, something their batsmen have done with style in the last two Tests.

"We've started very, very well in the last two games and managed to put Australia under pressure early," Vaughan said. "The team that starts best will have an advantage and that has been proved in this series.

"Australia are like any team in the world if you get on top of them, but it's a matter of trying to make that advantage count," he stressed. "In the last two games we've had we have managed to keep our concentration levels over a period of time and that's the way to beat good teams."

Exploiting the conditions will be crucial, too, especially if cloud cover persists. According to Nottinghamshire's director of cricket, Micky Newell, the ball tends to swing about when skies are leaden, while the pitch tends to be at its best on days two and three.

Yet bat first seems to be the percentage call, if only because facing Shane Warne in the fourth innings (stiff back or not), is always a difficult task.

Whatever the order of play, the anticipation is electric after the breathtaking ride of the last few Tests. In recent Ashes series, England has expected, but only the worst. Now they expect a changing of the guard, with captain Vaughan leading the way. ●DP

MCGRATH TWIST FAILS TO AFFECT OUR GOOD VIBES

Matthew Hayden

The scriptwriter of this epic series has conjured up more twists and turns ahead of the fourth Test.

Having enjoyed an excellent build-up, our strike bowler, Glenn McGrath, is under another fitness cloud. While it's a concerning situation, we all know just how resilient he is, following his comeback from injury ahead of the last Test, so to write him off this time around would be a big mistake.

We all know that he is in the hands of our very own miracle worker, team physio Errol Alcott, which certainly gives me the confidence that our veteran quick will be right. Glenn will do everything in his power to make sure he is ready to go at Trent Bridge this morning.

Today will be a memorable day for Australian cricket when Shaun Tait, our exciting young tearaway, becomes the 392nd player to wear the Baggy Green Cap.

We were looking up some records of Tests at Trent Bridge when it dawned on us that the great Bill Brown, Australia's oldest living Test cricketer, made his debut there in 1934. It's amazing how this can turn full circle, and some 71 years later, the youngest member of our touring party is doing the same.

The unique history of our great game and those that have come before us is something that is not lost on this team, and today Shaun will enter those amazing history books. It's something he can be very proud of.

Since leaving the scene of the last chapter of this captivating encounter, Old Trafford, we have enjoyed a wonderful few days which allowed us to recharge the batteries during our trip to Scotland, before putting together some quality time in the middle during our tour match against Northants.

That preparation, combined with the momentum generated by Ricky Ponting's match-saving innings in Manchester, has generated an exciting vibe among our group, and I feel confident that we are ready to do the business starting from ball one today.

The break between Tests, and the opportunities presented to us away from the playing arena during that time, gave me a perfect opportunity to reflect, not just on this series but on the bigger picture of life as an international cricketer.

As a youngster growing up in the Queensland country town of Kingaroy, a place known for little more than politicians and peanut produce, never could I have imagined that one day I would travel the world playing the game I love, let alone find myself in the midst of a contest as heated as this.

Even harder to believe would be some of the once-in-a-lifetime experiences afforded upon me, simply for being an Australian cricketer.

It has become an almost surreal existence for an ordinary Aussie bloke, and while life on the road presents plenty of ups and downs, including a huge amount of time spent away from family and friends, it also brings about some experiences that I'm sure I wouldn't have encountered had I not taken up this particular calling in life.

There's not a scrap of cricket memorabilia in my home, but proudly displayed on the wall of my parents' place is a picture of me meeting the Queen for the first time during the 1993 Ashes series. They were obviously so chuffed, but all that I remember from that meeting were the thoughts racing through my head as Her Majesty approached: "What am I, Matthew Hayden, a kid from Kingaroy, doing here, meeting the Queen?"

It's amazing the openings that cricket can present. Just last week, through the greater cricketing community, I fulfilled a lifelong dream by spending the day fishing in the Scottish Highlands, a world away from the intensity of this extraordinary Ashes series.

Fishing has been a huge part of my life, from the days of dangling a line with my brother Gary, to deep-sea fishing with my Queensland and Australia team-mates, Andrew Symonds and Andy Bichel. The water has always been a great source of energy for me.

It is without doubt my escape and I find it helps clear the mind of cricket clutter, while reinforcing how lucky we are to be leading this life. ●MH

Day 1
Trent Bridge
Rain frustrates England

A messy day of stop-start, after rain showers limited play to 60 overs, left first-day honours about level at Trent Bridge. It may even be that England are slightly disappointed with their eventual 229 for four after their strong start, yet it might have been much worse had Australia not dropped two catches, sent down 22 no-balls and been forced to make do without Glenn McGrath for the second time in the series.

Before the Test, both captains had stressed the importance of grabbing the initiative on the opening day. Unlike the previous three Tests, nobody has yet done that, though with Andrew Flintoff and Kevin Pietersen at the crease and looking dangerous, England will be hoping any advantage will be theirs by close of play today.

They might have achieved it sooner had Michael Vaughan not been winkled out by his opposite number, Ricky Ponting, for 58, five overs before the end of play. Dropped by Matthew Hayden off Michael Kasprowicz, Vaughan had been playing superbly until undone by a short, wide one from part-time Ponting.

Instead of crashing the ball through the covers off the back foot, he ended up tickling it to Adam Gilchrist, a horrible fate to suffer off a dibbly-dobbler. Ponting now has five Test wickets and his latest brought joy unconfined, perhaps because it was his first of the 21st century.

Australia's captain would also have been pleased with Shaun Tait's debut. Although there were no split lips or concussed batsmen strewn about Trent Bridge, Tait did take two wickets with his muscular swing bowling.

His first, Marcus Trescothick, came just after the second break for rain, the left-hander bowled off his pads after being beaten by some swing into his pads. Eight balls later, he had sent back Ian Bell, caught behind pushing at a ball just outside the off stump, a weakness that spoilt John Crawley's career and one that Bell needs to eradicate if he is to prosper at this level.

Before that strike, not much had gone right for Ponting, who again lost the toss to Vaughan. McGrath's withdrawal with a sore right elbow, after he failed a fitness test before play, will have jolted the confidence levels of the side. Australia are masters of inscrutable body language but the concerns of playing a re-jigged attack were not easy to mask as Trescothick and Andrew Strauss notched up the hundred stand.

Having taken full advantage of McGrath's absence in the second Test at Edgbaston, after the pace bowler had turned his ankle treading on a cricket ball, a repeat looked likely, with Trescothick striking the ball imperiously as he passed 50 for the third time in the series.

The knock took him past Jacques Kallis as

Teams

England	Australia
M E Trescothick	J L Langer
A J Strauss	M L Hayden
*M P Vaughan	*R T Ponting
I R Bell	D R Martyn
K P Pietersen	M J Clarke
A Flintoff	S M Katich
+G O Jones	+A C Gilchrist
A F Giles	S K Warne
M J Hoggard	B Lee
S J Harmison	M S Kasprowicz
S P Jones	S W Tait

the highest Test run-scorer in 2005. His tally stands at 924 runs, though he did pig himself against Bangladesh, scoring 345 runs in two innings against them. Yesterday he batted wearing a black armband in memory of Stuart Dove, a young man he first met at the Twenty20 game at the Rose Bowl, but who had recently died from cancer.

With Trescothick and Strauss looking in control and the pitch responding like a Trent Bridge featherbed of yore, England's domination looked total. They even had Shane Warne, on by the 18th over, resorting to the more sinister side of his art, which comprises a near endless stream of backchat with the batsman in the search for a wicket.

He got one too, though even he would struggle to claim it as part of a master plan as Strauss departed, caught at slip having bottom-edged a sweep on to his boot.

The breach might have become worse had the contagion of no-balls that has afflicted Australia in recent Tests not continued here. When you send down almost one every two overs, as Australia did until the new ball softened, there is bound to be a cost.

At Old Trafford, where Vaughan was bowled off a no-ball, it was 121 runs. Yesterday proved less costly with Trescothick adding just 10 more runs after Brett Lee had bowled him on 55 with one of 22 illegal deliveries he and the other

pace bowlers sent down in the 60 overs bowled yesterday.

The world record for no-balls in an single innings is 40, jointly held by England and Australia, both against the West Indies in the 1980s.

Significantly, West Indies were the best side in the world at the time and putting teams under the kind of pressure people now come to associate with Australia.

While the occasional no-ball is caused by tricky wind conditions or significant slopes (both mess with a bowler's rhythm), an outbreak is usually symptomatic of wider spread agitation among the team. Indeed, once a few wickets had settled Australia, the problem dried to a trickle after lunch when only four were bowled in 33 overs.

Spilled catches often have the same causes and Kasprowicz will still feel aggrieved that both came off his bowling, even if he was the one who floored Pietersen's punched drive when the batsman was on 14.

Soon after, with England on 197 for three, Pietersen survived a run-out after a mix-up with Vaughan gave Hayden the chance to hit the stumps from 30 yards. With everything but Strauss's dismissal going England's way, he missed the mark. But then Australia have been doing that all summer. ●DP

Day 1 Scoreboard

ENGLAND/FIRST INNINGS		M	B	4	6
M E Trescothick b Tait	65	138	111	8	1
A J Strauss c Hayden b Warne	35	99	64	4	0
*M P Vaughan c Gilchrist b Ponting	58	145	99	9	0
I R Bell c Gilchrist b Tait	3	13	5	0	0
K P Pietersen not out	33	113	89	4	0
A Flintoff not out	8	20	14	2	0
Extras (lb 4, w 1, nb 22)	27				
Total (4 wkts, 60 overs, 268 mins)	229				

FALL OF WICKETS: 1-105 (Strauss 21.4 overs); **2-137** (Trescothick 30.5) **3-146** (Bell 34.1); **4-213** (Vaughan 55.2)
BOWLING: Lee 16-1-75-0 (nb 7, 5-1-16-0, 4-0-28-0, 7-0-31-0); **Kasprowicz 18-2-56-0** (nb 13, 8-0-37-0, 10-1-19-0); **Tait 14-1-62-2** (nb 4, 5-0-26-0, 6-1-23-2, 3-0-13-0); **Warne 6-1-23-1** (5-1-22-1, 1-0-1-0); **Ponting 6-2-9-1** (w 1, one spell)
UMPIRES: Aleem Dar (Pakistan) & **S A Bucknor** (West Indies)

Ponting's percentages

Simon Briggs

In virtually every press conference of this tour, Ricky Ponting has made reference to "the little things". Otherwise known as "the one per-centers", Ponting's mini-obsessions consist of boring details like holding your catches and staying behind the popping crease when you bowl.

"We are saying all the right things in our team meetings," is another line Ponting loves to use. Unfortunately, saying finishes a poor second to doing. A total of 22 no-balls in the day's play, not to mention straightforward dropped catches from Michael Kasprowicz and Matthew Hayden, proved that Ponting's troops are worryingly cloth-eared where such conversations are concerned.

One of those 22 misfires found Marcus Trescothick chopping onto his stumps, taking several steps towards the dressing-room, then performing a slightly embarrassed U-turn. It was the third time Australia had taken a wicket with a no-ball during the series.

"They just don't work hard enough, I reckon," was the view of one Australian observer after Hayden's miss. Complacency is not a quality generally associated with Australia, but the evidence is becoming compelling. A team cannnot keep bowling no-balls in this quantity – 82 in the series so far – unless slack thinking and poor training habits have crept into the camp.

During the Old Trafford Test, Australian coach John Buchanan was asked to explain the rash of over-stepping. "We have put in place different measures to try to address that," replied Buchanan, whose own press conference habit is an addiction to clunky business-speak. "It is not happening, but we will keep working at it and hope in the next Test we reach zero tolerance."

Buchanan's words came back to haunt him last night, when one reporter asked him what exactly zero tolerance was supposed to mean. "What kind of question is that?" replied Buchanan, visibly bridling for the first time on the tour. After a little coaxing, he confirmed: "It means to get it to zero." But the graph right now is heading up, not down. ●SB

Woodworm's sales graph has looped the loop since Andrew Flintoff started smashing sixes with the company's willow. Bat sales usually tail off towards the end of a summer, as thoughts turn towards the football season, which is why Woodworm had expected their figures to drop by the usual third between July and August. But with help from Flintoff, they are on course to double instead. Woodworm's decision to put Flintoff and Kevin Pietersen on expensive lifetime deals seems a masterstroke.

Graeme Swann, England's 12th man on the first day, joined Nottinghamshire team-mate David Hussey for a drink after play in the tourists' team hotel. Enthused by the fervent support at the ground, he was explaining how great it is to be a cricketer at a time when everybody is following the game so closely. At which point an excited punter came up to him and asked: "Excuse me, but aren't you Brett Lee?"

Also flying off the shelves is the DVD of The Greatest Test Ever, which tells the story of the recent match at Edgbaston. "We have sent out 30,000 DVDs to stores like Woolworths," an ECB spokesman said. "But demand has been such that we are about to start another production run."

Follow my leader:
Steve Harmison and
Michael Vaughan are right
in step as they react to
Michael Clarke's dismissal
on the second evening.
Below: Australia's fans
maintain the pressure
on Geraint Jones's
wicket-keeping

Analysis

Simon Hughes

You would have got very long odds two months ago on the spectre of Glenn McGrath and Jason Gillespie ferrying on bananas and crumpets to the Australian team during the first day of this fourth Test. But it wasn't the only oddity of yesterday's play. Another was the sight of Shane Warne coming on to bowl with a lone slip and everyone else set back, and later six overs of apparently innocuous trundle from Ricky Ponting. The only predictable thing about this Ashes is its unpredictability.

To look at the Australian team at breakfast yesterday was to see a changed beast. No more are these men chomping on raw beef steak while salivating over the prospect of dismembering England again.

Now, after their humbling experiences, they are meeker, milder, eating fruit and yoghurt – a survival diet. They recognise their own mortality and the burgeoning appetites of their hosts. The hunters have become the hunted.

Instead of harrying their opponents into mistakes, they are sitting back and waiting for them. Brett Lee barely bowled a bouncer, the debutant Shaun Tait, who talked before the game about broken bones and split heads, bowled mainly a full length outside off stump. Michael Kasprowicz attempted to bore the batsmen out. Later, Ponting bowled a succession of deliveries that the batsmen could barely reach, trying to tempt them into an indiscretion.

It could be said that the approach worked. England, winning first use of a featherbed pitch, did not properly consolidate after rattling up 100 for no wicket by midday – 500 was there for the taking. In the equivalent Test here in 1989, Australia batted all day without losing a wicket. Sunshine in the morning rendered the pitch benign, and the England openers fed gluttonously on tasty morsels. Rain clouds in the afternoon fuelled the bowlers, then the sun came out again and Vaughan and Kevin Pietersen fashioned a quick 50 partnership. They are chalk and cheese at the wicket: Pietersen busy, electric, Vaughan calmer, more elegant. Somehow their liaison didn't hint at permanence. But few have in this extraordinary, shifting contest. ●SH

AUSTRALIA ALL REARGUARD ACTION

Martin Johnson

It happened in golf, when the Ryder Cup became so one-sided that Great Britain and Ireland expanded into Europe, and without wishing to sound too patronising, it might now be time for Australia to consider teaming up with a few close neighbours. New Zealand probably wouldn't be averse to the idea, Papua New Guinea isn't all that far away, and who knows? Oceania versus England in 2007 could even turn out to be a decent contest.

Pure fantasy of course, and this Australian team are a long way from being beaten yet, but the days when they put their foot on an opponent's throat and kept it there may be over. If they put their feet anywhere at all yesterday it was about a yard over the front crease, and if either umpire was able to lift his drink after play last night, it wouldn't have been with the arm they used for signalling no-balls.

The one area in which Australia remain undisputed world champions is the frequency with which they pat each other's bottoms, so often in fact that Channel 4 have done well to persuade the television watchdog to allow them to transmit their live pictures before the nine o'clock watershed.

There was a time when an Australian bowler began worrying about a team-mate getting fresh after he'd done something very good, like taking a wicket, but as that happens less and less frequently, he's now more concerned about the consoling pat on the bum when the ball is being retrieved from the second tier of the pavilion.

The risk of having your team-mates get a bit touchy-feely also rises sharply when you're making your debut, so with Shaun Tait achieving all three requirements yesterday – pulling on the Baggy Green cap for the first time, bowling some dross and also taking a couple of wickets – he must have wished he'd taken the field with a Wisden Cricketers' Almanack stuffed down the back of his trousers.

Tait had been compared to Jeff Thomson before the game, and for a while it looked as though he'd emulate the great man in at least one area, given that Tommo's bowling analysis on his Australian Test debut was nought for 110 against Pakistan at the Melbourne Cricket Ground.

Thomson once gave a television interview in which – in terms of expressing the pleasure it gave him to puncture the flesh of an opposition batsman – he came across like Hannibal Lecter. Tait, similarly, spoke of how it was part of his job to "hit" a batsman (although he did qualify this by stating that it wasn't his intention to kill anyone) and his confidence in this area had already been boosted by cutting open a Northamptonshire player's head earlier in the week.

However, Tait's understandably nervous opening burst was far too innocuous to raise the possibility of any more blood on the pitch, and the only serious danger of a spillage of human body fluid out there would have been the saliva from England's opening batsmen.

To his credit, Tait produced a particularly good delivery to get rid of Marcus Trescothick, whose innings of 65 took him past Trevor Bailey's record of 875 runs against Australia without actually scoring a century. The problem with Bailey reaching a century was whether you'd still be alive by the time he made it, which is not something you could ever say about Trescothick.

Trescothick's figures alone illuminate the way Test cricket has changed, especially in what used to be a sedate first session of a match. When the lunch gong sounded yesterday he'd scored 62, and hit eight fours and a six. This was positively pedestrian compared to his first-session statistics from Edgbaston (77 runs, 13 fours and two sixes) and to put those figures into contest, Geoffrey Boycott's bench mark as an opening Test-match batsman was 30 runs per session.

There are many reasons why England have at last managed to start competing with Australia after all these years, not least by taking up their own mantle of fast scoring, and you can throw in central contracts, the academy, and even dyed hair if you like. But the reason they're now starting to forge ahead, or at least appearing to, is the fact that no matter what you do – hit a six, take a wicket, drop a catch – you don't have to worry that 10 other blokes are going to run up and pat you on the behind. As a recipe for success, it's the bottom line. ●**MJ**

Day 2
Trent Bridge
England hunt down victory

Matthew Hoggard cast aside his role as occasional bowler in this series to reduce Australia to tatters at Trent Bridge, with three wickets in his opening spell. Hoggard's strike, coming as it did after Andrew Flintoff had hit his maiden Ashes century, helped reduce Australia to 99 for five by the close of play, some 378 runs shy of the 477 England made in their first innings.

With Adam Gilchrist on strike first thing this morning, England have a way still to travel, especially as the pitch appears to hold few demons. Yet there is no escaping the impression that Australia are being crushed in this match, and there is little their bluff and bluster can do to prevent that or the Ashes being taken from them.

"It's been demanding mentally," admitted Gilchrist after play. "England are doing to us what we've been doing to other teams for years. They've got the best attack I've faced in my Test career. Working together and hunting in a pack.

"We have to believe we can get it right some time before the end of the series and do enough. What with missing the odd chance and umpiring decisions going against us, it feels like we're in a vicious circle."

Their batting predicament here, after an anaemic display by the bowlers, was again caused by their plethora of left-handers being vulnerable to England's combination of swingers, with some jitters from the others thrown in. Australia will point, with some justification, to the controversial nature of the lbws won against them (two came off the inside edge and one looked a tad high), but the way their batsmen had been playing the swinging ball, it was only really a matter of time before the alignment was perfect.

The idiosyncrasies of this ground, with its recently built stands, were always likely to help Hoggard's brand of swing, the type still found in the MCC's coaching manual. Yet after just 56 overs in the previous three Tests, he could easily have been rusty and flunked the exam.

His threat was not immediately apparent. As when England batted, the new ball went gunbarrel straight and it was not until his fourth over that any curves became apparent. Whether it was gathering cloud cover or the lacquer coming off the ball, the effect was like a tranquilliser, rendering Matthew Hayden statuesque in his attempt to counter it – one that soon proved futile as he fell over an in-swinger and was lbw.

If there could be no complaints about that one, Ricky Ponting was less happy to trudge back to the pavilion when Jones hustled one past his forward prod. Channel 4's snickometer suggested his displeasure was well-founded.

In the next over, Damien Martyn also got a

On his knees:
Michael Kasprowicz finally dismisses Geraint Jones for 85, but this is his only wicket of a listless performance. He would be dropped for the Oval.

Left: Ricky Ponting digests his first-innings lbw decision, handed out despite a hint of an inside edge

bad decision, when Hoggard nipped one back, off inside edge on to pad. That bat-pad combination proved good enough for Justin Langer soon after, but he was caught at short leg by Ian Bell rather than fired out lbw by umpire Aleem Dar.

Hoggard might have added to his tally had Bell not dropped Simon Katich first ball, though the chance was a sharp one for short-leg. After that let-off Katich batted freely, adding 41 with Michael Clarke. Yet just as Australia were beginning to lose that put-upon look, Clarke was beaten for pace by Stephen Harmison to become the fourth lbw victim just before the close.

The secret to putting Australia under pressure is to have big runs on the board. There was no guarantee of this, especially when Brett Lee got rid of Pietersen in the fifth over of the morning. Yet enter Flintoff and Geraint Jones, the mighty and the mouse combination, to keep England's growing sense of destiny on course.

Flintoff's 102 off 132 balls turned him into a pukka all-rounder for the first time in his Test career, at least with regard to the traditional yardstick of possessing a batting average higher than the bowling one (33.35 to 32.77).

His no-nonsense demeanour marks him out as the people's hero, the kind of Englishman Voltaire found agreeable when he compared English society to a hogshead of ale: "Froth at the top, dregs at the bottom, but rather agreeable in the middle."

A favourite wherever he goes, he is not yet bound by the expectation to thrill his public every time he goes to the crease, at least not in the way he did at Edgbaston in the last Test. Yesterday he sheathed his broadsword and took out his bat, playing shots that even mortals might feel to be within their grasp. Apart from one six, casually swatted into the new stand off Shane Warne, he treated every ball on its merit, though that still left plenty to clatter to the boundary as Australia's bowlers strayed. Pity for England then that his first big forcing shot was his last, as Shaun Tait forced one past his mighty heave.

He did not venture alone, with Jones ably keeping him company as the pair added 177 for the sixth wicket, the highest stand of the series so far on either side, and one indicative of the gentle nature of the pitch and the erratic bowling on show. Australia only sent down

three no-balls yesterday (compared with 22 on Thursday). Yet by concentrating on the front line they forgot the line that goes with length, a basic requirement at Test level.

It was a fine effort from Jones, who made 85, not least because it was done in the back yard of the man he usurped as England's wicket-keeper, Nottinghamshire's Chris Read. His batting against Warne was particularly fine, especially on the back foot where he milked him through the covers. Indeed a first hundred against Australia looked certain until a rash shot against Kasprowicz ended with a return catch after the ball ballooned up off bat and pad.

With Jones gone, the last three wickets fell for 27 runs, with Warne taking the lot, including a stumping against Stephen Harmison that was pure slapstick. Although the tail wagged, another two runs would have made this the biggest England total since they last held the Ashes.

That it was not, losing out to the 478 for nine made at Edgbaston in 1997, will not stop the soothsayers from nodding sagely. The evidence for regime change is stacking up, with Australia's empire looking distinctly like a former one. ●DP

Day 2 Scoreboard

ENGLAND/FIRST INNINGS		M	B	4	6
K P Pietersen c Gilchrist b Lee	45	130	108	6	0
A Flintoff lbw b Tait	102	200	132	14	1
+G O Jones c & b Kasprowicz	85	204	149	8	0
A F Giles lbw b Warne	15	45	35	3	0
M J Hoggard c Gilchrist b Warne	10	45	28	1	0
S J Harmison st Gilchrist b Warne	2	7	6	0	0
S P Jones not out	15	32	27	3	0

Extras (b 1, lb 15, w 1, nb 25)	42
Total (123.1 overs, 510 mins)	477

FALL OF WICKETS: 5-241 (Pietersen 64.1); 6-418 (Flintoff 103.2); 7-450 (G Jones 112.5); 8-450 (Giles 113.1); 9- 454 (Harmison 115.1); 10-477 (Hoggard 123.1)

BOWLING: Lee 32-2-131-1 (nb 1, 5-0-23-1, 8-0-31-0, 3-1-2-0); Kasprowicz 32-3-122-1 (nb 2, 5-0-21-0, 4-1-20-0, 5-0-25-1); Tait 24-4-97-3 (3-0-21-0, 7-3-14-1); Warne 29.1-4-102-4 (10-0-39-0, 7-1-22-0, 6.1-2-18-3)

AUSTRALIA/FIRST INNINGS		M	B	4	6
J L Langer c Bell b Hoggard	27	95	59	5	0
M L Hayden lbw b Hoggard	7	41	27	1	0
*R T Ponting lbw b S P Jones	1	6	6	0	0
D R Martyn lbw b Hoggard	1	3	3	0	0
M J Clarke lbw b Harmison	36	91	53	5	0
S M Katich not out	20	50	41	2	0

Extras (lb 1, nb 6)	7
Total (5 wkts, 30.3 overs, 147 mins)	99

FALL OF WICKETS: 1-20 (Hayden 9.3); 2-21 (Ponting 10.3); 3-22 (Martyn 11.1); 4-58 (Langer 19.3); 5-99 (Clarke 30.3).

BOWLING: Harmison 5.3-1-25-1 (nb 2, 3-1-13-0, 2.3-0-12-1); Hoggard 11-3-32-3 (nb 1, one spell); S P Jones 9-3-22-1 (5-1-12-1, 4-2-10-0); Flintoff 5-0-19-0 (nb3, one spell)

Leviathan unbound: Andrew Flintoff had been all things to all men in this Ashes series – a Bothamesque hitter, a ferocious fast bowler, and a public figurehead. Now he showed his credentials as a pukka top-order batsman, stroking a glorious century to under-pin England's first innings

**Nerve-jangling:
Brett Lee and friends
enjoy the dismissal of
Ian Bell, caught in the
deep as England faltered
in their victory chase**

Days 3 & 4
Trent Bridge
England shred a nation's nerves

If England really are the new Australia, they have certainly inherited the jitters the world champions used to show chasing small totals. Set only 129 to win, Michael Vaughan's side spluttered their way to victory by three wickets and the precious 2-1 lead going into the final Test that surely makes them favourites to win the Ashes and one of the most compelling series of all time.

The tension, just as it has been in the previous two Tests, was spine-tingling and a wave of sweet relief washed over Trent Bridge at 6.30 when Ashley Giles clipped the winning runs through midwicket. Mind you, Vaughan and his men would have happily wracked their nerves all over again just to take a lead into the final Test at the Oval in 10 days' time, a match now set for epic status.

While the frayed nerves of those here as well as the millions glued to TV sets will take a while to calm, England will not care a jot about how they crossed the line – only that victory was theirs.

It did not always seem certain during a riveting final session of play as Shane Warne and Brett Lee, who touched 95 mph, huffed and puffed their way to exhuming any lingering doubts in England's psyche. It proved a gargantuan duel, too, the seeds of disbelief following the first few wickets growing to Redwood proportions by the time Andrew Flintoff was sixth out, clean bowled by Lee.

With Geraint Jones following soon after, the victim of the mounting pressure as he skied a drive to long off, England were 116 for seven and still 13 short of victory. Yet salvation was at hand in the form of bowlers Ashley Giles and Matthew Hoggard.

Unlike some of their predecessors in the batting order, Giles and Hoggard played the percentages and waited for the bad ball. When they came, in the form of a full toss from Lee to Hoggard, and a leg-stump half-volley from Warne to Giles, both were composed enough to put them away.

For once a tense endgame didn't look likely. Indeed, with England dismissing Australia for 387, their highest total of the series so far, and the pitch still playing well, Vaughan's men looked as if they might achieve what they had been threatening to do since losing the first Test at Lord's – and give the Aussies a good towelling. Yet with Ricky Ponting's side unable

to say die, at least not yet, the drama began to wind its way to another tortuous resolution.

England's batsmen, no doubt seduced by a four-day finish, made it hard for themselves. What no doubt began as positive intent quickly began to look like blind panic as top-order batsmen played shots more appropriate to a lost cause than a nailed-on win.

Having marshalled his side well in the field, especially after being a bowler down following Simon Jones' ankle injury on Saturday, Vaughan was as culpable as anyone when he tried to work Warne through midwicket from out of the rough only to edge to slip. Perhaps 173 overs in the field took its toll, but it was a very risky shot given the meagre reward (two runs at most) it might have brought.

Modern batsmen appear reticent to play the percentages any more. Whether this is boredom, or lack of confidence over their defensive technique, it appears that dot balls are for cissies. Even that arch blocker, Ian Bell, was lured into an indiscreet shot, though in his case nerves rather than machismo probably betrayed him as he top-edged his hook off Lee to Michael Kasprowicz at long leg.

His dismissal, following that of Strauss, caught by Michael Clarke off Warne at leg slip after a television replay confirmed the catch carried, left England 57 for four and threatened to undo all the sterling work of the bowlers, who had been forced to dig deep after making Australia follow on on Saturday afternoon.

Fortunately, a colossus called Andrew Flintoff, the man of the match, joined the hyperactive Kevin Pietersen to staunch the haemorrhage with a stand of 46 for the fifth wicket. The pair played sensibly, though that did not mean the emotions were calmed for Warne was putting every ounce of torque into stopping England's march. With the first three in England's line-up falling to him, the addition of Jones saw him reach his 50th Test victim for the year.

His efforts kept England's big-hitting duo in check, though Flintoff managed to loft him for a four over wide long on. Yet just as the pair looked to have the game sealed, Pietersen wafted at Lee and was caught behind. The wicket visibly lifted the pace bowler, who then produced the ball of the day, a vicious nip-backer at 93 mph, to knock back Flintoff's off peg.

Ahead at last:
Michael Vaughan enjoys the feeling of being the first England captain to take a lead over Australia since Mike Atherton in 1997

At this stage, Ponting was calling huddles after every wicket, no doubt reminding his team what India had done to Australia in Calcutta four years ago, overcoming the disadvantage of following on to win the match.

Invoking painful memories can often have a powerful effect and old England might have folded. But Vaughan and Duncan Fletcher have built a team not only hungry for success but who back themselves fully, as Giles and Hoggard showed when they steered the uncertain ship home.

According to Steve Waugh, in an interview yesterday on Radio Five Live, Australia have lost that hunger. He also pointed out that yesterday's pre-lunch session was the biggest of the series, though all seem to have taken on massive proportions since the opening match at Lord's. Waugh might have been proved right had Australia, 222 for four overnight and 27 runs light of making England bat again, managed to reach lunch without losing a wicket. They almost did it, too, until Clarke wafted at Hoggard and was caught behind.

Without Jones, who will continue to receive treatment for the anterior impingement to his right ankle, England's bowlers were forced to toil, especially by Simon Katich, whose fine innings was ended by yet another dubious lbw, this time courtesy of Aleem Dar.

A merry spree by Warne and a more circumspect knock by Lee meant England would have to sweat a bit to win, though few predicted the buckets that were finally shed en route to yesterday's potentially epoch-making victory.

It is not the first time England have enjoyed a one-match advantage in an Ashes series since they last held the urn 18 years ago, but it is the first time they hold one with the realistic possibility of winning the big prize, something England's women managed to achieve on Saturday.

To follow suit, the men will have to extend, or hold on to their lead under the big gasometer of SE11. Be there if you can. ●DP

4th Test Scoreboard

CLOSE DAY 1: England 229-4 (60 overs, Pietersen 33, Flintoff 8)
CLOSE DAY 2: Australia 99-5 (30.3 overs, Katich 20)
CLOSE DAY 3: Australia (2nd) 222-4 (67 overs, Clarke 39, Katich 24)

ENGLAND/FIRST INNINGS		M	B	4	6
M E Trescothick b Tait	65	138	111	8	1
A J Strauss c Hayden b Warne	35	99	64	4	0
*M P Vaughan c Gilchrist b Ponting	58	145	99	9	0
I R Bell c Gilchrist b Tait	3	13	5	0	0
K P Pietersen c Gilchrist b Lee	45	130	108	6	0
A Flintoff lbw b Tait	102	200	132	14	1
+G O Jones c & b Kasprowicz	85	204	149	8	0
A F Giles lbw b Warne	15	45	35	3	0
M J Hoggard c Gilchrist b Warne	10	45	28	1	0
S J Harmison st Gilchrist b Warne	2	7	6	0	0
S P Jones not out	15	32	27	3	0
Extras (b 1, lb 15, w 1, nb 25)	42				
Total (123.1 overs, 510 mins)	477				

FALL OF WICKETS: 1-105 (Strauss 21.4 overs); **2-137** (Trescothick 30.5) **3-146** (Bell 34.1); **4-213** (Vaughan 55.2); **5-241** (Pietersen 64.1); **6-418** (Flintoff 103.2); **7-450** (G Jones 112.5); **8-450** (Giles 113.1); **9-454** (Harmison 115.1); **10-477** (Hoggard 123.1)
BOWLING: Lee 32-2-131-1 (nb 8, 5-1-16-0, 4-0-28-0, 7-0-31-0, 5-0-23-1, 8-0-31-0, 3-1-2-0); **Kasprowicz** 32-3-122-1 (nb 13, 8-0-37-0, 10-1-19-0, 5-0-21-0, 4-1-20-0, 5-0-25-1); **Tait** 24-4-97-3 (nb 4, 5-0-26-0, 6-1-23-2, 3-0-13-0, 3-0-21-0, 7-3-14-1); **Warne** 29.1-4-102-4 (5-1-22-1, 1-0-1-0, 10-0-39-0, 7-1-22-0, 6.1-2-18-3); **Ponting** 6-2-9-1 (w 1, one spell)

AUSTRALIA/FIRST INNINGS		M	B	4	6
J L Langer c Bell b Hoggard	27	95	59	5	0
M L Hayden lbw b Hoggard	7	41	27	1	0
*R T Ponting lbw b S P Jones	1	6	6	0	0
D R Martyn lbw b Hoggard	1	3	3	0	0
M J Clarke lbw b Harmison	36	91	53	5	0
S M Katich c Strauss b S P Jones	45	90	66	7	0
+A C Gilchrist c Strauss b Flintoff	27	59	36	3	1
S K Warne c Bell b S P Jones	0	1	1	0	0
B Lee c Bell b S P Jones	47	47	44	5	3
M S Kasprowicz b S P Jones	5	7	6	1	0
S W Tait not out	3	23	9	0	0
Extras (lb 2, w 1, nb 16)	19				
Total (49.1 overs, 242 mins)	218				

FALL OF WICKETS: 1-20 (Hayden 9.3); **2-21** (Ponting 10.3); **3-22** (Martyn 11.1); **4-58** (Langer 19.3); **5-99** (Clarke 30.3); **6-157** (Katich 39.2); **7-157** (Warne 39.3); **8-163** (Gilchrist 42.2); **9-175** (Kasprowicz 43.2); **10-218** (Lee 49.1)
BOWLING: Harmison 9-1-48-1 (nb 3, 3-1-13-0, 2.3-0-12-1, 0.3-0-1-0, 3-0-22-0); **Hoggard** 15-3-70-3 (nb 4, 11-3-32-3, 4-0-38-0); **S P Jones** 14.1-4-44-5 (nb 1, 5-1-12-1, 4-2-10-0, 5.1-1-22-4); **Flintoff** 11-1-54-1 (nb 8, w1, 5-0-19-0, 6-1-35-1)

AUSTRALIA/SECOND INNINGS (Following on)		M	B	4	6
J L Langer c Bell b Giles	61	150	112	8	0
M L Hayden c Giles b Flintoff	26	58	41	4	0
*R T Ponting run out (G J Pratt, sub)	48	135	89	3	1
D R Martyn c G O Jones b Flintoff	13	55	30	1	0
M J Clarke c G O Jones b Hoggard	56	210	170	6	0
S M Katich lbw b Harmison	59	261	183	4	0
+A C Gilchrist lbw b Hoggard	11	20	11	2	0
S K Warne st G O Jones b Giles	45	62	42	5	2
B Lee not out	26	74	39	3	0
M S Kasprowicz c G O Jones b Harmison	19	28	26	1	0
S W Tait b Harmison	4	21	16	1	0
Extras (b 1, lb 4, nb 14)	19				
Total (124 overs, 550 mins)	387				

FALL OF WICKETS: 1-50 (Hayden 13.4); **2-129** (Langer 34.0); **3-155** (Ponting 44.1); **4-161** (Martyn 46.1); **5-261** (Clarke 94.2); **6-277** (Gilchrist 98.5); **7-314** (Katich 119.2); **8-342** (Warne 112.3); **9-373** (Kasprowicz 119.2); **10-387** (Tait 124.0)
BOWLING: Hoggard 27-7-72-2 (nb 1, 7-2-25-0, 6-3-11-0, 2-0-8-0, 12-2-28-2); **S P Jones** 4-0-15-0 (2-0-8-0, 2-0-7-0); **Harmison** 30-5-93-3 (nb 1, 4-1-15-0, 7-0-29-0, 4-1-10-0, 2-0-7-0, 4-1-3-0, 9-2-29-3); **Flintoff** 29-4-83-2 (nb 9, 7-2-23-1, 3-1-6-1, 3-0-4-0, 5-0-8-0, 8-1-33-0, 3-0-9-0); **Giles** 28-3-107-2 (9-0-34-1, 5-0-10-0, 3-1-18-0, 6-2-9-0, 5-0-36-1); **Bell** 6-2-12-0 (nb 3, 3-0-11-0, 3-2-1-0)

ENGLAND/SECOND INNINGS		M	B	4	6
M E Trescothick c Ponting b Warne	27	23	22	4	0
A J Strauss c Clarke b Warne	23	68	37	3	0
*M P Vaughan c Hayden b Warne	0	8	6	0	0
I R Bell c Kasprowicz b Lee	3	37	20	0	0
K P Pietersen c Gilchrist b Lee	23	48	34	3	0
A Flintoff b Lee	26	62	34	3	0
+G O Jones c Kasprowicz b Warne	3	8	13	0	0
A F Giles not out	7	13	17	0	0
M J Hoggard not out	8	20	13	1	0
Extras (lb 4, nb 5)	9				
Total (7 wkts, 31.5 overs, 168 mins)	129				

FALL OF WICKETS: 1-32 (Trescothick 5.1); **2-36** (Vaughan 7.1); **3-57** (Strauss 13.5); **4-57** (Bell 14.1); 5-103 (Pietersen 24.1); 6-111 (Flintoff 26.4); **7-116** (G Jones 28.0).
BOWLING: Lee 12-0-51-3 (nb 5, 8-0-35-1, 4-0-16-2); **Kasprowicz** 2-0-19-0 (one spell); **Warne** 13.5-2-31-4 (one spell); **Tait** 4-0-24-0 (one spell)
UMPIRES: Aleem Dar (Pakistan) & **S A Bucknor** (West Indies)
ENGLAND won by 3 wickets, MATCH AWARD: A Flintoff

Australia paying heavy price for arrogance

4th Test comment
Simon Hughes

The Australians are suffering from shock. Not the shock of losing the fourth Test. It is more than that. It is the shock of being constantly challenged on a cricket field like they've been never been challenged before. By the English, moreover, the cricket team whose collective knees buckle at the mention of the word 'Ashes'.

Now they are under siege, as they perceive it: from England, the press, the public, the umpires, the match referees. Everyone and everything is against them, even the Almighty (injuries, losing crucial tosses) and, with the exception of one or two, notably Shane Warne and Brett Lee, they don't know how to respond.

They don't know how to respond because they didn't remotely expect it. As this series has unfolded, it has become abundantly clear that they totally underestimated their opponents. They arrived with a Plan A, to batter the bowlers and suffocate the batsmen to death, and that was it. There was no contingency for potential hurdles, no Plan B.

No one in the Australian camp read the signs from last September onwards that this England were not like the ones before, who would cower in a corner at the first sight of Matthew Hayden's rippling physique at the crease or Warne twirling the ball menacingly in his fingers.

They didn't really acknowledge that some of this England team were serious adversaries. Michael Vaughan was the only one they respected. They wrote off that one-day win at Edgbaston in the semi-final of the Champions Trophy as a flash in the pan.

Clearly, none of the reports of that match alerted Australians to the fissures appearing in their once impregnable team or the potential for the burgeoning English side to pour through them. Or if they did, key influences chose to ignore them.

Channel 9, long time home of Australian cricket, did not bother to bid for the home rights to this series, not recognising it as a contest worthy of disrupting their evening schedules (the minority SBS station filched them instead and have achieved unprecedented ratings.) Australia arranged a light schedule between Tests, where, on previous tours, there had been a full programme. Ex-Australian players dismissed England's chances out of hand, Australian news agencies sent the bare minimum of reporters, there was no sense that the Ashes was going to be anything other than a routine extermination of English endeavour.

This attitude was prevalent in the team right through the height of summer. They refused to see the obvious deterioration in Jason Gillespie's bowling, or the vulnerability of Hayden's batting. Mike Hussey, their most consistent and resourceful batsman in the one-day series, was released at the end of it to play for Durham. Shane Watson, a talented all-rounder who could have provided another bowling option in the Tests, was similarly let go, to Hampshire. Four bowlers had always been ample in the past. Why would they need five now?

At a sponsors' event before the first Test, I suggested to two Australian selectors – Merv Hughes and David Boon – that England could win the series. They looked at me with amusement and sympathy, concluding I must be slightly mad. "But who are going to get your runs and wickets?" Hughes challenged. "Well, who are going to get yours?" I should have replied.

The players remained unconvinced of England's potency right up to the beginning of the second Test. England might have made a few sparks fly, they conceded. But would they be able to sustain this through a five-Test series. Nah mate. Not a XXXX of a chance. England's heavy defeat at Lord's did nothing to dispel that notion.

Ricky Ponting and Glenn McGrath talked of a 5-0 whitewash, and the Australians had a casual week afterwards. Rain affected the match at Worcester, before the second Test at Edgbaston. Ponting's decision to field first there, even after the freak injury to McGrath, indicated how little they respected England with the exception, perhaps, of Warne, who at least had an inkling of what might come.

That lack of respect has bitten them, and bitten them hard. They have limped through the last three Tests, clinging to the only thing they know – confrontation, meeting the enemy head on. There have been few attempts to adapt their strategies in the on-going struggle. Many of the top order have consistently lost their wickets in similar ways, illustrating the discipline of the England bowlers to execute their plans, and the inflexibility of the batsmen's thinking. Even now, some of them stand at the wicket looking perplexed, unable to comprehend the failure of their tried and trusted method. Moderate bowling attacks round the world have suckered them into a false sense of security.

Credit, of course, is due to England for their sustained excellence, particularly from the bowlers. All the Australians now concede that, armed with an older ball, Andrew Flintoff poses an unprecedented threat, especially to left-handers. They find his combination of hostile pace, an awkward angle from round the wicket, persistence and significant movement allied to excellent control very difficult to deal with. Courtney Walsh, whose bowling Flintoff's most closely resembles, was never as effective round the wicket, or as consistently fast.

The embodiment of this threat was Flintoff's over to Gilchrist after lunch on Sunday at Trent Bridge. Realising that this serious affliction would not subside, Gilchrist at last retaliated. Like a wounded animal making a last dash for freedom, he carved two audacious boundaries off the over. Flintoff smiled in acknowledgment, whistled a ball past Gilchrist's edge, then watched as Australia's erstwhile dasher walked in front of a Hoggard delivery in the next over and was lbw.

The Australians know what they're up against now. Is it too late? Ponting's irascibility at Trent Bridge suggests that he thinks it is, almost. They're backed into a corner. But this beast still has lethal claws and now that England have wounds of their own, this is going to be a fight to the death. ●SH

Out of the shadows: Matthew Hoggard had been a bit-part player for the first three Tests, but rose to answer England's call with five wickets at Trent Bridge. Here he dismisses Michael Clarke on the fourth afternoon

Team bonding:
England get to know
each other better on the
dressing-room balcony
after their pulsating win

Flintoff fired up for final act

4th Test afterword
Derek Pringle

The seven tortuous steps England took at Trent Bridge might not have led to heaven had Brett Lee got his first ball to Matthew Hoggard swinging in like the one that castled Andrew Flintoff. Lee was straining every sinew to reach maximum velocity as Australia sensed an improbable get-out clause, a fearsome proposition for most batsmen let alone a tailender who reckons he never saw it.

"Bizarrely, I was very confident," said Hoggard the day after England took a 2-1 lead in the Ashes. "It was surreal. Every thing seemed to be in slow motion once I crossed the boundary rope – even Brett Lee. At least he did after the first ball, which I didn't really see. After I survived that one I thought, here we go."

England still needed 13 more runs following the demise of Geraint Jones, England's last recognised batsman. With only three wickets in hand, it was collywobbles time for the third Test in a row, at least until Hoggard, with his stolid companion Ashley Giles, shepherded England home.

If they were experiencing the same neurotic twitches and palpitations the rest of us had to endure through that final hour in Nottingham, they seemed to have gone by the time the pair reached the crease. "When you're waiting in the dressing room you can't hold a bat you're so tense," Giles admitted. "It's like, what do I do with this thing. I couldn't even feel my legs. But once you get out there instinct takes over and you just get on with it."

With Lee at one end and Shane Warne the other, the threat was clear and ever-present. Yet Giles seemed to take Warne, and Hoggard Lee, though neither admits to being totally in control.

"Whether it's Hoggy or Michael Vaughan facing, if Lee gets one of those inswingers right, and in the blockhole, it's going to be tricky to keep out," Giles said. "Yet Hoggy played him brilliantly, including that brilliant cover-drive for four."

With even Australia choking in the past chasing small totals, England were not exactly immune. That they eventually prevailed reveals much about the depth of character and belief within the side, two factors that have come to the fore under Vaughan's captaincy.

"It's certainly very different now than when I and Freddie Flintoff began our England careers in 1998," Giles said. "The set-up was very disjointed back then and I didn't really understand my role in the side.

"Now that we have central contracts, we're basically another county team – we play that much cricket together that we know each other that well. We develop as cricketers together, too. Obviously Freddie has come further than I have, but it's great that I've been there with him and seen him develop into the best cricketer in the world."

As befitting a man dominating the series, Flintoff was centre stage in all the team photos plastered over the front pages of yesterday's newspapers, looking as demented as Jack Nicholson during his "Heeeere's Johnny" scene in The Shining. It is the all-rounder's first Ashes series and his contribution since Lord's has been tectonic, more an unstoppable force of nature than a smashing lad who once bowled and batted a bit for Lancashire. "I'm pinching myself at times," Flintoff confessed yesterday.

"I've always wanted to play in an Ashes series and I've waited and waited to play in one and I just can't believe how good it actually is."

"I've never felt like this before playing cricket. When I got out on Sunday I sat up in the dressing room and was nearly sick. It was unbelievable, and I got quite emotional at the end when Ashley knocked the winning runs off. We've got one more game left at the Oval and I've got one more game in me, hopefully, and a few more overs and a few more runs."

Australia will talk up the defeat as another instance where they almost snatched victory after being comprehensively outplayed for most of the match. Yet this was England showing nerves rather than an Australian renaissance, though that may come if Glenn McGrath can take his form from Lord's, where he took nine wickets, to the Oval showdown in nine days' time.

One of their problems is that they cannot stop griping about substitute fielders, dodgy umpiring decisions and bad luck, despite their captain, Ricky Ponting, saying they must. In fact Ponting appears to be the worst offender, whinging again yesterday to a Melbourne radio station about Duncan Fletcher's use of athletic fielders not in England's original squad.

Certainly, the sense of injustice is running deep, as Ponting revealed when he asked Hoggard whether he had hit the ball after Lee appealed for an lbw during the high drama of Sunday evening. The ball, which hit Hoggard's foot, would have missed leg-stump, though apparently umpire Steve Bucknor told Lee he had rejected the appeal because he felt the batsman had hit it.

Quite why Ponting had to get involved, other than confirm his growing sense of paranoia, is not immediately apparent. It could be that he is using these perceived slights to stoke the ire that once came naturally to him and his team and which many observers feel has gone missing in action this summer. If it is, the final Test at the Oval could be an even hotter ticket than it already is. ●DP

Ponting keeps up tirade over substitutes

4th Test review
Simon Briggs

Ricky Ponting, Australia's captain, yesterday returned to the same emotive issue that cost him 75 per cent of his Trent Bridge match fee.

In an interview with a Melbourne radio station, Ponting described England's use of fielding substitutes as "an absolute disgrace".

Just two days after being charged with bringing the game into disrepute, Ponting is a brave man to fire such criticism at his opponents.

Ranjan Madugalle, the ICC match referee, has chaired several discussions on the subject this summer without feeling the need to take direct action. If he happened to find Ponting's words objectionable, Madugalle could charge him again under the ICC playing code, which demands that players make no "inappropriate criticism" of the opposition.

As Ashes rows go, fielding subs may seem a little dry compared with the Bodyline tour of 1932-33, when England's vindictive bowling tactics provoked an international incident. Yet this obscure point of order is fast becoming the biggest flashpoint of the series so far.

Ambushed by a resurgent England, the Australians have focused their anxiety on a variety of peripheral issues. They have complained about England's aggressive throwing in the field – which they seemed to find as threatening as Harold Larwood's bodyline bowling – not to mention the team's lack of sympathy when Ponting was clonked on the head by Steve Harmison on the first morning of the series. And they reckon Poms whinge.

Australia's latest objection is that England keep sending their bowlers off the field and replacing them with subs. Not just any subs, mind you, but fielding specialists who move like greyhounds and hit the target as accurately as a spitting cobra.

"I think it's an absolute disgrace the spirit of the game is being treated like that," Ponting said. "It is within the rules, it's just not within the spirit of the game which we are trying to uphold."

As he left the field after being run out by Gary Pratt's lithe pick-up and throw, Ponting could not resist firing a tirade in the direction of the England dressing room. In the interview, he explained how the incident had escalated when he walked through the pavilion gate and saw England coach Duncan Fletcher standing on the balcony and smiling.

"Fletcher has known right the way through the summer this is something we haven't been happy with, but it's continued," Ponting said. "He knows it's something that has got under our skins and I've had enough of it, and I let him know that, and most of his players too."

Ponting believes the game should be played by the men selected for the match. If one side uses home advantage to call up slick substitutes, that tilts the playing field in their favour. But home advantage has always been a factor in cricket, as in any sport. As former captain Steve Waugh said at the weekend, Australia have not been averse to using the odd supersub in their own back yard.

While Ponting claims that England's bowlers are going off the field for a massage to help them loosen up before they start their spells, the home camp say they are simply visiting the toilet and changing their shirts. A player uses just as much energy running up and down the stairs to the dressing room, they argue, as he would standing at fine leg. And in any case, didn't Michael Clarke stay off the field for three whole days at Old Trafford before batting without a runner in the second innings?

The use of fielding substitutes is clearly a touchy subject with players and administrators around the world. A press release from the International Cricket Council yesterday admitted that discussions had begun over "clarifying the role of the 12th man". Comments have been invited from both the Test captains and the umpiring panel, with a view to a possible rule change in October.

England have certainly become a little more ruthless in using home advantage since the days when they offered visiting teams a coin-toss to decide which make of cricket ball to play with. Yet none of these issues would ever have surfaced here if Australia were carrying all before them as usual. ●SB

Warne left stumped by his rotten luck

4th Test review
Martin Johnson

It's generally accepted that Australia have not had their fair share of good fortune in this series, and you can't get much more unlucky than Shane Warne was yesterday. "Stumped Jones?" No wonder he left the field shaking his head. If you were to compile a list of unlikely entries in a scorer's book, it would be right up there alongside "bowled Strauss" or "caught Pietersen."

Those who say you make your own luck in sport could point to the fact that, in the midst of what ought to have been a dogged rearguard action, Warne was halfway down the pitch waving his bat at thin air. However, on all the available evidence, Warne was entitled to believe that, with Geraint Jones behind him, halfway down the pitch was just about the safest place to bat.

But for two more weekend additions to a summer of gaffes, England would have conceded 47 runs fewer than they did, and the coronary-inducing potential for making a total horlicks of their fourth innings target would have been reduced to almost nil. Watching England staggering, rather than sailing, across the winning line, ought to have made the selectors realise that the Ashes can still be lost as long as Jones remains a missed stumping waiting to happen.

Even those who say his batting makes up for his wicketkeeping might have been reviewing that opinion last night. Just when he had a chance to steer England calmly into harbour, Jones pranced down the pitch to Warne and spooned a catch to mid off. Cool head in a crisis? You could have boiled a kettle on it.

Jones is a long way from being the first wicketkeeper to break into a Test side on the strength of his batting, but he shows absolutely no sign of being able to turn himself – like Rodney Marsh, Ian Healy, Jim Parks, and Alec Stewart – into a highly proficient stumper. Even when he was known as 'Iron Gloves', Marsh's gauntlets were like a pair of goose-down duvets by comparison.

Jones drops enough of his own catches to make you shudder, never mind dropping other people's, as he did yesterday when he dived right across first slip. However, it wasn't in the same league as his missed stumping on Saturday, when Jones spent so long juggling with what appeared to be a live electric eel that Michael Clarke could have had the turning circle of the Queen Mary and still made it back.

What on earth was Andrew Strauss prattling on about in his Sunday newspaper column (on the back of Jones' first-innings 85) that he was "pleased to see Geraint silence the doubters". Spare us. Everyone knows Jones can bat – if he couldn't, he wouldn't even get a game for the country of his birth – Papua New Guinea – solely as a wicketkeeper.

After Ricky Ponting's outburst about English substitute fielders on Saturday, it is tempting to say that it's a bit rich for Australians to refer to Poms as whingers, and in any event, what were the batsmen doing trying to steal a single to Gary Pratt, a bloke they knew to be a high-class fielder? Ponting did apologise, presumably realising that there was more than one Pratt involved in his run out.

Among England's various plans for the Oval, it might be worth attempting to further upset the Australian captain by employing a substitute keeper along with their various substitute outfielders. The usual claim is that someone needs to go to the toilet, although this really doesn't hold water, so to speak, because wicketkeepers never appear to be affected in this way. If some of them have iron gloves, they've all got iron bladders, in which case Michael Vaughan might be overheard at breakfast during the final Test saying: "Come on Jonesey, have another flagon of orange juice".

There is nothing in the playing regulations to prevent England from using whoever they like as a substitute fielder. There is nothing in the small print to say he has to be English (they used a Danish player from the MCC groundstaff last summer) or even human. They could presumably put an octopus in the covers, although to make it blend in with modern fashion, it would have to take the field with a dyed blue tentacle and a pair of sunglasses.

Ponting has a point, though, and perhaps it would be fairer not only to allow the visiting captain to select anyone on the ground to take an absent fielder's place, but also make him stand wherever he chooses.

It would mean Ponting could make his selection from the Barmy Army enclosure, and demand the sub be placed at short leg without a helmet.

With any luck, by the end of a five Test series, they might have been reduced to a Barmy Platoon. ●MJ

England's pace assault stirs memories of the legendary West Indians

4th Test comment
Derek Pringle

Comparisons can sometimes help us to make sense of the bewildering world we live in, but this Ashes series has thrown them up like confetti following England's incredible performances since the Lord's Test.

Are Michael Vaughan's team the new Australia? Are Australia the old England? With Flintoff fired up for the final act, is Freddie the new Ian Botham? Is cricket the new football? All have been floated as people seek context for the rush of hyperbole cricket is attracting. Now there is another. Is England's fast-bowling quartet the equivalent of the West Indies of the 1980s, a period in which their dominance was absolute?

With Australia's batsmen looking so uncomfortable, it is a question worth asking. Apart from Matthew Hoggard's brisk medium pace, the other three in the equation, Flintoff, Stephen Harmison and Simon Jones, all have the unremitting pace of the great West Indies combos, probably best represented by Malcolm Marshall, Michael Holding, Joel Garner and Andy Roberts.

Others, like Courtney Walsh, Curtly Ambrose and Colin Croft, also played major parts during that period between 1980-95,

when the West Indies won 20 out of 29 series (none against Bangladesh or Zimbabwe) and drew the other nine.

Similarities exist in style and Harmison, with his gangling approach and fast arm, is almost pure Ambrose, though he lacks the latter's nagging accuracy and occasional strops. Once the cricket treadmill began to turn more quickly, Ambrose cut his pace to prolong his career.

Unlike Marshall and Holding, whose pure athleticism made them appear as silent assassins, Flintoff's snorting rhino charge to the crease does not disguise itself. You know it's going to be quick and that mistakes will either hurt you, or cost you your wicket.

At the moment Flintoff has the grim trio (at least for batsmen) of fast-bowler's assets – presence, hostility and accuracy. He also possesses an immense power that is transferred into the ball, which hits the pitch with enormous energy.

In that respect, and especially the way his stock ball is angled in at right-handers, his action is part Walsh and part Sylvester Clarke, the latter a huge, barrel-chested fast bowler from Barbados who terrorised entire teams during his nine years with Surrey. Clarke played only 11 Tests, mostly on flat decks in India and Pakistan, but there is a generation of county batsmen who know what Ricky Ponting's men are going through when big Freddie has his tail up.

Jones the Steam is less easily twinned, though his sudden improvement (as shown by his 18 wickets this series) has made England a far more potent force since their winter tour of South Africa. His muscular frame and rollicking approach have no obvious analogue among the fast bowlers in the great West Indies sides, though his ability to swing the ball, both conventionally and reverse, is something Roberts could do.

Roberts used to prevent batsmen from

seeing which side the shine was on as he ran in to bowl – something that would give them an advantage in predicting which way it would swing.

There is much cricket to be played before the comparison, if ever, becomes valid. Jones' record – 59 Test wickets at an average of 28.2 – is way off Roberts' 202 at 25.6 let alone the 376 wickets by Marshall or the incredible 519 taken by Walsh. Staying injury-free is the main prerequisite, and all of England, and Wales, will be hoping and praying Jones will now stay consistently fit for the next five years.

England's other bowlers don't match up on the figures either. Garner took his 259 Test wickets at 20.97, while Harmison's 137 have so far cost him 28.06 a wicket. You could argue that the disparity is due to the attacking mindset of today's batsmen, who score more readily than their counterparts 20 years ago. Perhaps, but the increased risk of losing their wicket should even out the average cost.

If there is a comparison, it is best made at the collective level. During the match at Trent Bridge, Adam Gilchrist spoke of the relentless nature of England's speed machine and how it places pressure on Australia's batsmen. Although protective equipment is better now, the constant physical threat of fast bowling wears down a batsman's resistance, something Graham Gooch had first-hand experience of.

"England don't quite have the physical intensity of the West Indies attacks, which were unique in that they had four express bowlers to bowl all day long if necessary," Gooch said. "But this is the most penetrative attack I've seen England field for over 20 years.

"In Flintoff they have the best fast bowler currently in world cricket. Apart from bowling fast, he hardly ever bowls a bad ball. That would win him the most valuable player award even before you consider his batting." ●DP

**5TH TEST MATCH
THE OVAL
08 – 12
SEPTEMBER**

THE ASHES SERIES 2005

McGrath can walk the walk

The Oval
Test preview
Derek Pringle

Not since the War Of Jenkins' Ear has so much been riding on one man's body part as that currently placed upon Glenn McGrath's dicky right elbow.

Jenkins lost his ear after years of boundary disputes between Britain and Spain in the early 18th century. Now, if recent claims are to be believed, nothing less than the Ashes rides upon the fortunes of McGrath's sore elbow and its willingness to allow its owner to send down at least 50 probing overs at the Oval some time between Thursday and next Monday.

The match contains potentially momentous outcomes for both sides should England, 2-1 up in the series, not lose. While joy would be unconfined for Michael Vaughan's team and the rest of the country at their first Ashes series win since 1987, Australia would have to cope with the unthinkable ignominy of relinquishing the urn after 18 years of monopoly. For a country predicated on sport, it is a terrifying thought and unknown territory for the 35-year-old McGrath and the rest of the Australian team.

The tall pace bowler, often called Pigeon by team-mates in reference to his skinny legs, certainly believes he can be the difference between Ashes surrender and their retention for a record ninth time. He has even said as much whenever prompted, which has been often as Australians begin to absorb the awful truth of their predicament with just one Test remaining.

If he has convinced himself of his readiness to thwart the Poms, he will also need to convince his captain. Yesterday, as just a handful of batsmen took the option to attend voluntary nets, Australia's selectors called up paceman Stuart Clark, currently playing for Middlesex, as cover. Unless subterfuge is in the air, McGrath is going to have to do more than carry a shopping bag down Oxford Street to prove his fitness.

Given his contemptuous predictions of a 5-0 whitewash after Australia's win in the first Test at Lord's, it is tempting to dismiss his latest spin of England's impending demise at the Oval as those of last year's bully still trying to cling to power. Yet, anyone with 513 Test wickets in the bag, and needing another seven to beat Courtney Walsh's record tally for pace bowlers of 519, has surely earned the right to believe his own propaganda.

The empirical evidence, that he is the difference between the two sides in this riveting series, also stacks up. When he has played this series, as at Lord's and Old Trafford, Australia won the first and drew the other. They have lost only when he has been absent, first with a sprained ankle at Edgbaston and then with a tender right elbow at Trent Bridge, though rain in Manchester and Ricky Ponting's rearguard century had a greater effect on securing the draw than he did.

His return for the biggest crunch match of recent times would certainly boost Australia's flagging morale. The tetchiness that McGrath often directs at batsmen in the middle – though mostly to gee himself up – has multiplied and been spilled over the boundary's edge. Ponting's rant at Duncan Fletcher about substitute fielders and Simon Katich's outburst at spectators after receiving a poor lbw decision, are all side vents to the pressure building inside the Australian dressing room.

England's batsmen should not quake even if he does play. Ian Bell's trenchant claims that England want him in the side, so Australia have no excuses when they lose, is not as barmy as it appears. McGrath has little match fitness to speak of in the last three weeks. Even a bowler of his calibre and experience needs to feel some rhythm when he bowls. It is rarely found in nets either, as Australia's generous no-ball tally reveals.

The pressure for him to deliver, as on players like Andrew Flintoff, will be enormous. Lucky for him he has the kind of simple, efficient and repeatable bowling action that can withstand the wobbling nerves.

Like so many of Australia's great sportsmen, he is a country boy with all the have-a-go wholesomeness that entails. His home town of Narromine in New South Wales is outback country, but like towns cut from similar fabric it has nurtured a perspective and honesty often lacking in those from urban areas.

Certainly McGrath never looks depressed, at least not over cricket. Last weekend he conducted his 12th man duties at Chelmsford with humour and dignity, when it would have been just as easy to sulk in the dressing room.

On song, McGrath is a bowler for all seasons and conditions. His slingshot wrist action, which adds at least a yard of pace to his arm speed, is the secret weapon that provides the bounce and seam movement with which he so often undoes his victims. His action, if not his intentions, is so pure that bio-mechanists and bowling coaches use it as the paragon upon which modern fast bowling is taught.

By regularly dismissing Brian Lara and Sachin Tendulkar throughout his career, McGrath has targeted the best current batsmen and won more often than not.

On Thursday at the Oval, elbow permitting, he will target England's Ashes ambitions – the one pigeon in that part of London capable of making a serious mess. ●DP

PRESSURE IS HAVING AN ANGRY NATION ON YOUR TAIL

Martin Johnson

Ashes fever is now so virulent that spectators at the fifth and final Test will probably turn up wearing surgical masks. However, Keith Miller, one of the great legends of Ashes cricket, once called upon his wartime experiences to invite a hyperventilating interviewer to put the entire concept of a stick and ball game into context. "Pressure," said Miller, "is having a Messerschmitt up your arse."

This may not, though, be enough to prevent the Australian cricket captain from wondering whether the wrong result might force him to reach for the pearl-handled revolver or, given the venue, stick his head inside one of the Oval gasometers. He may indeed have cause to recall Miller's airplane analogy next week, but only by leaving the queue for the Qantas flight for Sydney and heading instead for the Aeroflot check-in to Siberia.

Ricky Ponting will carry the can if Australia don't win at the Oval, as his is not a nation which embraces sporting failure – especially against this opposition – with a "c'est la vie" shrug of the shoulders. An entire generation of Australians has grown accustomed to breakfast table conversations along the lines of: "Anything in the paper today dear?" "Nah, the Poms lost again at cricket, but nothing you'd describe as news."

They're not quite as unforgiving as the Indians, who once pelted Ravi Shastri's house with stones after he was perceived to have scored too slowly in a World Cup match. However, even if Mrs Ponting may not feel the need for a precautionary flick through the double-glazing section of the Tasmanian Yellow Pages, she'd be as well – just in case things go badly – to look up the number of the Missing Persons Bureau.

Going into hiding would be a drastic step, but it's been done before, when Keith Murdoch, a New Zealand rugby union prop forward, was sent home early following an altercation with a hotel bouncer (who came off considerably worse) after the 1972 Wales v All Blacks international in Cardiff.

As reporters and television crews gathered in the arrivals hall at Auckland airport, the passengers disembarked with no sign of Murdoch. It turned out he'd got off in Australia and wasn't discovered until several years later working in a remote Outback mining town. The chances are, though, should Australia part company with the Ashes some time over the next five days, that Ponting will decide against taking up carpet weaving in Tashkent for a few years until the heat dies down. It doesn't happen too often, but when it does Australia has a fine tradition of dealing with sporting disaster. Namely, pretend it never happened.

When England last won the Ashes, so long ago now it was pre-Barmy Army, the series in Australia began with all manner of grisly predictions for Mike Gatting's team, whose form in the build-up to the series had the media in both camps wondering whether they were capable of lasting five days against the Toowoomba Girl Guides XI.

The host broadcaster, Channel Nine, gleefully interviewed their various fast bowlers, with vacant peroxide blonde presenters playfully urging them to go easy on the Poms in case the series produced a record number of "retired hurts". Well, they were half right. Evasive action was definitely required when the Australian pace attack was in full cry, but only among the spectators when Ian Botham was batting.

When it finally dawned on them that the cricket team barely capable of bowling a hoop downhill actually belonged to them, the Australian media wiped their hapless cricketers off the back pages and replaced them with Pat Cash and their victorious Davis Cup tennis team. It was still possible to find the cricket scores in the newspapers, but only with a magnifying glass.

Ergo, if the lead item on the Australian sports headlines at the end of this match involves someone from Wagga Wagga winning a welly-whanging tournament in Winnipeg, it will mean that England have regained the Ashes.

There is, of course, a match still to be won (or drawn), but so unremitting has the drama been that the nation has united in protest about Test cricket being removed from the terrestrial TV preservation list and sold off to satellite subscription.

It is hard to believe now, but not so long ago the most suitable outlet for broadcasting stirring England performances against Australia would have been the History Channel. ●MJ

Day 1
The Oval
England's grip on urn loosened by Warne

Teams

England	Australia
M E Trescothick	J L Langer
A J Strauss	M L Hayden
*M P Vaughan	*R T Ponting
I R Bell	D R Martyn
K P Pietersen	M J Clarke
A Flintoff	S M Katich
P D Collingwood	+A C Gilchrist
+G O Jones	S K Warne
A F Giles	B Lee
M J Hoggard	G D McGrath
S J Harmison	S W Tait

If England should get their hands on the Ashes urn for the first time in 16 years, the first feel should be given to Andrew Strauss. Australia are just shading this deciding match after Shane Warne took five wickets, but without Strauss's majestic 129, England's prospects of not losing here would be far bleaker.

Strauss was seventh man out, caught at silly point off pad then bat, after being worn down by Warne's enigma variations. With England's extra batsman Paul Collingwood following soon after, the job suddenly looked incomplete, though a late flurry of runs from Geraint Jones saw England to 319 for seven at the close.

Jones made a crucial 85 in the previous Test at Trent Bridge, and England will take everything he and the tail can get them when they resume today on an Oval pitch and outfield chock full of runs.

Given England's rocketing ambition of the last few weeks, Strauss' knock could conceivably end up as the most important innings of the summer. His runs were certainly needed, and without their soothing balm Australia might have ridden roughshod over England's batting after Warne took four wickets, three of them in the morning session.

It was a classical Test century full of controlled strokes, with Strauss reaching three figures in the last session of play. Though the fly-swatting celebration is modern, Strauss bats as if from another era, one where centre partings were in vogue.

Unlike some of his more gung-ho team-mates, he appears to know his limitations and rarely attempts to exceed them. He also knew here that one big score, especially after England won the toss, could bat Australia out of the match, a view only Andrew Flintoff appeared to share.

While others chose to take Warne on with shots of increasing degrees of difficulty, they accorded him due respect, at least until after tea when a calculated assault against him saw Flintoff bring up his fifty with three fours in successive balls. Big Freddie later lofted him for a mighty six into the new stand, but mostly Warne kept a lid on England's scoring rate.

Together, Strauss and Flintoff made 143 for the fifth wicket until Flintoff edged Glenn McGrath to Warne at first slip. It was England's second highest partnership of the series, though its true value is yet to be determined.

Warne has been indefatigable this summer, which has been one of the most absorbing and frenetic on record. The dark rumblings about the schisms in his personal life have not affected him as they did Graham Thorpe, who took an extended break from the game to cope. Instead, Warne seems to have channelled his demons into his bowling for even seasoned watchers have been surprised by the sustained

The 12th man:
Paul Collingwood, England's supersub, becomes the only player to be drafted into the Test team after the beginning of the series

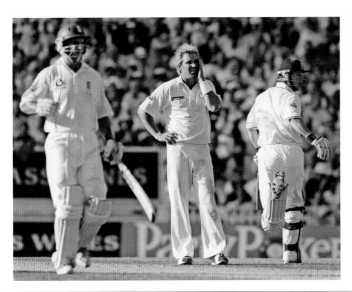

One that got away: Shane Warne appears astonished that Paul Collingwood has just taken runs off his bowling

nature of his brilliance in this series.

Yesterday, as so often this summer, he used the energy of the occasion to impose his will and skill on batsmen having little trouble with the brisker components in Australia's bowling attack. Before Warne came on in the 14th over, Australia were leaking runs at five an over. His first over, which cost nine runs, did little to stem that, but once he had settled, the situation was not long in coming to the boil.

Warne works batsmen and umpires as an ageing lothario might work a cocktail party, using every ruse in the book to get what he wants, which in daylight hours is English wickets. With his suspenseful stroll to the wicket, he ratchets up the suspense to make every ball an event that has to be coped with. But if that undoubtedly takes its toll on Warne's shoulder, it also wears down the batsman, as even Strauss will vouch.

With little help from the pitch, he managed to get Marcus Trescothick to slice a late cut to slip, though Matthew Hayden's low two-handed catch was a beauty for a big man.

If that was something of a donation, following Trescothick's silky-smooth start, Michael Vaughan was just as generous, especially as Warne set a fielder at midwicket just for the very shot the captain played – a jittery pull off a ball too full for the stroke.

With Ian Bell dyslexic when it comes to

reading Warne, few would have been surprised when he was lbw to another slider, albeit one that was probably sliding by leg-stump. It was a straight one that also dismissed Kevin Pietersen, though given the length of time he spent staring at the pitch, you would have thought Warne had bowled him a hand grenade.

The bling king among England players, Pietersen is being loaned £50,000 earrings for this match. Mind you, Warne has probably got him trumped there, too, the rocks adorning his lugholes big enough to attract more than a passing interest from Elizabeth Taylor.

If the rendition of Jerusalem before play was supposed to stiffen resolve, England, 131 for four when Pietersen departed, were in danger of going the same way as the walls of Jericho. Fortunately for the eager crowd basking in the September sunshine, Strauss and Flintoff spotted the danger.

This is an abnormal match even in the rarefied world of Test matches, and as such can buckle the strongest wills. Happily for England, Strauss and Flintoff remained steadfast, something the bowlers must emulate when they are called upon later today. ●DP

Day 1 Scoreboard

ENGLAND/FIRST INNINGS		M	B	4	6
M E Trescothick c Hayden b Warne	43	78	65	8	0
A J Strauss c Katich b Warne	129	353	210	17	0
*M P Vaughan c Clarke b Warne	11	25	25	2	0
I R Bell lbw b Warne	0	8	7	0	0
K P Pietersen b Warne	14	39	25	2	0
A Flintoff c Warne b McGrath	72	161	115	12	1
P D Collingwood lbw b Tait	7	26	26	1	0
+G O Jones not out	21	51	40	4	0
A F Giles not out	5	35	22	0	0

Extras (b 4, lb 6, nb 7)	17
Total (7 wkts, 88 overs, 390 mins)	319

FALL OF WICKETS: 1-82 (Trescothick 17.3 overs); **2-102** (Vaughan 23.5) **3-104** (Bell 26.0); **4-131** (Pietersen 33.3); **5-274** (Flintoff 70.1); **6-289** (Collingwood 76.3); **7-297** (Strauss 79.4.)
BOWLING: McGrath 19-5-48-1 (w 1, 7-1-21-0, 4-1-8-0, 4-0-15-0, 3-2-4-1, 1-1-0-0); **Lee 17-3-68-0** (nb 3, 4-1-21-0, 6-0-23-0, 6-2-20-0, 1-0-4-0); **Tait 15-1-61-1** (nb 3, 2-0-15-0, 2-0-7-0, 1-0-11-0, 4-0-14-0, 6-1-14-1); **Warne 34-4-118-5** (18-3-55-4, 16-1-63-1); **Katich 3-0-14-0** (one spell)

Analysis
Simon Hughes

Before the Test Ricky Ponting expressed his relief that Glenn McGrath would be fit because he represented two bowlers in one. In fact it was Shane Warne who proved, for the umpteenth time yesterday, his double value. He is, as we all know, the world's greatest

wicket thief, an artful dodger of a bowler who distracts the batsman with all kinds of byplay, then makes off with his jewels. But he can be a Scrooge too, dissuading batsmen from being too thrifty. The combination of the two is the single reason Australia still have a toehold in this series.

On the first day of this momentous Test, he played both roles. Brought on in the 13th over, when England had rattled up 62-0, he initially went for a few runs. The England batsmen have targeted him since the first morning at Edgbaston, lofting him over the top, sweeping him, using their feet to him, trying to break

his spirit. Briefly it worked as Trescothick and Strauss took him for five an over. He grimaced a few times: his shoulder was playing up. The dismissal of Trescothick to a craftily disguised overspinner changed all that. Vaughan, after one or two promising shots, chipped to midwicket, Bell was lbw, and just after lunch Pietersen played all round a straight one. Warne's five overs for 26 had become 11-2-34-4.

None of his deliveries, it must be said, were remotely unplayable. In fact only one of them – Trescothick's – could be said to have done anything at all. He had no right to take one wicket never

mind four in the space of a few overs. Warne's genius is in forcing batsmen into mistakes when the conditions are totally in their favour, as well as wreaking havoc when they're ideal for him. He does this by quickly under-standing the nature of the pitch, and then adapting his versatile bowling to fit. ●SH

"After all the fanfare, the glitter and the posturing, after the singing of Jerusalem and the hoisting of the flag, it was somehow gratifying that the first day of this supercharged Test match should be seized by England's most understated player. When marketing men exult over the new fashion for cricket, over the magazine profiles and the designer clothes, one name they rarely mention is that of Andrew Strauss. An admirable player, if not a bar-emptier, Strauss repels the limelight as surely as his namesake Andrew Flintoff attracts it."
Simon Briggs

Above: Flintoff was influential yet again, striking 72 in a vital partnership with Strauss before Glenn McGrath finally removed him
Above right: Warne lets his feelings show after rattling Kevin Pietersen's stumps. The boot would be on the other foot in the second innings

Day 2
The Oval
Australia play patient game

Australia's cricketers must have greater confidence in the Met Office than the rest of us, judging by their decision to abandon play for bad light at the Oval after tea yesterday. In a game Ricky Ponting's side must win to retain the Ashes, 80 minutes' batting time was passed up before rain eventually ended play early with just over half of the scheduled overs bowled.

Either Ponting believes he has England just where he wants them, after Justin Langer and Matthew Hayden put on an unbroken stand of 112 for the first wicket, or that he is willing to wait for more favourable light in the hope that any lost time can be made up over the remaining three days. If it is the latter he may find that dusk is rather more abrupt in September.

With England making 373, a below-par score on this marvellous pitch, Ponting's team are certainly ahead in the game. A few quick wickets this morning can change that, though where they might come from will have kept Michael Vaughan up for most of the night. England's bowling attack has not looked so toothless for a long time and the captain was beginning to look like Stan Laurel at his most put upon.

The half-day belonged to Australia, though England's last three wickets did manage to add 54 runs. For the second time in two days a compact left-handed batsman has dominated the summer's most important stage. What

Andrew Strauss did for England on Thursday was matched, if not yet in runs, by Langer, another who values hard graft above a heady 15 overs of fame.

Langer finished unbeaten on 75, an innings that veered from the sublime to the ridiculous as fine shots mingled with ghastly ones. He was never as aesthetically challenged as Hayden, who seemed intent on lying doggo for as long as possible. His 32 has so far taken 96 balls, a sure sign he has passed over hitting his way back into form in favour of occupying the crease.

A tenacious cricketer, Langer is a product of the school of hard knocks – though in his case mainly from cricket balls to the head. Last time he played against England at the Oval, he suffered concussion after being struck by Caddick, though he did make a hundred.

He has taken pain this series too, especially from Stephen Harmison. Hardly a match has gone by without Langer rubbing his chest or peering at a dent in his helmet. Yet there was no reprise of that yesterday despite healthy bounce in the pitch.

Part of the reason was that Harmison was only nudging the mid-80s mph – a curious effort given England needed him to make an early statement of intent. If ever there was a time for him to charge in and be at his terrifying best, this was it.

With Langer taking more than the odd risk

**Slow-hand Matt:
Matthew Hayden struck
a career-saving hundred,
but the funereal pace of
his scoring allowed England
to take too much time out
of the game**

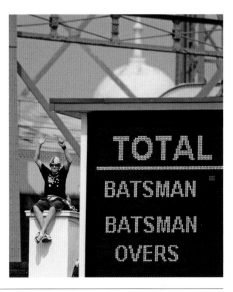

against Harmison early on, it looked as if Australia had a plan to unsettle him. With Simon Jones absent, Australia will have targeted him rather than Andrew Flintoff, an altogether harder nut to crack.

Langer also went after Ashley Giles, striking the left-arm spinner for two sixes in his first over, a ploy Australia hatched earlier in the series to prevent Giles from allowing the quicker bowlers a rest.

It did not work then, mainly because a five-man attack has enough fresh limbs to keep bowling, but now they are four it makes sense. Vaughan, having whisked Giles off immediately, soon brought him back at the other end, where the bigger boundary is less easy to clear.

Flintoff is England's Shane Warne, though in his case he is trying to carry the hopes of a rapt nation as well as England's bowling. But even he could not work a wicket, as England went an entire session without taking one for the first time this series.

The reverse-swing that has served him so well in previous matches has not been seen here, perhaps a product of closer policing by the umpires over the ruses used to abrade one side of the ball. When Flintoff deliberately threw the ball in so that it bounced on the pitch well short of Jones, it resulted in an unofficial warning from Billy Bowden.

Like England's use of substitute fielders, Flintoff's actions are not against the laws of the game, but they are probably against the spirit. Certainly umpires in county cricket have decided that any throw from the outfield that bounces more than twice will be considered under the umbrella of unfair play, and as such can be met by a change of ball.

Two difficult catches were presented by Langer, the first flying head-high past Strauss in the gully, the other parried by Marcus Trescothick going high to his right at a wide first slip. That chance came off the bowling of Paul Collingwood, who reached the same pace as Matthew Hoggard as he scurried in from the Pavilion End. With his higher arm action he got more bounce, which is what caused the edge.

In the morning session, Hoggard, along with Giles and Harmison, had managed to eke out important runs following the early dismissal of Geraint Jones, bowled by Brett Lee with the ninth ball. With admirable savvy Giles scored 32 until he was out lbw to Warne.

This his sixth of the match, takes Warne to 34 for the Tests, a tally that equals his best against England in a series, the previous being set in 1993, a six-Test series in which Warne unveiled his wonder ball to Mike Gatting.

By equalling that record now he has proved that he is bowling as well as ever. Had England faced any other spinner yesterday, this game would now be in the bag. ●DP

Day 2 Scoreboard

ENGLAND/FIRST INNINGS		M	B	4	6
+G O Jones b Lee	25	58	41	5	0
A F Giles lbw b Warne	32	117	70	1	0
M J Hoggard c Martyn b McGrath	2	46	36	0	0
S J Harmison not out	20	25	20	4	0
Extras (b 4, lb 6, w 1, nb 7)	18				
Total (105.3 overs, 472 mins)	373				

FALL OF WICKETS: 8- 235 (G Jones 89.3); **9- 345** (Hoggard 100.2); **10- 373** (Giles 150.3)
BOWLING: McGrath 27-5-72-2 (w 1, 8-0-24-1); **Lee 23-3-94-1** (5-0-13-1, 1-0-13-0); **Warne 37.3-5-122-6** (3.3-1-4-1)

AUSTRALIA/FIRST INNINGS		M	B	4	6
J L Langer not out	75	149	105	8	2
M L Hayden not out	32	149	96	4	0
Extras (b 2, nb3)	5				
Total (0 wkts, 33 overs, 149 mins)	112				

BOWLING: Harmison 8-1-21-0 (nb 1, 5-1-14-0, 3-0-7-0); **Hoggard 7-1-21-0** (nb 1, one spell); **Flintoff 7-2-20-0** (nb 1, 4-1-11-0, 3-1-9-0); **Giles 7-0-31-0** (1-0-14-0, 6-0-17-0); **Collingwood 4-0-17-0** (one spell)

**Heels over head:
Justin Langer takes a
different perspective
on life after evading a
particularly vicious Steve
Harmison bouncer. Later in
the same over, he played
onto his stumps**

Days 3 & 4
The Oval
England have upper hand after Australia blunder over light

Nip and tuck may finally be giving way to tick and tock in this ding-dong series. With a minimum of 98 overs play in the final Npower Test left today, a final twist cannot be ruled out, but time is running out for Australia after England's batsmen spent most of yesterday afternoon playing Shane Warne on their computer screens rather than in the middle, after bad light caused play to be suspended for over 50 overs.

With umpires eventually calling time at 6.15pm, England will be by far the happier of the two sides, though it is not yet beyond the bounds of either Warne, or the higher Being tweaking the plotlines in this Ashes contest, that England could be bowled out some time this afternoon, leaving Australia to chase 220 in 35-40 overs. As one gentleman yesterday summed it up on a placard outside the Oval tube: "Wanted – One Ticket For English Masochist."

At the moment Michael Vaughan's side, having lost Andrew Strauss to a bat-pad catch as Warne got one to bite out of the rough, enjoy a lead of 40 runs after finishing the fourth day on 34 for one. Ahead, definitely, but not exactly home and hosed – at least not according to the precedent set by the last three Tests, which have kept both sides interested until the last gasp of play.

Apart from the opening Test at Lord's, these sides have been as close as identical twins, a contention borne out when you compare the average runs per wicket of the two sides throughout the series. At the moment, England shade it with their 31.67, but Australia's 31.52 could be ahead if wickets tumble in the first two sessions today.

They might have already sneaked it but for some decisive bowling by Andrew Flintoff (five for 78) and Matthew Hoggard (four for 97), after Australia were forced, by their need to win this match, to bat in poor light, something England, by dint of their 2-1 lead in the series, had the luxury of avoiding.

It was only Flintoff's second five-wicket haul in Tests, following one against the West Indies 18 months ago – a fact that proves his excellence is not always measured in wickets. Facing him with his tail up is a mettle test in bright sunshine let alone the murk that descended on the Oval yesterday, and with Hoggard reviving the swing and nip that saw him destroy South Africa in Johannesburg last winter, the batsmen were up against it.

Yet, superbly though the pair bowled to share nine of the 10 wickets to fall, Australia lost their last seven wickets for 44 runs in 90 balls. Having taken 434 balls to lose their first two wickets, it was a tactical boob that could yet cost captain and coach their jobs,

**Looking for answers:
Ricky Ponting cannot
understand why Ashley
Giles has not been given out
caught behind off Glenn
McGrath. Like many losing
sides, Australia rarely
seemed to get the breaks**

Counting them out: Andrew Flintoff is determined that Matthew Hoggard should share his applause as they leave the field at the close of Australia's innings. The modest Hoggard is underplaying his own efforts, as he actually claimed four victims

should the Ashes change hands for the first time in 16 years later today.

With the light poor and with no bright weather in sight, Australia should have set their sights on batting until tea, not least because England's batsmen were always likely to be offered the light should the low cloud persist.

Instead, not long after Flintoff had removed Damien Martyn with a brute of a short ball in the third over of the morning, a message was brought out via 12th man Stuart MacGill. Judging from the shot-a-ball response from Matthew Hayden and Michael Clarke, the order was not to occupy the crease. The masterminds of the plan should be called to account.

In good seeing conditions, you could understand why such an aggressive approach might put pressure on England. But when the opposition are going to head for the sanctity of the pavilion at the first sign of a light meter, it was just plain barmy, especially as Australia's bowlers could now be working on a team still in deficit rather than 40 runs in front.

They'd have needed to bat well, especially as Flintoff's movement off the seam was beginning to cause consternation. His ball to dismiss Hayden, lbw for 138, was near-on unplayable for a left-hander, having the same effect as a 90mph leg-break.

Hoggard was almost as effective, though some of the shots being played were optimistic given the amount of swing and seam. Some butterfingers, first by Flintoff at second slip and then by Geraint Jones diving to his right, saw Michael Clarke twice reprieved off him. His perseverance was rewarded when first Clarke, and then Adam Gilchrist were trapped lbw.

When England went out to bat just before 2pm, light was always going to be an issue, which is why Warne was brought on after just one over from Brett Lee. His effect was instant when Strauss was out to his fourth ball. Then a bouncer to Vaughan from McGrath, a decision almost as dumb as the one that saw Australia throw their wickets away earlier in the day, caused the umpires to immediately offer the light to England's captain.

It was not refused, and while play did resume again briefly, the standing ovation received as Vaughan and Marcus Trescothick headed for the dressing room, rather than the usual boos, showed that even spectators are prepared to make sacrifices to see the Ashes returned to England. ●DP

Day 3 Scoreboard

AUSTRALIA 277–2 at close of play
(J L Langer 105, M L Hayden 110no) Langer passes 7,000 Test runs, Hayden completed 6,000

Delayed start due to rain
Only 45.4 overs bowled due to bad weather

Day 4 Scoreboard

Langer and Hayden parternship of 185 is Australia's best opening stand at the Oval

AUSTRALIA 367 all out
A Flintoff 4-30, M J Hoggard 4-44

ENGLAND 2ND INNINGS 34–1
(M E Trescothick 14, M P Vaughan 19). Trescothick reachd 1,000 Test runs in 2005

Analysis
Simon Hughes

It was Lancashire and Yorkshire in harmony at the Oval yesterday. The marauding Freddie one end; the galumphing Hoggy the other. The raging bull and the determined mule. Until the last two Tests, Hoggard has had a quiet series.

Michael Vaughan had tended to use him in short bursts with the new ball, and then leave him to graze in the outfield while the old ball specialists did their work.

But Hoggard continued to contribute, where a lesser man would have retreated into himself, and picked up useful wickets. Justin Langer and Matthew Hayden have both twice been defeated by his late swing, and several times he has successfully bored out Michael Clarke with a sequence of widish deliveries luring him into an indiscretion. At Trent Bridge he became the first seam bowler in Test cricket to trap Adam Gilchrist lbw.

It illustrated the strength of this bowling attack, that an escape from Flintoff's clutches doesn't necessarily lead to prosperity. It was the big skinhead's sustained hostility that set up the remote possibility of an England lead; but it was the subtle persistence of his shaggy haired colleague that made it a reality.

It was just reward for his perseverance and good humour too, for, on Friday he was denied several lbw appeals that on another day would have been successful. Later he produced a classic outswinger to dismiss Glenn McGrath. It was the first time McGrath had been out in this series. Another strange eventuality in this surreal summer.

Quietly, methodically, Hoggard has established the best strike rate this year of any leading bowler in world cricket. He has 47 wickets this calendar year, at a rate of one every 6.2 overs. Now all he has to do, in all probability, is hold out for half a dozen overs some time after tea tomorrow, the Ashes will be England's and he will be smelling of Roses. Now that's got to beat walking the dogs on Ilkley Moor. Then again in the words of one tabloid, its not all over til the fat laddie spins. ●SH

Playing for time:
with Australia desperate
to force a result, Andrew
Flintoff is far from
unhappy about the bad
weather that wipes out
a day-and-a-half's play
at the Oval

Man of the people:
Andrew Flinoff enjoys the
electric atmosphere at
the Oval. The fans did their
best to cheer England over
the line, even applauding
every time the covers
came onto the field

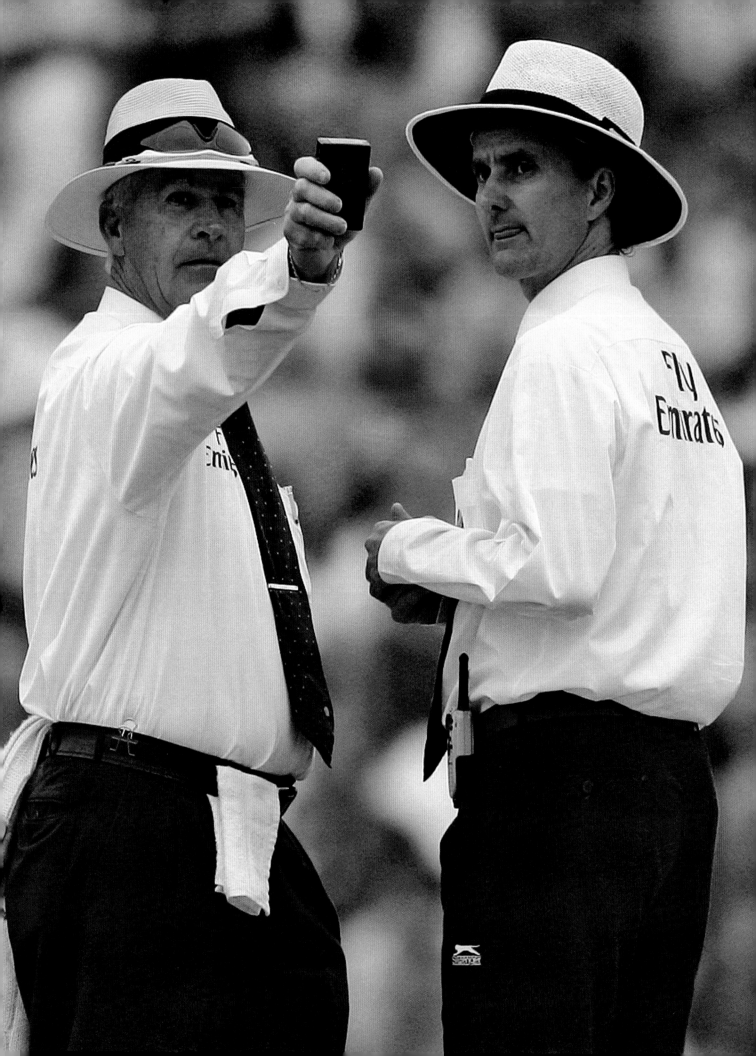

THREE CHEERS FOR THE CHARGE OF THE BAD LIGHT BRIGADE

Martin Johnson

There have been many bizarre sights in the long history of England and Australian conflict, including, believe it or not, a lunchtime ceremony in which the Mayor of Bendigo embraced the "general" of the Barmy Army and handed over a commemorative plaque in exchange for an official Barmy T-shirt. However, it is probably safe to say that not even that compares with a Test match crowd giving a standing ovation to a pair of umpires for leading the players off a cricket field for bad light.

It was further proof, if any were needed, that no sacrifice is too great when it comes to winning back the Ashes. Depriving spectators of their cricket normally results in a cacophony of booing and an outfield knee deep in seat cushions, but not in the potentially momentous circumstances which await today.

Some of yesterday's cheering spectators may even have paid the £1,000 a pair being asked for seats on Ebay, and so united is the nation in England's cause that today's ticket touts outside the Oval tube station will probably be operating the England and Wales Cricket Board's bad-weather refund policy in reverse. Five hundred quid if it looks like bright sunshine and plenty of cricket, or £1,000 if it is forecast to rain all day.

Not surprisingly, the Australians spent most of their time conveying the impression that they were on Bondi Beach, while England squinted towards the pavilion in an attempt to convince the umpires that the sinister building they could just about make out through the darkness only required a burst of forked lightning to turn it into Castle Dracula.

There was no bias in the umpires' decision to twice come off for bad light – they were merely obeying the laws of cricket. If you consult the Wisden Almanac, they actually end with "Law 42: Unfair Play", but while it's not actually written down, everyone knows that there's a Law 43: "If At All Possible, Thou Shalt Not Play."

Test matches may have changed out of all recognition in recent years, but certain traditions die hard. Namely, if a passing fluff of cotton wool is spotted overhead, it is mandatory for everyone to return to the dressing room for a pot of tea, a slice of cake and a game of cards.

The relevant law used to be fairly specific, in that a batsman was required to be in physical danger, but as this precise stipulation was regularly ignored, it was changed to allow the umpires to bring the players off if the light were considered "not suitable". They also gave them meters, the workings of which remain a mystery. "What was the reading when you came off?" Rudi Koertzen was asked on Channel 4 yesterday. And Rudi replied, in that spirit of openness and spectator-friendly PR for which the game is rightly famous: "I can't tell you that."

Dickie Bird, the most celebrated bad-light umpire of all, rarely looked upon a dark cloud as anything less than a total eclipse of the sun, and his reputation was such that he was booed off in a Test at Headingley when an underground water pipe burst and soaked the bowler's run-up. Dickie led the teams off in glorious sunshine, and as the punters hurled abuse, he yelled back: "Don't blame me. I'm not a plumber!"

Yesterday's light was never very good, and when they took the first drinks break, you half expected the respective 12th men to bring out jugs of carrot juice. On the other hand, it was nothing like as dark as on the occasion, in the 1970s, the result of a Gillette Cup semi-final was announced live on the Nine O'Clock News. When one of the players suggested it might be dark, the umpire, Arthur Jepson, said: "You can see the moon, lad. How far do you want to see?"

What was puzzling about the umpires' final decision to take the players off yesterday was that it appeared to be precipitated by Michael Vaughan playing and missing at a Shane Warne leg-break. It was as though Warne had never done this sort of thing before, and that if Vaughan had missed it, it must have been because he hadn't seen it.

Only 89 of the weekend's 196-over allocation was possible, which was tough luck on Australia, and there will be sympathy for them in what has been the most chivalrous of series. However, you'll get slightly better odds on a squadron of pigs being spotted over the gasometer today than a sporting declaration from the England captain. ●MJ

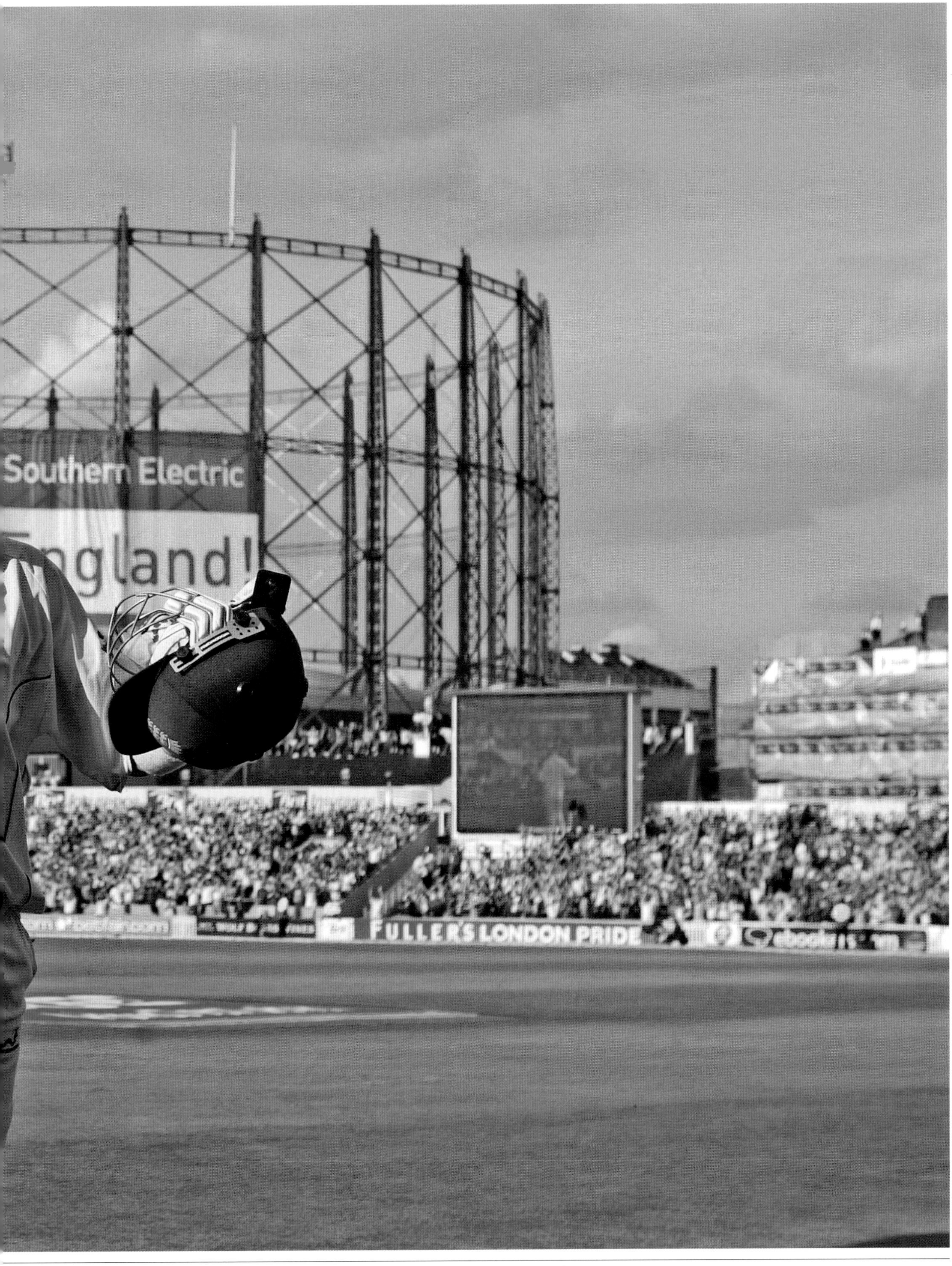
Southern Electric
FULLERS LONDON PRIDE

Day 5
The Oval
England's Ashes

It used to be the dream that disappeared on waking, the yearning that had no release, and the trophy that England teams could neither win, borrow nor steal – at least not since 1989. Then, amid tumultuous scenes at the Oval yesterday, the Ashes fell back into English hands, the little brown urn finally secured after an astonishing century by Kevin Pietersen made the final Test safe from one last Australian ambush.

Pietersen's high-octane innings did not prevent the moment being sealed with a whimper though, after Australia openers Justin Langer and Matthew Hayden accepted the offer of bad light.

With the visitors needing an impossible 338 runs from 17.2 overs, the move simply sealed the draw prematurely, though Michael Vaughan, perhaps wanting to savour the moment in front of another capacity crowd, seemed more than a little aggrieved.

Vaughan's annoyance was short-lived and once he had given the replica urn a peck on the cheek and held it aloft to roars of delight, he and the team appeared overjoyed as they did a lap of honour to renditions of Jerusalem and Land of Hope and Glory – a combination that with all the flags and confetti made the occasion feel like a cross between a Wembley Cup final and Last Night at the Proms.

Eight Ashes series had been lost before this 2-1 win. It has been fully deserved too, and after their defeat in the opening Test at Lord's, England's has been the bolder and more persuasive cricket, a combination that has relied on finding the right man at the right time. Yesterday, that man was Pietersen, who ever since he brought his combination of bling and bluster to this England side has threatened to produce something sensational, though thrill-seeker that he is, he left it until the attention of the entire country, as well as the insomniac parts of Australia, were on him before producing it.

In the context of the game, which England needed to make safe by batting out most of the day, it was a reckless but glorious ride, most of it at breakneck speed. By the time Glenn McGrath ended it, clean bowling him with the second new ball for 158, he had struck seven sixes and 15 fours, nearly all whistle clean off the middle of the bat.

Given the extraordinary events of this series,
it would be easy to be blase about Pietersen's deeds. But as they have done ever since they got their noses in front during the Edgbaston Test, England once more faltered as the main prize hove into view as McGrath and Shane Warne probed for scar tissue in England's collective psyche one last time.

But Pietersen is wired up differently to most and does not do caution or self-doubt, as he revealed when hooking 93mph bouncers from Brett Lee high into the crowd at long leg. Although he is more likely to reveal the dark roots in his blond streak than the English ones in his make-up, he clearly cares, though perhaps not to the extent that he chokes up as some of his team-mates have done.

Arriving at the crease after McGrath had removed Vaughan and Ian Bell in successive balls to leave England 69 for three, Pietersen survived the hat-trick ball, but only just as the bouncer missed his glove by a whisker before striking his upper arm. With the whole team appealing for the catch, the pressure on umpire Billy Bowden was enormous, but his intransigence proved to be the right decision – one of several hairline ones the umpires got spot-on during the day.

If that near-miss could be put down to Pietersen's skill, he also enjoyed some luck, being dropped on nought and 15. The first chance came off Warne, as Pietersen edged to Adam Gilchrist, and the second to Warne, as he edged a drive off Lee to first slip. If the first was tricky the second was standard fodder and shouts of "Warney's dropped the Ashes" echoed around the Oval for the rest of the day.

While it is indisputable that the mistake cost them dear, without Warne Australia would have been pole-axed this summer. Worrying times for Australia then that he and McGrath, who took three for 85 yesterday, are into the last phases of their careers.

Warne finished with six wickets to bring his tally to 40 for the series. While that is not an Australian record for an Ashes series (Terry Alderman took 42 and 41 in the 1980s and Rodney Hogg 41 before that), he did beat Dennis Lillee's record for the most Ashes victims over a career, now set at 172.

He almost rallied his team for one last attempt to claw back their proud Ashes legacy, following the dismissal of Marcus Trescothick and Andrew Flintoff, caught and bowled after

The man who gave his all: Shane Warne (far left) finally accepts the inevitable after a match in which he took 12 wickets but dropped the catch that could perhaps have saved the Ashes

A damp conclusion: as the ground staff hover, umpires Billy Bowden and Rudi Koertzen prepare to remove the bails and declare the match a draw. Few spectators have any idea what is happening

Warne had lured him into an indiscreet drive.

The double strike left England looking distinctly insecure on 126 for five at lunch. Fortunately for them Warne's mastery of Pietersen here was limited to the first innings only. While others groped and smothered his spin, the skunk-haired one treated him with disdain, twice sweep-slogging him for six over mid-wicket before biffing him straight for another two sixes as the mood took him.

It was the stuff of fantasy, ably abetted by a sturdy 59 from Ashley Giles, who added 109 runs with Pietersen for the eighth wicket, an Oval record against Australia. Although both eventually perished and the team were bowled out for 335, all threat had been defused and the game, and with it the series, was in the bag.

England have won the Ashes – a statement that has a magnificent ring to it. ●DP

5th Test Scoreboard

CLOSE DAY 1: England 319-7 (88 overs, Jones 21, Giles 5)
CLOSE DAY 2: Australia 112-0 (33 overs, Langer 75, Hayden 32)
CLOSE DAY 3: Australia 277-2 (78.4 overs, Hayden 110, Martyn 9)
CLOSE DAY 4: England 34-1 (13.2 overs, Trescothick 14, Vaughan 19)

ENGLAND/FIRST INNINGS		M	B	4	6
M E Trescothick c Hayden b Warne	43	78	65	8	0
A J Strauss c Katich b Warne	129	353	210	17	0
*M P Vaughan c Clarke b Warne	11	25	25	2	0
I R Bell lbw b Warne	0	8	7	0	0
K P Pietersen b Warne	14	39	25	2	0
A Flintoff c Warne b McGrath	72	161	115	12	1
P D Collingwood lbw b Tait	7	26	26	1	0
+G O Jones b Lee	25	58	41	5	0
A F Giles lbw b Warne	32	117	70	1	0
M J Hoggard c Martyn b McGrath	2	46	36	0	0
S J Harmison not out	20	25	20	4	0

Extras (b 4, lb 6, w 1, nb 7)	18
Total (105.3 overs, 472 mins)	373

FALL OF WICKETS: 1-82 (Trescothick 17.3 overs); 2-102 (Vaughan 23.5) 3-104 (Bell 26.0); 4-131 (Pietersen 33.3); 5-274 (Flintoff 70.1); 6-289 (Collingwood 76.3); 7-297 (Strauss 79.4); 8-235 (G Jones 89.3); 9-345 (Hoggard 100.2); 10-373 (Giles 150.3)
BOWLING: McGrath 27-5-72-2 (w 1, 7-1-21-0, 4-1-8-0, 4-0-15-0, 3-2-4-1, 1-1-0-0, 8-0-24-1); Lee 23-3-94-1 (nb 3, 4-1-21-0, 6-0-23-0, 6-2-20-0, 1-0-4-0, 5-0-13-1, 1-0-13-0); Tait 15-1-61-1 (nb 3, 2-0-15-0, 2-0-7-0, 1-0-11-0, 4-0-14-0, 6-1-14-1); Warne 37.3-5-122-6 (18-3-55-4, 16-1-63-1, 3.3-1-4-1); Katich 3-0-14-0 (one spell)

AUSTRALIA/FIRST INNINGS		M	B	4	6
J L Langer b Harmison	105	236	146	11	2
M L Hayden lbw b Flintoff	138	418	303	18	1x5
*R T Ponting c Strauss b Flintoff	35	82	56	3	0
D R Martyn c Collingwood b Flintoff	10	34	29	1	0
M J Clarke lbw b Hoggard	25	120	59	2	0
S M Katich lbw b Flintoff	1	11	11	0	0
+A C Gilchrist lbw b Hoggard	23	31	20	4	0
S K Warne c Vaughan b Flintoff	0	18	10	0	0
B Lee c Giles b Hoggard	6	20	10	0	0
G D McGrath c Strauss b Hoggard	0	5	6	0	0
S W Tait not out	1	5	2	0	0

Extras (b 4, lb 8, w 2, nb 9)	23
Total (107.1 overs, 471 mins)	367

FALL OF WICKETS: 1-185 (Langer 52.4); 2-264 (Ponting 72.2); 3-281 (Martyn 80.4); 4-323 (Hayden 92.3); 5-329 (Katich 95.0); 6-356 (Gilchrist 101.1); 7-359 (Clarke 103.3); 8-363 (Warne 104.5); 9-363 (McGrath 106.0) 10-367 (Lee 107.1)
BOWLING: Harmison 22-2-87-1 (nb 2, w 2, 5-1-14-0, 3-0-7-0, 9-1-39-1, 3-0-15-0, 2-0-12-0); Hoggard 24.1-2-97-4 (nb 1, 7-1-21-0, 7-0-32-0, 3-0-16-0, 7.1-1-28-3); Flintoff 34-10-78-5 (nb 6, 4-1-11-0, 3-1-9-0, 5-3-5-0, 2-1-2-0, 2-0-13-0, 3.4-1-8-1, 14.2-3-30-4); Giles 23-1-76-0 (1-0-14-0, 6-0-17-0, 3-0-13-0, 11-0-30-0, 2-1-2-0); Collingwood 4-0-17-0 (one spell)

ENGLAND/SECOND INNINGS		M	B	4	6
M E Trescothick lbw b Warne	33	151	84	1	0
A J Strauss c Katich b Warne	1	16	7	0	0
*M P Vaughan c Gilchrist b McGrath	45	80	65	6	0
I R Bell c Warne b McGrath	0	1	1	0	0
K P Pietersen b McGrath	158	288	187	15	7
A Flintoff c & b Warne	8	20	13	1	0
P D Collingwood c Ponting b Warne	10	71	51	1	0
+G O Jones b Tait	1	22	12	0	0
A F Giles b Warne	59	162	97	7	0
M J Hoggard not out	4	44	35	0	0
S J Harmison c Hayden b Warne	0	2	2	0	0

Extras (b 4, w 7, nb 5)	16
Total (91.3 overs, 434mins)	335

FALL OF WICKETS: 1-2 (Strauss 3.4); 2-67 (Vaughan 22.4) 3-67 (Bell 22.5); 4-109 (Trescothick 33.1); 5-126 (Flintoff 37.5); 6-186 (Collingwood 51.5); 7-199 (G Jones 56.5); 8-308 Pietersen 82.5); 9-335 (Giles 91.1); 10-335 (Harmison 91.3)
BOWLING: McGrath 26-4-85-3 (nb 1, 5-0-13-0, 8-2-24-2, 5-1-7-0, 8-0-41-1); Lee 20-4-88-0 (nb 4, w 1, 1-1-0-0, 2-0-9-0, 8-0-57-0, 5-1-14-0, 4-2-8-0); Warne 38.3-3-124-6 (w 1, 5.2-0-15-1, 0.4-0-4-0, 31-3-101-3, 1.3-0-4-2); Clarke 2-0-6-0 (one spell); Tait 5-0-28-1 (w 1, 4-0-27-1, 1-0-1-0)

AUSTRALIA/SECOND INNINGS		M	B	4	6
J L Langer not out	0	3	4	0	0
M L Hayden not out	0	3	0	0	0

Extras (lb 4)	4
Total (0 wkts, 0.4 overs, 3 mins)	4

BOWLING: Harmison 0.4-0-0-0
UMPIRES: B F Bowden (New Zealand) & R E Koertzen (South Africa)

MATCH DRAWN (England win series 2-1)

MATCH AWARD: K P Pietersen
SERIES AWARD: A Flintoff & S K Warne
COMPTON/MILLER MEDAL: A Flintoff

New England must aim for true greatness

5th Test afterword
Derek Pringle

The law of the sporting jungle is different to the one that persists in nature, as England's cricket team are about to find out after winning the Ashes back off Australia. They may have beaten the world champions over a bruising series, but to take their crown they need to create a legacy – a challenging prospect now that the hunter has become the hunted.

Although there is time to bask in the glow of what has been an uplifting and extra-ordinary summer of cricket, the next challenge is never far away. For Michael Vaughan and his heroic team that will mean winning against Pakistan and India in their own dusty backyards this winter.

Should they win in India for the first time since 1984/5 (an even longer gap than between Ashes victories), the next major hurdle will be the Aussies on their home patch, after Pakistan and Sri Lanka have toured here next summer. Thus the endless quest for the true and lasting greatness enjoyed by Australia over the past decade goes on.

The lifespan of Vaughan's Ashes team, providing they do not suffer serious injuries, could be four to five years. Given the usual improvements most players make until their early thirties, it is not difficult to see them dominating world cricket over that period, especially if a talented spinner could be unearthed to back up and then replace Ashley Giles, who at 32 has less petrol in the tank than most of his team-mates.

Giles will have a central role to play this winter, and is a better bowler than when he last visited the subcontinent. Other than him,

the county cupboard appears bare, though Northamptonshire's Monty Panesar has his advocates. The counties do not help by employing overseas spinners.

With their calm, calculating coach, Duncan Fletcher, committing himself at least until that World Cup, key personnel will also remain in place.

Seven months ago, despite beating South Africa 2-1 in a five-match Test series, only a brave few would have foreseen England being talked of in these terms. Over dinner in Johannesburg one night, even Vaughan agreed with the assessment that unless England improved on their performances there, the Aussies would have them on toast come the Ashes. Well, improve they did and when someone as battle hardened as Shane Warne admits Australia were beaten by the better side, you know something very special has taken place.

The transformation may appear remarkable but it can mostly be traced to three things – the eventual realisation by Andrew "Freddie" Flintoff that he is the world's best all-rounder; the arrival of bling king Kevin Pietersen; and the quantum leap made by Simon Jones from a wayward tyro his captain was loath to trust, to strike bowler with laser-guided swing.

Involved at last in his first Ashes series, after injury kept him out of the previous two, Flintoff admitted that he placed too high a price on the first Test at Lord's, which England lost by 239 runs. Although he twice showed Adam Gilchrist how he would get him out throughout the series, by going around the wicket to deny Australia's most destructive batsman room to cut and carve the ball through the off side, he batted as if with rigor mortis.

Fortunately for England, a short break with his wife and baby daughter to Bovey Castle in Devon placed matters into perspective and Flintoff returned for the second Test vowing to be himself.

England won by two runs to level the series, but it was Flintoff, in an outstanding all-round performance in which he made 68 and 73 and took seven wickets, who imprinted himself on the match. He also lent the series its most enduring image when he bent to console a distraught Brett Lee after he was left as Australia's last man standing.

Flintoff finished with 402 runs and 24

wickets. The latter, especially when added to the 18 wickets taken by Jones and the 17 by Stephen Harmison, means the trio accounted for 59 of the 89 Australian wickets to fall.

Although their individual records were not as impressive as the 40 victims snaffled by Warne, the trio proved, as the West Indies did time and again in the Eighties, that relentless fast bowling, especially with reverse swing attached, is often more effective than top-class spin. Runs were still needed to give the bowlers something to work with and Pietersen topped the list with 473 runs at an average of 52.

His 158 on the last day of the Oval – which extinguished any late plans on Australia's part to level the series – was the most extraordinary of the series.

Before that Marcus Trescothick and Andrew Strauss did a fine job as England's openers, though they, more than anyone, benefited when Glenn McGrath turned an ankle treading on a ball before the second Test.

After taking nine wickets at Lord's in the opening Test, McGrath, who also missed the fourth Test with a sore elbow, never really rediscovered that menace.

Fletcher's part in the victory is undeniable, but his obsessive secrecy makes it difficult to gauge. His impassive and calm nature during moments of crisis probably makes him a father figure for many, something Mike Brearley was for Ian Botham in the 1981 Ashes series, generally reckoned to have been the most exciting until this one blew it into the ether.

He certainly breaks the game down for players so that they focus only on the truly important, spoon-feeding them the kind of bite-sized chunks most easily digested in a fraught atmosphere of a Test match.

With Vaughan cut largely from the same cloth, at least outwardly, England's dressing room is a no-blame area even when the going gets tough.

For the past 16 years against Australia England had been as Sisyphus was, getting the boulder halfway up the slope before rolling back to where they started, their perceived progress back to square one.

This time, a young, vibrant team who have combined aggression with flair have not only got the boulder to the top of the hill but managed to squash Australia beneath it. For the moment, that is worth celebrating. ●DP

Michael Vaughan heads a new generation of legends

5th Test afterword
Simon Hughes

Hutton, Compton, Edrich, May, Graveney, Bailey, Evans, Laker, Lock, Trueman, Bedser. All became cricket legends after England regained the Ashes for the first time in 18 years at the Oval in 1953. Fifty years on substitute in the hall of fame Vaughan, Trescothick, Strauss, Bell, Pietersen, Flintoff, Jones G and Jones S, Giles, Hoggard and Harmison, with a little help from Collingwood. Not yet an invincible team but an incredible one of heart and soul and remarkable reserves of strength and desire.

The impassioned scenes they generated after the match – the joyous faces and the raucous singing and the flinging of paraphernalia into the air – have never been seen before at a cricket ground. Standing in the middle the hairs on the back of your neck were stirred and tears of happiness leaked into your eye.

The last day had everything. Supine strokes from Vaughan and Trescothick, English fallibility from Bell and Jones, a last hurrah from the brilliant Warne and the relentless McGrath, an innings of near genius from Pietersen, the yeomanry of Giles and exceptional umpiring.

Pietersen's audacious innings took the game away from Australia. It was Compton who hit the winning runs in 1953 and Pietersen is his modern reincarnation. His batting is a mixture of Mohammad Azharuddin and Viv Richards. Quite a combination.

Why have England triumphed? Reason one: their four-pronged pace attack was too varied and hostile for Australian's much-vaunted top seven. Flintoff's dominance of that old ball destroyer Adam Gilchrist symbolised this superiority.

Reason two: Michael Vaughan's inventive field settings backed the bowlers up brilliantly and muted the Australian bats. They were unable to dominate the bowling as they would have liked and few of them seemed to find an alternative approach.

Reason three: the ageing Australian bowling, on the other hand, relied heavily on Warne. In six of the 10 innings he took the first England wicket – which both reflected his continuing mastery and the relative impotence of the rest of the attack – and he only got the chance to bowl last on a wearing pitch once.

Reason four: Marcus Trescothick's composure at the top of the order, a man unflustered by any situation and making consistent contributions without ever managing that coveted century. Reason five: Pietersen's extraordinary talent and ridiculous self-confidence with the bat. Reason six: England's cohesion and greater inner strength, a product of central contracts and an excellent back room staff, that engineered the tight wins at Edgbaston and Trent Bridge.

Ultimately England had two match winners – Flintoff and Pietersen – to Australia's one, Shane Warne. To lose their advantage here yesterday, would have been unjust. The right team won. What a side, what a series, what a story. ●SH

POST SERIES REFLECTIONS

THE ASHES SERIES 2005

Post series reflections
Derek Pringle

Some champions are toppled by natural causes others by the better man, but few go quietly especially when a trophy as symbolic as The Ashes is at stake. Over a five-Test series this summer, Australia, the pre-eminent team in world cricket for the past decade, were beaten 2-1 by an England side no longer content with being their inferiors.

Those are the bare bones of it, but they do not reveal the thrilling, passionate tug-of-war that saw The Ashes wrenched from Australia's grasp for the first time since 1989, an act many are convinced produced the greatest Test series in history. Certainly the four Tests after Lord's were riveting contests that refused to yield their result until the very last gasp had been wrung from both players and spectators.

The sustained drama of the event moved people from Barbados to Brisbane, and most points between. Even the start of the football season could not quell its fervour, for this was the only show in town. Why else would two hundred thousand people turn out to catch a glimpse of the country's latest sporting heroes as they took their hangovers on an open-top bus ride around London the morning after?

Even Australians, notoriously churlish whenever the mother country celebrates success, saluted Vaughan's men. The excitement felt during this volatile series is already having a knock-on effect Down Under with the Melbourne Cricket Ground taking over 600 bookings for the Members' dining room on Boxing Day 2006 – the opening day of the 4th Test in the next Ashes series.

Given the Aussies' overweening dominance during their sixteen-year monopoly of the urn, England's victory was as momentous as the cricket played in achieving it. Ironic then, that few among Michael Vaughan's team, which spills over to include coach Duncan Fletcher and his support staff, believed they could win this time around. Australia 2006/7 had been their aim, which shows that even those in control can be wide of the mark when a team is in the ascendancy as England have been since triumphing in the Caribbean 18 months ago.

It was a rare misjudgement from Fletcher, who saw the rest of his plans bear fruit in a summer cocktail that ended up intoxicating millions. Meticulous in the same way Clive Woodward was during England Rugby's World Cup triumph, Fletcher must take credit for

giving his players the blueprint for beating Australia.

Having the instructions is one thing, possessing the players to carry them out quite another, especially the bowling attack which needs to take 20 wickets a match – the minimum condition for victory in modern Test cricket. Batsmen win awards; bowlers win matches.

So, how did England fast-track their ambitions, and were Australia caught off guard by their own arrogance and complacency? Most of the Aussies involved would claim a 'No' to the second question, but when Cricket Australia sent over the series trophy (the big Waterford crystal one not the little brown urn which almost never leaves Lord's) in a box with duty and postage already paid for the return trip, the charge is not easily dismissed.

Nor are the claims of 5-0 by Glenn McGrath or the decision by Ponting to put England into bat at Edgbaston in the 2nd Test, moments after losing his champion opening bowler to injury. Dress it up how you will, but that blunder allowed England – one-nil down after the opening Test – to get back into a series that might easily have been decided had they been made to bat last against Shane Warne on a wearing pitch.

For a great side used to having its way with an opponent, Australia returned home with question marks over a number of key positions, including captain and coach. Only Warne and Brett Lee could be proud of their performances, which were every bit as impressive as England's main players. Without Warne, Australia would have been hammered, something not even a born optimist would have predicted.

The first glimpse that Vaughan's team might have the means to beat their own 2007 Ashes deadline came during the semi-final of the ICC Trophy against Australia, the previous September. A fifty-over game, England won it comfortably by six wickets, their aggression with both bat and ball felt not only by Australia and Ricky Ponting, who broke his hand, but all those watching. Little wonder that Fletcher used the win as an aide memoire this summer – emphasising again and again that the victory had been clinical and emphatic rather than some jammy fluke.

Nine months later, on 13 June, England

added to their slender but growing portfolio of successes against Australia by winning the Twenty20 match at Hampshire's Rose Bowl. Playing in a format new to international cricket, Ricky Ponting and his coach John Buchanan tried to make light of the drubbing after losing their first seven wickets in 20 balls. What they can't have missed but perhaps chose to ignore was another ruthless display by an England team intent on setting down a marker.

In Fletcher's two previous Ashes campaigns, both lost 4-1, his players were often beaten before the game began – intimidated by opponents certain of their superiority. This time Vaughan and his team set out determined not to be bullied by the swaggering power plays. And yet the Twenty20 match, apart from unleashing Kevin Pietsersen on an unsuspecting world, was so much more than just a plucky stand by the underdog. In those brief moments of mayhem, Australia revealed that they too were vulnerable to a robust and well-executed plan.

Aggression is a word tossed about lightly in sport, but in cricket its constituency lies mostly with fast bowlers and big-hitting batsmen. Unlike Nasser Hussain in previous Ashes series, Vaughan had three very quick bowlers in Stephen Harmison, Andrew Flintoff and Simon Jones, all of them capable of 90 mph – the speed at which a batsman's bluster turns to bluff.

When all are fit and firing, as they were for almost four of the five Tests this summer, it gives England something they have mostly lacked since the move to covered pitches over thirty years ago – the priceless ability to bowl sides out on flat pitches.

All three quicks had been present on the previous winter's tour to South Africa, where England won the Tests 2-1, but only Flintoff performed with any distinction. Harmison, so deadly in the West Indies ten months earlier, and in the return series that followed, was wayward and distracted. Meanwhile, Jones was used mainly as a last resort, his captain plainly not trusting him when the pressure was on.

The pre-Ashes hype, and the crowd's gathering euphoria at England's early successes in the NatWest Series and Twenty20, seemed to galvanise them into a trident of real potency, especially after Jones revealed he'd mastered conventional swing to go with the reverse swing that had long been the mainstay in his armoury.

His 18 wickets in the first four Tests dismantled the theory that the late start to the series, which began on 21 July, would prove disastrous for England (whose bowlers needed early season pitches with moisture in them to prosper) and perfect for the Wizard of Oz, Shane Warne.

Well Warne did thrive in the dry late summer conditions, finishing the series with 40 wickets, but so did the reverse swingers. Jones and Flintoff can now claim unalloyed mastery of this lethal technique. In fact, the only pitch that seamed was Lord's and Glenn McGrath, perfectly attuned to the ground's unique geomorphology, out-bowled everyone there.

Another benefit of reverse swing is that it demands a full length from bowlers or it will not work. This automatically reduced the amount of balls to which Australia's batsmen could play the cut or pull shot, traditional strengths and the main run-scoring strokes for many of the top order. Damien Martyn, a back foot player of great panache, was particularly nonplussed and finished the series with an average of 19.7, paltry compared to the 76.4 he'd managed in the Ashes series here four years earlier.

From the second Test on, England's pace bowling strategy basically revolved around two balls – the bouncer and full-pitched swinger. The first invited the hook, the second the drive, shots neither safe nor controllable against balls either at the head or changing direction at high speed. It proved mightily effective too, with Australia failing to pass 400 in an innings during the series – a major coup given their preference for playing an extra batsman instead of five bowlers as England did for four of the five Tests.

The relentless attrition on mind and body of facing three quick bowlers on rotation simply wore batsmen down. The ploy wasn't new, having been used to even greater effect by the pace quartets of the great West Indies sides of the 1980s, but after years of coping with just one or two quality bowlers per opponent, Australia were unprepared for the extra demands.

England hit them hard too, the sheer ferocity of their in-your-face hostility bringing unforced errors from a team used to running the game. At Lord's, Harmison revealed his hostile

intentions early on by striking Justin Langer a nasty blow to the elbow with the second ball of the opening day. Not long after, the team then revealed theirs by ignoring Ponting after another bouncer from Harmison had split his cheek, a wound that requiring stitching.

Ponting made much of England's lack of concern after Australia won the match in emphatic fashion by an innings and 239 runs, implying even that a natural justice had been served by the result. A reformed drinker and brawler, Ponting has tried to get Australia to shed their win-at-all-costs image. No longer happy to be respected for their tough unflinching brand of cricket, they want to be loved too.

It is a difficult balancing act and one that saw Australia's skipper fall spectacularly from the moral high ground during the 4th Test at Trent Bridge, another nail-biter won by England. Run out for 48 in the 2nd innings by a direct hit from substitute fielder Gary Pratt of Durham, Ponting let fly with the verbals at Duncan Fletcher as he left the field. Compared to Vaughan's regal calm this was the tantrum of a man feeling fate's cold hand against him, along with the umpires, crowd, media etc ...

The euphemistic version with expletives deleted, is that Ponting accused England and their coach of sharp practice, partly because Pratt was a young whippet not named in the original squad, and partly because England's bowlers were fielding substitutes when taking comfort breaks. Neither are illegal under the International Cricket Council's regulations, but the subtext is that England were abusing the spirit of the game by allowing bowlers to nip off for a change of clothes and a quick massage.

England were quick to counter that Pratt was on for Jones, who'd left the field and gone to hospital for a scan on his right ankle. An injured player can be substituted but not if he came into the game with a pre-existing injury. Jones had been given a pain-killing jab in his ankle before the match, which suggested there was a problem – in which case a replacement should not have been allowed.

Ponting probably had a point anyway though his tirade, made in full earshot of the members' enclosure at Trent Bridge, cost him dear. It was not the £3,800 (which constituted 75 percent of his match fee) that mattered, but the fact that he was losing control. After the series was lost at the Oval, Ponting had the

grace to share a beer with Pratt, handing the tyro his batting spikes as a memento.

The edginess wasn't confined to the captain. Jason Gillespie, already under extreme pressure after England's batsmen had decided to assault Australia's second-string bowlers, complained about heckling from the crowd. For England's players victimised in the past by the baying mobs in Australia, it was hypocritical in the extreme, though Gillespie was saved further torment when he was eventually dropped for young fast bowler Shaun Tait.

The crowds, revved up each morning by a rousing rendition of William Blake's Jerusalem, sustained a rare intensity of support, session after session. After years of one-sided Ashes encounters, they sensed a real contest and responded with football-like fervour. After the series Vaughan paid his respects, saying they'd been England's 12th and 13th men.

It wasn't just the jingoism among spectators that made Australia realise they were up against more than eleven Englishmen in whites, fearsome prospect though that became. Starting with the mickey-taking in the media over the ghost in the Lumley Castle, which had genuinely spooked some of the players staying there, the visitors then fell victim to a dirty tricks campaign during the NatWest Series.

Certainly there seemed little substance to claims that Matthew Hayden had sworn at school children forming a guard of honour with flags bearing the cross of St George. The Australians, clearly unhappy with the symbolism of a flag-lined tunnel, tried to skirt around the edges, a move that led to accusations in the next match that Hayden had barged one child out of the way. Although the Aussie camp felt the stories were coming from shadowy figures at the England and Wales Cricket Board, the only GBH committed during the summer was by England's fast bowlers and Brett Lee.

That mischief aside, the series was generally praised for the spirit in which it was played, a fine advert for the game as football disappeared into its customary morass of foul language and petulant behaviour. Uncompromising in their exchanges with bat and ball, the players of both sides came to respect one other. Even the post-match beer, a tradition that had been on the wane since Allan Border forbade it on the 1989 Ashes tour, was resurrected. →

Breaking out the bubbly:
Andrew Flintoff and Kevin
Pietersen, England's
man of the series and man
of the match, lead the
celebrations at the Oval

The sporting chivalry led to the summer's most enduring image, one that headmasters and newspaper leader writers will feed off for months. The photograph, taken at Edgbaston, depicted Flintoff stooping to place a commiserating arm around Lee who'd batted his team to within two runs of victory. The moment, as victor and vanquished became inseparable, resurrected the oft-fractured link between sport and sportsmanship.

Following England's humbling defeat at Lord's, the 2nd Test at Edgbaston proved to be the most exciting and crucial match of the entire series, though those that followed would also lay their claim. It was certainly close, with molecules deciding the eventual outcome as Harmison took the final wicket.

The margin between success and failure can be minute and had last man Michael Kasprowicz got a smidgen more contact onto Harmison's bouncer with his glove, an action that would have directed the ball to the fine leg boundary rather than to wicket keeper Geraint Jones, England would have gone 2-0 down. And that, as they say, would probably have been that, at least until 2006/7.

Birmingham often brings out the best in England cricketers. This time it sparked Flintoff, though not before Marcus Trescothick and Andrew Strauss had made the most of Ponting's decision to insert England after McGrath had sprained his ankle treading on a cricket ball before the start. McGrath missed the 4th Test too, the other England won. But while it might be tempting to apply cause and effect and say he was the difference between England winning or not, he wasn't the force he'd been earlier in the summer.

Happily for England, Flintoff grew in stature and following a poor debut Ashes Test at Lord's, in which he admitted feeling anxious, big Freddie suddenly became a tour de force with bat and ball. Ian Botham's 1981 summer of miracles has long been seen as the apogee of all-round performance, but he rarely dominated with both bat and ball in the same match. At Edgbaston, Flintoff took seven wickets and made two vital half-centuries in what proved an immense all-round performance and the finest of his career.

Forged in the white heat of such a close encounter, England saw a better Flintoff emerge. A man possessed of immense

instinctive talent anyway, he took it to the next level by using his head – a combination that led to his thinking man's century at Trent Bridge. With him as the team's beating heart, and with the discovery of a more pro-active spinner than the stoic Ashley Giles, England could dominate world cricket for the next three of four years, though given his long history of injuries luck will be required.

Most Test players produce their most telling performance midway through their careers, yet 25-year old Kevin Pietersen will do well to exceed the 158 he made in the 2nd innings of the final Test at the Oval if he plays until he is forty.

Many will find Pietersen, one of four boys born in Pietermaritzburg, unacceptably foreign despite a British mother, and his intentions unacceptably mercenary. Yet there is little difference to his predicament – save the fact that South Africa is no longer denied Test status – than that faced by Allan Lamb and Robin Smith, both capped many times for England.

Pietersen was the missing piece of England's batting jigsaw. The cultural distance between him and most of those willing the Ashes upon England probably freed him to play that amazing knock, a heady mixture of calculated risk and reckless gamble. Only Botham and perhaps Flintoff could have matched its audacity, though neither has struck seven sixes in a Test innings before, especially with their team so precariously placed.

A man who has never knowingly undersold himself, Pietersen will believe he can trump it, but without the adulation, adrenalin rushes and churning excitement of the battle, nothing will probably feel quite the same ever again. This is the challenge now on, not just for him, but also Vaughan and the remainder of the team as they travel to Pakistan and India for the winter.

For a decade Australia set the cricketing agenda. As with all great dynasties it was only a matter of time before one of the following pack caught them up and beat them.

After a breathtaking summer of cricket England was that team. But if that is worth celebrating with ticker-tape parades and all night benders, many more series need to be won, particularly away from home, before they can claim Australia's crown as the best team in the world. ●DP

Post series reflections
Martin Johnson

It's a short hop from Captain Marvel to Captain Cock-Up, as readers of an English Sunday newspaper discovered during the Michael Atherton-led tour to Zimbabwe in 1996. "Super England Silence Critics!" screamed the back page headline as the visitors seemed to be recovering from a dismal start to the tour. Seven days later, however, when it became clear that things were just as bad as we suspected, it had changed to: "He'll Ath To Go!"

So it was after the pulsating Ashes series of 2005. As Michael Vaughan stood atop an open topped bus in Trafalgar Square, Ricky Ponting was arriving back in Australia with famous old cricketers like Dennis Lillee inviting him to reach for the pearl handed revolver. One captain ended up carrying the urn, and the other carrying the can.

After Australia's victory in the first Test at Lord's, when England appeared to take the field with the accumulated baggage of eight previous Ashes humiliations, Ponting was asked whether the gulf between the two sides was as wide as ever. He gave it a moment's thought before replying: "I'd guess you'd have to say it's vast, yes." Oh dear.

The defining moment of Ponting's captaincy came during the Trent Bridge Test, when he let fly with a flurry of expletives after being run out by England's substitute fielder, before going on to whinge about what he considered to be the home team infringing the spirit of the game in their use of a specialist 12th man.

Ye Gods. In days gone by England would have pinched this idea from the Australians, so ruthlessly did they go about their business. In the 1989 series, when Robin Smith asked if he could have a glass of water after being struck a painful blow amidships, the Australian captain Allan Border snarled at him: "What do you think this is? An effing tea party?"

It was the same Border who watched dispassionately when his badly dehydrated batting partner in a Test match in Madras, Dean Jones, threw up in the crease and asked his captain whether he could go off. Border replied: "If you like, but make sure the next man in has got a bit more ticker." Jones stayed out to make a double century.

Steve Waugh had the same cold blooded streak, but under Ponting, the old strut and swagger, and superior body language, seemed to go missing. He even got upset when Vaughan declined to inquire about Ponting's health when he was struck on the visor by Steve Harmison at Lord's, whereas a Border or a Waugh would have taken it as a compliment that England had latched on to the old Australian blueprint. A shared beer or two off the field, but totally ruthless on it.

Ponting was numbingly defensive in his tactical approach, made a bad error after winning the toss at Edgbaston, and his body language was almost entirely negative. The Australian captain spent much of the series wearing much the same expression as King Canute when the eccentric old monarch realised that the tide was up around his nostrils, and not about to turn merely by royal decree. After Lord's, you got the impression that Australia had begun to believe in the Canute principle of forcing the other team to bend to their regal will, and were stumped for an answer when the opposition failed to oblige.

The New Zealand all-rounder Chris Cairns had said of Waugh's Australia: "My mum could captain this lot", by which he meant that they were so powerful in all the key individual areas that all the bloke in charge was required to do was rotate his quick bowlers at one end, and bring on Shane Warne at the other. However, with England's newly discovered determination not to tug the forelock requiring something more cerebral, it quickly became clear that there might not have been much to choose between Ponting and Mrs Cairns.

One of the most important parts of captaincy is exuding confidence in the players you have around you. Ponting did quite the opposite, especially with out of form bowlers such as Jason Gillespie, and newcomers like Shaun Tait. When a ball disappeared to the boundary, the Australian captain would run up and pat them on the bottom, which far from being a gesture of faith, mostly conveyed the subliminal message: "Er, do you really think the wide long hop to Flintoff is a good idea, mate?"

The key to Vaughan's captaincy is that not only does his body language suggest total confidence in his team-mates, but that he's pulled off the difficult trick of remaining one of the boys while eliminating all doubt as to who's actually in charge. Vaughan's doctrine to his troops is to enjoy their cricket, which they clearly do, and he himself has been an unwitting ally in one particular area. His own fielding, which is a puzzling source of dressing room hilarity for a batsman who's destroyed some of the world's best attacks with a combination of nimble footwork and razor sharp eyesight. However, when the ball is heading Vaughan's way in the field, you're never quite sure whether he's going to drop it, or fall over before he has the chance to.

If there was one moment which summed up what kind of team spirit England have developed under Vaughan, it was when the players were off the field for lunch at Edgbaston. The captain, who had just taken a catch to remove Ponting, and then run out Damien Martyn with a direct hit, suddenly heard Steve Harmison pipe up: "I don't know. Australia must be the unluckiest side in the world. A Vaughan catch and a run out in the space of half an hour? We're certs to win the Ashes."

Vaughan's philosophy about the job is simple, and based on an awareness of the world outside cricket. Visits to handicapped children in hospital have put the pressures of leading England on a cricket field into a healthier perspective. "How tough is your job?" he was asked. "Not very," he replied. "Being an NHS nurse is what I'd describe as a tough job."

He's not an egghead captain like Mike Brearley, but he does appear to have Brearley's knack of knowing how to treat individuals differently. As Brearley once said: "Man management is a bit like gardening. Some plants need fertilizing, others need pruning."

The one thing England had during this series was a plan for every situation. Not a single Australian batsman took guard this summer – as Vaughan deployed his fielders in often unusual areas – without realising that England had a strategy for him. Sounds obvious enough, but this is an area in which England have previously belonged to the "please sir, the dog ate it" school.

And yet we still come back to luck. Had Mike Kasprowicz been given not out at Edgbaston (and television replays suggested he was unlucky), and Kevin Pietersen not been dropped twice early on at the Oval, it might all have turned out differently. Both captains ended up wearing dark glasses, but for one of them it was to hide the after effects of the celebrations, and for the other, to disguise the hurt in his eyes. It could so easily have been the other way around. ●MJ

He's urned it:
Michael Vaughan (main pic)
emphasised enjoyment and
perspective. Ricky Ponting
(inset) failed to exude any
confidence in the players
around him

Post series reflections
Simon Hughes

At the very end of this compelling, pugilistic, nerve-shattering series, there was a touching scene. It was the Sunday night at the Oval, play had been called off for the day, and press and TV interviews were being conducted on the boundary edge. A familiar figure suddenly dashed past the camera crews, straight across the field and up into the media centre on the opposite side of the ground: Shane Warne.

His sole aim was to pop into the Channel 4 commentary box to wish Richie Benaud good luck for his last day of commentary on British television. Benaud no doubt wished Warne all the best for his last Test bowling spell in England. He ought to have mentioned his slip catching too. But for a rare drop at slip the next day, when his mate Kevin Pietersen was on 15, Warne could have pulled off the unthinkable for Australia, and here, the byword would now be inquest rather than conquest.

Ever since Warne first came to prominence in the early 1990s, he and Benaud have always had a special relationship. Less teacher-pupil, more father-son. Warne occasionally seeks reassurance about his bowling from his great leg spinning predecessor which Benaud is happy to dispense. They are not especially close, but there is that mutual understanding of the baffling leggie's art, two master conjurers conspiratorially exchanging tricks like members of the magic circle.

Benaud and Warne – the most distinctive names in the modern game – two men united by the rare skill of being able to bowl two identical-looking balls that can spin in opposite directions. Both record holders in their own right too. Benaud has played in or watched more Test matches than anyone in history (well over 500 so far) Warne has taken more Test wickets than anyone in history (623 and counting.) There must be something about the pleasure of twirling a ball down mischievously at less than 50mph that keeps you young. Undoubtedly Warne's emergence into the Australian team gave Benaud a new lease of life in the commentary box. Here was his subtle art, which had lain largely dormant for 20 years – except on the sub-continent – resurrected. Magnanimity personified, Benaud would always say Warne was the best leg spinner he had ever seen (and he's seen a few.)

You could probably go further than that and say Warne is the best bowler there's ever been.

Never mind that he holds the world record for Test wickets taken, it's hard to imagine anyone else so consistently tying batsmen in knots at any stage of any game on any surface. Look at this Ashes series just gone. Hardly any of the pitches suited him, he only got to bowl once in the last innings (at Trent Bridge.) Yet still he gave all the batsmen kittens, produced balls that spun so much that Channel 4's Hawkeye computer system rejected them as physically impossible, and took 40 wickets in the five Tests. And that was after England's batsmen had had exhaustive stints at every Test against a machine, Merlyn, specially designed to replicate his bowling. Commentators ran out of superlatives for Warne. Benaud's 'quite mervellus that' was regular and heartfelt. They are of course vastly different men, reflecting their age, but their attitude too. Benaud is meticulous, systematic, a creature of habit. He rises early, walks daily to keep himself fit, eats healthily, is perennially neat and punctual and keeps himself to himself. An information-junkie, consuming papers and on-line information with gusto, he spends hours a day hunched over his laptop. His commentary style is legendarily understated, and based on the maxim that why use 20 words when five will suffice.

Apart from in the commentary box, he is rarely without his delightful wife Daphne and invariably refers to himself as 'we.' Warne is the diametric opposite. He is a glamour puss, a fly by night, a risk taker, a born entertainer. He craves attention, adulation. He likes gambling and night life and it was once said that his idea of a balanced diet was a cheeseburger in each hand. On the field he has hunches, he will try anything to get a wicket. A brilliant reader of the game, he is the best captain Australia never properly had. As a result he is a virtuoso, an exceptional performer, though according to tabloid revelations during the summer, this doesn't extend to activities in the bedroom. He and his wife Simone are going through an acrimonious separation.

This summer, both Warne and Benaud left us performances to savour. Benaud, a habitual enthusiast, finds the unpredictable patterns of the game endlessly fascinating, and was at his succinct best at critical moments of games. His commentary as Harmison's bouncer tickled Kasprowicz's glove at Edgbaston was the most prefect précis of the situation: 'Jones!....Bowden! ... Kasprowicz – the man to go. Harmison has done it. Despair! ... on the faces of the batsmen. And joy! ... for every England player on the field.' At Trent Bridge, as England lurched and stumbled towards their victory target of 129, he simply called the score, and how many to win, but made certain to regularly point out that if even Australia lost, they could retain the Ashes by winning at the Oval. Perhaps his most valuable asset as a commentator is he keeps everything in perspective.

Not surprisingly there was a flurry of activity around him for his last Test, after a remarkable 42 years behind the mike. There were book signings to be done, radio and TV appearances to give, farewell dinners to attend, cameras following him everywhere. Still he calmly delivered his lines to set up the last day ... 'Morning everyone, stirring moments these...' and retained his poise when his brief farewell speech ... 'it's been a privilege ... and a great deal of fun ...' was interrupted by Pietersen's wicket '... but not for the batsman!' He finished with a simple handover to Mark Nicholas and Tony Greig and retired to the back of the box.

At times during the summer it had felt like Warne v England, and that was certainly true at the Oval. Rapidly able to size up a pitch, he realized there would be little spin for him in the first innings, so kept England in check with cleverly disguised over-spinners that extracted extra bounce instead. His six wickets were solely responsible for keeping England's advantage to a minimum in the first innings. In the second, when there was some assistance, he spun out Trescothick for the umpteenth time, could have had Pietersen for nought and winkled out Flintoff to leave England perilously placed at 126-5. It was only Pietersen's audacity that stole the show. And finally, when England's triumph was safe, he still produced one more wonder ball to bowl Giles and remind us all of the genius he has bequeathed on the game. Benaud and Warne will be back of course, Benaud to visit friends and watch some cricket, Warne to play for Hampshire. But never again on our airwaves will we hear those mellifluous tones saying, 'Mervellus deliveree from Warne....just too good!' And cricket will be the poorer. ●SH

'Cricket will be the poorer':
the apparently inde-
fatigable Shane Warne
finally shows signs of
weariness as he leaves the
Oval with long-time strike
partner Glenn McGrath.
Warne says he has played
his last Test in England

PLAYER
PROFILES

THE ASHES SERIES 2005

AUSTRALIA
R T PONTING

BATTING AVERAGES	M	I	NO	Runs	HS	Avge	100	50	Ct	St
R T Ponting	5	9	0	359	156	39.88	1	1	4	-

BOWLING AVERAGES	O	M	R	W	Avge	Best	5w	10w
R T Ponting	6.0	2	9	1	9.00	1-9	-	-

Ricky Ponting knew all about public humiliation before arriving in England for the 2005 summer. But even his youthful admission to having an alcohol problem must have felt like an easy ride compared to the pain of becoming the man who lost the Ashes. Through his talent as a batsman and leading Australia to the 2003 World Cup, Ponting had made up for the excesses of his early days. The man who was once knocked unconscious by a Sydney doorman and forced to admit a battle with the bottle had matured into a world-class leader.

But England managed to do more than dole out a couple of black eyes. After four months of exhausting action, Ponting was forced to slink back into Australia as a beaten man. Beaten by a rejuvenated England, beaten by his own bowlers and finally beaten by his side's rigid thinking. As the ticker tape and confetti rained down on England's celebrating players at the Oval, Ponting was forced to admit: "We were never as good as England and they deserved to win the Ashes."

Such humility was a credit to Ponting the man, who since succeeding Steve Waugh in 2003 had done his best to change the Australian image. 'Mental disintegration' had been given a human face under Ponting.

He lost his cool only once. His four-letter tirade at the England dressing room after his mistake of taking on the substitute fielder Gary Pratt at Trent Bridge cost him a chunk of his match fee. "Ponting did apologise, presumably because he realised there was more than one Pratt involved in his run out," wrote Martin Johnson.

Ponting found his captaincy in England stretched to new limits both by his own side and the opposition. When he arrived the talk was of the itinerary suiting Australia perfectly. But their insistence on two-day county matches left little room for experimentation away from the glare of Test cricket.

Michael Vaughan out-thought Ponting with his bowling changes, field placings and perhaps most importantly, was consistently able to conjure a vital trick out of thin air. Where Vaughan made things happen, Ponting was often happy to bide his time. He had no extra dimension to his captaincy. Perhaps that is the downside to having the brilliance of Shane Warne and Glenn McGrath at your disposal, they take on the irksome burden of having to produce the unexpected.

His support bowlers let him down, but the refusal to act on Jason Gillespie's poor form showed a lack of ruthlessness. Where once the Australian selectors ended careers with impunity, they now showed a softer side and Ponting was effectively left a bowler short.

There were stories of a stand-up row with Warne during the Edgbaston Test, hotly denied by Australia, but as the tour progressed it seemed the leg-spinner was often conducting proceedings on the field. It was Warne's pep talk to Brett Lee that inspired him to bowl ferociously fast in the second Test.

At the end of the fifth Test, Ponting refused to admit to his biggest blunder. His decision to bowl first at Edgbaston just minutes after losing McGrath to an ankle injury allowed England to change the tempo of the series. "Ponting winning the toss and putting England in was a piece of good fortune. It was never a putting-in pitch. It was flat, there was no pace, no bounce and no movement," wrote Geoffrey Boycott. He was right, England made 407 and could move on from the heavy defeat at Lord's.

"It was either madness or arrogance," to bowl first was Mark Nicholas's verdict. Australia could not help themselves, England were vulnerable and had to be crushed. Ponting could not alter his thinking and instead of having Shane Warne bowl last on a wearing pitch he instead had his champion spinner batting in the fourth innings of the match, desperately trying to salvage a sensational win for his side.

But the captaincy was not Ponting's only problem. England also invaded his personal space, the place where he could always find solace from his troubles – the batting crease. Ponting's brilliance as a batsman had earmarked him for Australia selection from an early age and he started the tour with an average of 56.97. His ability to dominate attacks had impressed many, but Boycott had spotted weaknesses. "Ricky Ponting is fallible. He plays straight stuff to the on side and cuts or pulls anything short, so you've got to get him doing what he doesn't want to do early on and stop his pet shots."

England followed that advice to the letter. Andrew Flintoff and Matthew Hoggard gave him little room to play his strokes and a combination of short balls and yorkers were often his undoing.

His Borderesque rearguard at Old Trafford, where he saved the Test with a gritty 156, was described as "arguably the captain's innings of the 21st century," by Derek Pringle. But Ponting suffered from the same malaise that struck down his colleagues in the Australian top order. He ended the series averaging 39.88 and cursing his inconsistency. He was hurt on the first morning of the series, when his cheek was cut by Steve Harmison, and the bowlers continued to probe away, nibbling at his confidence as England targeted the opposition captain, for so long a favourite Australian tactic.

As the light faded at the Oval and in turn on Australia's Ashes challenge, Ponting was left to reflect on where it all went wrong. Calls for his resignation had replaced the familiar sound of compliments and the Ashes had turned a full circle.

Ponting returned to Australia talking of lessons learned. For so long the student, England had turned into the teachers. "We can learn a little bit from the way England have played and their off-field set up," said Ponting, his admission reflecting the changing times.

AUSTRALIA
M L HAYDEN

BATTING AVERAGES	M	I	NO	Runs	HS	Avge	100	50	Ct	St
M L Hayden	5	10	1	318	138	35.33	1	-	10	-

"Would the real Matthew Hayden please stand up", asked the Daily Telegraph during the final Test at the Oval.

He responded with 138, but the fact it was 42 runs more than his combined effort in previous innings spoke volumes for Hayden's miserable tour. A big man, a big hitter and an even bigger sledger, Hayden's downfall was sweet for an England side he beat into submission on the previous Ashes tour.

But in truth, Hayden had not been playing well for some time. His century at the Oval was his first for 17 Tests and the man who once held the world record highest Test score was staring at the end of his career before the final match.

The reason? Hayden was simply out-thought by England. He fell into Vaughan's trap at Edgbaston where he slapped his first ball to short extra cover, and as the failures mounted, he was unsure whether to stick or twist.

"The Incredible Hulk Matthew Hayden has been stopped in his muscular tracks by the England bowlers' and fielders' general refusal to kowtow to him," wrote Simon Hughes. "His intimidatory batting has been slowly eroded by the buffeting from three 90mph pacemen."

Runs against county attacks gave a little reassurance but when confronted with lateral movement at Test level he consistently came up short, particularly against Matthew Hoggard's late swing. At Old Trafford he was totally dumbfounded by Flintoff's attack from around the wicket, and was then bowled behind his legs when Flintoff switched his line. With Simon Jones missing from the England attack at the Oval, Hayden cashed in although his century was the slowest of his career, taking 303 balls.

Failure there would have left him with plenty of time to complete the follow-up to his best-selling cookery book.

AUSTRALIA
J L LANGER

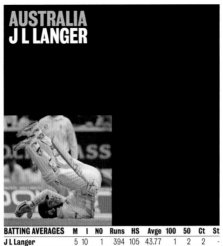

BATTING AVERAGES	M	I	NO	Runs	HS	Avge	100	50	Ct	St
J L Langer	5	10	1	394	105	43.77	1	2	2	-

Before the Ashes tour Langer and Hayden dominated attacks around the world as they blended two differing styles into one successful mix. But against England's quintet of pace, Australia's golden couple hit the rocks.

Langer clearly felt his mate's pain, helping him with relaxation techniques and words of advice at tough times, and his delight in Hayden's century at the Oval was clear.

His own hundred in that Test brought back memories of his career saving century at the Oval four years previously and ensured he topped his team's batting averages. Langer was Australia's most consistent batsman but he also acted out of character by failing to convert good starts into match winning scores.

While his team-mates were engaged in the one-day series, Langer was at home in Perth sharpening up his boxing skills. Inside the ring he hoped to improve his footwork but during the Ashes series he quite often found himself backed into a corner and fighting on the ropes. Flinty and something of a throwback to the days of old fashioned doughty Australian openers, Langer relished the challenge.

But even though he passed fifty three times, he could not carry the fight on his own. A hundred went begging at Edgbaston as Simon Jones gave his first display of reverse swing, and another was squandered at Trent Bridge when Ashley Giles teased and tempted Langer once too often.

At the Oval, Langer outscored his opening partner as he mixed the sublime with the ridiculous. Classic strokes were followed by awful ones, and once again he took several blows to the body. Those boxing lessons must have come in very handy.

AUSTRALIA
D R MARTYN

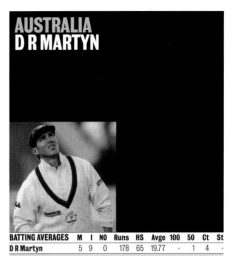

BATTING AVERAGES	M	I	NO	Runs	HS	Avge	100	50	Ct	St
D R Martyn	5	9	0	178	65	19.77	-	1	4	-

He began the Ashes series as Australia's form player, the model of consistency for 18 months. He ended it above only Gillespie, Tait and Kasprowicz in the batting averages – a motley crew of tail end blockers, old stagers and a young hopeful.

The crumbling of Martyn's form was built on a couple of poor umpiring decisions but several lazy dismissals suggested a poor attitude. When you bat as effortlessly as Martyn, the mistakes are construed as complacency, the bad shots as mental weakness.

England's disciplined lines caused him trouble throughout the series and his careless pull at the Oval brought an appropriate end to his series. "Damien Martyn, such a regal batsman when in full flow, has had his crown confiscated," wrote Simon Hughes. Hitting ordinary attacks around the world had built a false sense of security that was whipped away by England's hunger.

Martyn was cool under pressure at Lord's where his second innings partnership with Michael Clarke put Australia in charge. He scored 65 but his next seven innings yielded only 111 runs.

Two poor leg before decisions, at Old Trafford and Trent Bridge, went against him with television replays proving an inside edge. The fates were conspiring against Martyn as his future as Australia's No 4 became a matter for debate.

He fell victim to Giles's version of the ball of the century at Old Trafford where a delivery that pitched outside leg turned sharply to hit the top of off stump. England's much-maligned spinner had beaten the coolest and calmest member of Australia's middle order – a microcosm of the Ashes series.

AUSTRALIA
M J CLARKE

BATTING AVERAGES	M	I	NO	Runs	HS	Avge	100	50	Ct	St
M J Clarke	5	9	0	335	91	37.22	-	2	2	-

BOWLING AVERAGES	O	M	R	W	Avge	Best	5w	10w
M J Clarke	2.0	0	6	0	-	-	-	-

It all started so promisingly. Success at Lord's, where he played beautifully to score 91 in the second innings, confirmed all the hype about Michael Clarke, variously labelled the new Steve Waugh, the next Michael Slater and an Australian captain in waiting.

He was to end the series with one thing in common with fellow New South Welshman Waugh. Both lost their first Ashes series. Early defeats against England did not harm Waugh too much and Clarke will have learned a great deal from his troubles. Patience perhaps being the chief lesson.

He took on Flintoff at sledging during the Edgbaston Test and came off worse. Sidetracked into his battle with Flintoff, Clarke was then bowled by a magnificent slower ball from Steve Harmison in the second innings of that great Test. It was a moment that turned the match firmly England's way. At that point Clarke, 30 not out, was edging Australia closer to their target and threatening to fulfil the pre-series prophecies of being Australia's match winner.

That Harmison delivery changed it all so abruptly. A back spasm reduced Clarke to a shuffling bit part during the Old Trafford Test. He spent the majority of the match lying flat on his back at the team hotel and a history of lumbar problems is a worry for the future.

He recovered his fitness in time for the fourth Test but looked troubled by anything that moved off the straight as Australia followed on. A generation of Australian players never experienced such a humiliation, yet Clarke was in the middle of it all on his first Ashes tour.

He responded with a gutsy second innings performance as along with Simon Katich he scored a half century. Clarke eschewed attack in favour of defence, but in the end couldn't resist taking aim at a wide ball. The nick was faint, the resulting roar from the crowd was not.

AUSTRALIA
S M KATICH

BATTING AVERAGES	M	I	NO	Runs	HS	Avge	100	50	Ct	St
S M Katich	5	9	0	248	67	27.55	-	2	4	-

BOWLING AVERAGES	O	M	R	W	Avge	Best	5w	10w
S M Katich	12.0	1	50	1	50.00	1-36	-	-

The cool exterior cracked under pressure when he was given out leg before at Trent Bridge, ironically his best Test. Katich was busy building a match saving innings when he was given out lbw despite the ball pitching outside leg stump. He was cross and swore his way back to the pavilion losing a chunk of his match fee in the process. The son of a Perth murder detective had shown a hot-headed, angry streak.

His performances at Trent Bridge, where he scored 45 and 59, ensured he clung onto his place at the Oval but the failure of Australia's bowlers put his place in jeopardy. The long-term tactic of six batsmen, and in turn Katich's future, were far from assured at the end of the series.

Reverse swing was clearly a problem; he was bowled shouldering arms by Flintoff at Old Trafford and consistently shuffled his way across the crease. Katich's feet were stuck in glue and England's attack never felt threatened by his presence.

Until the Ashes tour, Katich was accustomed to walking out to the crease with a weight of runs already on the board. England threw him into an alien environment and he struggled to adjust. Despite extensive county experience, Katich never felt comfortable against a swinging ball.

"Simon Katich doesn't know what to leave and what to play," wrote Boycott "When Flintoff bowls around the wicket he either leaves it and has his off pole knocked out or plays at balls two foot wide." An all too familiar Australian failing.

AUSTRALIA
A C GILCHRIST

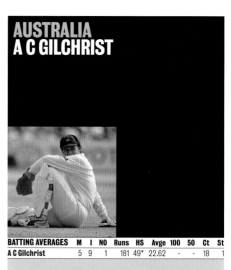

BATTING AVERAGES	M	I	NO	Runs	HS	Avge	100	50	Ct	St
A C Gilchrist	5	9	1	181	49*	22.62	-	-	18	1

Coping with the world's most destructive batsman had been an impossible task for England during the previous two Ashes series. He averaged more than 60 in Ashes Tests and a string of England bowlers had become notches on his holster.

A century in the final one-day match suggested Gilchrist had found his range but instead all he had done was meet his match. Flintoff was the one given the unenviable task of stifling Gilchrist. By bowling around the wicket to off-side fields, it seemed Flintoff had little room for error. In truth, it was Gilchrist who could ill afford to make mistakes. Catches were held in the gully and slips as Gilchrist ended the series with an average in keeping with mere mortals. A swinging ball proved an insurmountable task and sticky feet refused to move.

With the runs drying up, Gilchrist's keeping also looked scrappy. Two costly dropped catches at Old Trafford characterised a sloppy performance by a keeper with plenty on his mind.

Gilchrist tried attack and defence and his troubles were summed up in the second innings at Trent Bridge. "Gilchrist at last retaliated," wrote Simon Hughes. "Like a wounded animal making a last dash for freedom, he carved two audacious boundaries off the over. Flintoff smiled, whistled a ball past Gilchrist's edge, then watched as Australia's erstwhile dasher walked in front of a Hoggard delivery in the next over and was lbw."

Without the greatest safety net in world cricket Australia's middle order looked vulnerable. Whereas in the past Gilchrist had steered them from disaster and made up for early failings, he was too preoccupied with his own troubles to carry the team.

Australia's vice-captain failed to produce the performances when his side were most in need and it is no coincidence that in the two series Gilchrist has lost, he averaged in the low 20s.

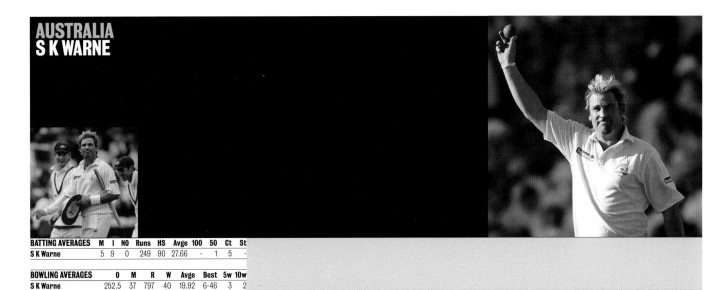

BATTING AVERAGES	M	I	NO	Runs	HS	Avge	100	50	Ct	St
S K Warne	5	9	0	249	90	27.66	-	1	5	-

BOWLING AVERAGES	O	M	R	W	Avge	Best	5w	10w
S K Warne	252.5	37	797	40	19.92	6-46	3	2

It is perhaps only through the pain of parting that England supporters finally appreciated how much they will miss Shane Warne when he lays his slider to rest.

He stood so far above every other member of the Australian side on his final Ashes tour that he often looked like a giant surrounded by toddlers. "If Australia had decent bowlers to back him up they would be walking away with this series," said Geoffrey Boycott during the final Test.

At the Oval, Warne stretched his tally in the series to 40 wickets and surpassed Dennis Lillee's record of 167 Ashes wickets. His 600th Test wicket was already in the bag, taken at Old Trafford in the third Test. "In any sensible reckoning of sporting achievement Warne belongs in the most select company along with Muhammad Ali, Jack Nicklaus, Pele, and dare I say it, Don Bradman," wrote Michael Parkinson.

All of them heroes, all of them champions. For Warne, a man troubled by personal problems but an addict hooked on winning, to bow out of Tests in England as a beaten man was chastening. "I couldn't have given any more," was his verdict and one beyond question.

England's triumphant bus journey through the streets of London coincided with Warne's 36th birthday. Although not met with out-and-out celebration or serious flag waving in Trafalgar Square, Warne's Ashes series was worth toasting.

Through a combination of turning leg breaks mixed with a deadly straight ball – Warne destroyed rumours of decline. "Increasingly Warne was used to dry up an end while the seamers wheeled away opposite him," wrote Mark Nicholas of Warne's days under Steve Waugh. "Thus the great blond bamboozler began to bowl defensively and now that he finds it difficult and wearing to bowl with the dip, swerve and spin of his youth, he competes with his mind as much as his fingers."

It would have been excusable if Warne's mind had not been on the cricket. His English summer with Hampshire began with the news that his marriage to wife Simone was over. But regardless of the problems he has faced in his private life, Warne has always been able to retreat to safety on the field, and the Ashes tour provided him with a chance to reconcile his life as well as prove to the Australian public he could be more than a subject for scandalous newspaper reports.

While Glenn McGrath ruled the Lord's slope once more, Warne chipped away at the England batsmen in the first Test and finished with six wickets, narrowly missing out on etching his name onto the honours board for the first time. "Shane Warne confounded predictions, he confounded expectations and occasionally he confounded the laws of trigonometry," wrote Simon Hughes.

The only batsman to attack him with any success was Kevin Pietersen, the Hampshire team-mate Warne had urged England to select. Pietersen judged Warne as much on length as anything else and hit him hard, very hard.

But for Warne the challenge was only just hotting up. England turned to a lump of steel, a bowling machine called Merlyn, in attempt to counter Warne's threat. In the end their cause was aided by circumstance. The injury to McGrath at Edgbaston left Warne as Australia's sole threat with the ball and he came mighty close to delivering the Ashes.

Victory for Australia in the second Test would end lingering English resistance but Warne was denied the chance to bowl in the final innings of the match, when the pitch would have been at its most receptive, because Ricky Ponting wanted to flex his muscles. England batted first, Pietersen flayed Warne again.

Warne tried everything. He played to the crowd, he goaded the batsmen and he tried to intimidate the umpires. "He spent so long shrieking for lbws he could miss the next Test with laryngitis," said Martin Johnson.

He took 10 wickets in the match and Australia would have been defeated by the kind of margins they inflict on others if he had not inspired some tailend resistance on the final day. His 42 gave Australia belief and left England breathing the biggest sigh of relief when Steve Harmison took the last wicket with two runs to spare.

Again and again Warne tried to reverse momentum. His obdurate batting at Old Trafford saved Australia from the follow-on and when all was lost at Trent Bridge he inspired the kind of panic in the England dressing room not seen since Australia were stunned at Headingley in 1981.

"It was Warne's infectious enthusiasm, nothing else, which kept Australia alive and his sheer bloody mindedness that made the game so tight," said Mark Nicholas. With England requiring 129 to win they were 32 for one when Warne took a wicket with his first ball. Andrew Strauss and Michael Vaughan followed before Geraint Jones cracked under Warne's pressure, but in the end even he could not save the condemned.

And so on to the Oval, the scene of so many Ashes last stands. The great Don waved goodbye at the ground, his triumphant farewell wrecked by a delivery from Warwickshire leggie Eric Hollies. While Bradman bagged a duck he did at least win that Test in 1948, Warne would have gladly taken such a finale.

As it was, he was again at his brilliant best, bowling unchanged on the final day as he tried to take Australia to victory. He took 12 wickets in the match and left Australia on the edge of success when he clung onto a low caught and bowled chance off Andrew Flintoff.

But Warne was to fall victim to a cruel irony. "Warney dropped the Ashes," sang the Oval crowd after he missed a straightforward catch when Pietersen was on 15. The man whose cause he had championed to inflict the ultimate punishment. It was a moment 'Warne, the great mover-on in life will find difficult to forget," wrote Nicholas.

"I had a lump in my throat," said Pietersen when Warne congratulated him on his 158 and proved irrefutably he had conquered the art of losing as well as winning.

AUSTRALIA
B LEE

BATTING AVERAGES	M	I	NO	Runs	HS	Avge	100	50	Ct	St
B Lee	5	9	3	158	47	26.33	-	-	2	-

BOWLING AVERAGES	O	M	R	W	Avge	Best	5w	10w
B Lee	191.1	25	822	20	41.10	4-82	-	-

Ignored for two years by Ricky Ponting, Brett Lee was clearly not a man to be trusted in Test cricket. But with a combination of guts, skill and fiery pace Lee re-established his place in the Australian side.

"It is not going to be a summer of orthodox swing and seam," predicted Simon Hughes at the start of the series. "It is going to be a summer of hit the deck and old-ball manipulation. For Australia, Lee is the man."

At times he was the only man. Lee bowled consistently 10mph quicker than his seam colleagues and his youth and fitness ensured he made it through all five Tests. Being the right side of 30 was a rare commodity in the Australian side and it was Lee's enthusiasm which carried the attack to England. Without McGrath, Warne needed a foil and Lee was the only viable alternative. His 20 wickets may have cost 41 each but he often willingly sacrificed his figures for that extra ounce of pace.

His over to Kevin Pietersen just before lunch on the final morning of the series was pure sporting excellence. It was brutal, bruising cricket with the Ashes at stake. "It was either him or me," said Pietersen.

Lee also plays the game with a smile on his face and is no stubborn blocker in the Gillespie mould. He had spent his early career stood at the other end and watched Gilchrist belt the ball around. He had clearly learned a few tricks. Steve Harmison was twice hit out of the ground at Trent Bridge as Lee ate into England's first innings lead. At Edgbaston he was battered and bruised, taking all that England could throw at him as he and Kasprowicz almost delivered a sensation. England were impressed and Lee had earned widespread respect.

"Brett Lee has entered the arena with all pistons firing, and claimed some useful scalps, but he is not Dennis Lillee and never will be," wrote Hughes. Lee may lack the quality of a genuine great but his Ashes summer was one he will remember with affection.

AUSTRALIA
J N GILLESPIE

BATTING AVERAGES	M	I	NO	Runs	HS	Avge	100	50	Ct	St
J N Gillespie	3	6	0	47	26	7.83	-	-	1	-

BOWLING AVERAGES	O	M	R	W	Avge	Best	5w	10w
J N Gillespie	67.0	6	300	3	100.00	2-91	-	-

Gillespie and Glenn McGrath were clearly not taking the Twenty20 match against England at the Rose Bowl very seriously. Both wore headbands and tried to imperson-ate the Australian bowlers of the Seventies. "Isn't it just a laugh this Twenty20 stuff?" Not for England.

Gillespie was attacked brutally as England sensed he had lost an edge to his bowling. His pace had dropped off and England circled a wounded animal. Kevin Pietersen smacked Gillespie out of the ground in a one-dayer at Bristol the following week and when Bangladesh got stuck into him the omens were clear.

But the mateship and team ethic that had served Australian cricket so well for so long ensured Gillespie was shown some loyalty. He was selected ahead of Kasprowicz at Lord's and survived through to the third Test at Old Trafford.

"Gillespie used to fly at batsmen, and his deliveries skated off pitches and hurried through defences," wrote Simon Hughes. "Now he lollops to the wicket and the zip generated from an explosion at the crease has largely gone. With his hippie hair and spindly legs he looked last weekend at Bristol like an ageing rocker who had lost his way to Glastonbury."

Three wickets in three Tests spelt the end. Gillespie was leaking runs and with him in the attack, Australia were unable to build up any pressure. Only his obdurate tailend batting was of any use to the side.

"It's all right saying that Gillespie has a good reputation," wrote Boycott. "All players have to live on facts and figures and Gillespie's are not very good at this moment. When that happens you have to face facts."

Australia did and Shaun Tait took Gillespie's place for the final two Tests. Dizzy was left to carry the bananas and crumpets at Trent Bridge along with the injured Glenn McGrath, surely the most successful 12th men in recent history.

AUSTRALIA
M S KASPROWICZ

BATTING AVERAGES	M	I	NO	Runs	HS	Avge	100	50	Ct	St
M S Kasprowicz	2	4	0	44	20	11.00	-	-	3	-

BOWLING AVERAGES	O	M	R	W	Avge	Best	5w	10w
M S Kasprowicz	52.0	6	250	4	62.50	3-80	-	-

Scrapped with Gillespie for a place in the first Test but in the end had to be satisfied being McGrath's understudy.

He replaced the great man at both Edgbaston and Trent Bridge, but failed to live up to the task. For a man experienced in county conditions, he mystifyingly failed to fire in England with both his line and length disappearing as quickly as his figures.

His eventual tally amounted to only four wickets and he never really found any rhythm on the tour. He will be best remem-bered for his courageous 20 in the fight for victory with Brett Lee at Edgbaston.

If he had managed to eke out the final two runs, Kasprowicz would have been a hero but a short ball from Steve Harmison wrecked the good work. Television replays proved his hand was off the bat when he was struck on the glove. Lives are changed by such close calls and Kasprowicz admitted his dismissal will live with him forever.

AUSTRALIA
G D McGRATH

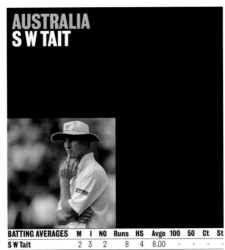

BATTING AVERAGES	M	I	NO	Runs	HS	Avge	100	50	Ct	St
G D McGrath	3	5	4	36	20*	36.00	-	-	1	-

BOWLING AVERAGES	O	M	R	W	Avge	Best	5w	10w
McGrath	134.0	22	440	19	23.15	5-53	2	-

When he stretched to collect a stray rugby pass before the start of the second Test the series was about to change. McGrath stepped on a stray cricket ball and was left ashen faced and in agony. Australia, more importantly, were left without their champion seamer and suddenly looked very vulnerable.

McGrath was no doubt furious his final Ashes tour ended in defeat and injury. This ultimate competitor had predicted a 5-0 win for Australia, a throwaway remark the Oval crowd enjoyed reminding him about on the final morning. From the first morning of the series to the last, McGrath had travelled an eventful path.

It may be a long way from Dubbo to Lord's but the boy from the bush was born to rule the home of cricket. The Lord's slope is his favourite hunting ground, a strip of earth Simon Hughes said McGrath would 'happily roll up and carry round with him forever.' And it supplied him with that most enviable of records when he picked up his 500th Test wicket by dismissing Marcus Trescothick with the first ball after tea on day one of the first Ashes Test .

Not only did McGrath haul Australia to victory, he also enjoyed destroying English morale. The Poms had got uppity and McGrath had knocked them back down.

But it all changed while McGrath was sat on the sidelines. He managed to recover in time for the Old Trafford Test but was wicketless in the first innings through a combination of dropped catches and bad luck. All of sudden, McGrath looked a little vulnerable and it became clear that away from Lord's, he was not going to pose the same threat.

While McGrath's ankle injury was a freak, the elbow strain that kept him out of the fourth Test was a worrying development. At the age of 35, McGrath began to show signs of wear and tear and Australia again lost in his absence. McGrath ended the series on the losing side but not once did England beat an Australian team boasting his skills.

AUSTRALIA
S W TAIT

BATTING AVERAGES	M	I	NO	Runs	HS	Avge	100	50	Ct	St
S W Tait	2	3	2	8	4	8.00	-	-	-	-

BOWLING AVERAGES	O	M	R	W	Avge	Best	5w	10w
S W Tait	48.1	5	210	5	42.00	3-97	-	-

Handed his baggy green cap by Michael Slater before the start of the fourth Test and told never to take it for granted. Starting out on a losing side probably left an unforgettable mark.

Tait was the wild card, a selectorial gamble forced by Gillespie's woeful form. The summer before he had been bombed out of the Durham side due to a no-ball habit, but wickets for South Australia confirmed his place in the touring party.

With a low slingy action reminiscent of Jeff Thomson, Tait showed an ability to bowl devilish deliveries. His downfall was the dross that often sandwiched the decent.

He dismissed Marcus Trescothick and Ian Bell during his first day in Test cricket but England knew they only had to bide their time. A half volley was often only a ball or two away.

His pace, up in the mid-90s at its peak, made up for Gillespie's lack of zip but when Australia needed wickets on the final day of the series, Ponting was slow to turn to the new boy.

ENGLAND
M P VAUGHAN

BATTING AVERAGES	M	I	NO	Runs	HS	Avge	100	50	Ct	St
M P Vaughan	5	10	0	326	166	32.60	1	1	2	-

BOWLING AVERAGES	O	M	R	W	Avge	Best	5w	10w
M P Vaughan	5.0	0	21	0	-	-	-	-

With the evening sun spreading across the Oval and his England cap soggy with champagne, Michael Vaughan was asked a simple question. "What does it feel like to be the man who lifted the Ashes?" Journalists were hoping for a passionate sound-bite that would make a back page headline, instead they were given a small insight into why Vaughan is such a popular captain in the England dressing room.

"I'm just the lucky one, the guy who got to pick up the little urn," said Vaughan in the Bedser Lounge just feet away from where he was handed the trophy. No arrogance, no conceit but plenty of modesty. In Vaughan's vision of England there are superstar players but no superstar egos. Even within Kevin Pietersen's oceans of self-confidence, there is room for modesty and the importance of putting the team first.

After the spiky, combative captaincy of Nasser Hussain, Vaughan has brought a different face to English cricket. He dashed off from a Test match in 2003 for the birth of his daughter Tallulah Grace, and throughout the Test series wore green and white wristbands for his own charity. He is a modern man in possession of the oldest job in English sport.

Vaughan's glorious summer will live with him forever and he realised moments after winning the Ashes that he was enjoying a once-in-a-lifetime feeling. "I've never experienced anything like it and I'm not sure cricket can reach these heights again," he said.

The journey towards those peaks of public affection began before Vaughan assumed the captaincy. The base camps were in Adelaide, Melbourne and Sydney, where three years previously Vaughan had scored three Ashes centuries and earned Australian respect. He also watched and learned. He saw how Australia, under Steve Waugh, attacked an England side confident of causing an upset. He also noted how England lapsed back into familiar insecurities at the first sight of Aussie intimidation.

In 2005 that would change. The bully was about to be bullied. England, with Vaughan at the forefront, attacked Australia from the first moment at Lord's. Under Vaughan's instruction, England players did not politely enquire into the health of Ricky Ponting or Matthew Hayden after they had been struck by short balls. England's tactic of throwing the ball towards Australian batsman was pioneered by Vaughan, who threw the ball so wildly at Shane Warne that he had to dive for cover.

It ensured Vaughan a mouthful from Ponting when he came out to bat. Vaughan stared him down and said he was no "Steve Waugh in the sledging stakes." A cruel riposte, and indicative of England's new ways.

But the big boy talk could not hide England's failings at Lord's. They tried too hard to be the boss and were left humbled by a heavy defeat. The Michael Vaughan that had pulled and driven a glorious trail across Australia in 2002-3 looked frail and fraught at the crease.

"He was a mess technically," said Geoffrey Boycott. "He was shuffling about too much, getting caught on the crease, and bringing his bat down from first slip to mid on. He must make runs. He's the focal point of the team, and to win the Ashes we need him to be at his very best."

Two further failures at Edgbaston and it was time for everyone to panic over the England captain's form. Everyone, that is, except Vaughan. At Edgbaston he had shown the value of keeping calm under pressure.

With Australia's last pair of Brett Lee and Mike Kasprowicz eking towards an astonishing victory on the Sunday morning, Vaughan kept the message simple, "just one more, boys." This showed great self-control and strength of mind in the face of such agonising tension, for Vaughan knew the Ashes were gone if England lost. The relief was summed up in the moment of victory with Vaughan punching the air while being held aloft by Andrew Flintoff.

"As Vaughan's leadership has grown in stature so the team have grown with him," said Simon Hughes. "To Nasser Hussain's passion he has added perspicacity, to his resilience he has added ruthlesssness. To his ambition he has added achievement."

The series may have been levelled but Vaughan had suffered two further failures, and was beaten by a straight one from Brett Lee in the second innings, prompting Martin Johnson to write: "All summer people have been picking up their morning papers to see a photograph of Vaughan, head over the bat in classic defensive pose, while all the time scratching their heads in the suspicion that something is missing, and then they realise what it is. Vaughan's off stump."

He needed runs at Old Trafford. He also needed some luck. Both came his way. Bowled by a no-ball from Glenn McGrath on 41 and dropped by Adam Gilchrist, Vaughan made the most of his chances. His classic cover drive returned as he grew in confidence and 166, his highest score as England captain, gave his side the edge.

"Vaughan's innings was a microcosm of his summer," wrote Hughes. "Sketchy at first, swishing at thin air. He said later his bat felt like a straw. A leg stump half volley from Brett Lee transformed it into a scythe."

There was criticism of Vaughan's field-placings, particularly in the slip cordon, as England failed to finish off Australia in Manchester, but they were the only muted concerns over his captaincy.

In the final two Tests, with both field placings and deployment of his bowlers, Vaughan consistently overwhelmed Ponting's outdated practices. If a bowler was failing to deliver, Vaughan whipped him out of the attack after two overs rather than giving him the regulation six. His plans for individual batsmen, in particular Matthew Hayden and Adam Gilchrist, were successful to the letter.

"Vaughan has a broader imagination and is better at stimulating his players – and he has used both skills to decisive effect," wrote Simon Hughes.

The result was that Vaughan clutched his hands around the four inch Ashes urn and had to endure a night on the town with Freddie Flintoff – probably his greatest physical challenge of the summer. From behind dark glasses and with exhaustion cracking his voice, Vaughan spoke the following day about legacies and future challenges.

The England captain was sounding distinctly Australian.

ENGLAND
M E TRESCOTHICK

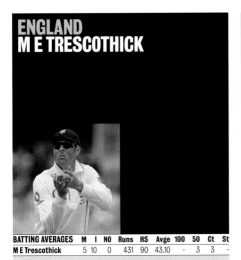

BATTING AVERAGES	M	I	NO	Runs	HS	Avge	100	50	Ct	St
M E Trescothick	5	10	0	431	90	43.10	-	3	3	-

His technique may be uncomplicated and his approach to batting simple, but Trescothick managed to rise above Australian barbs by becoming the summer's most effective left-hand opener.

During his previous two Ashes series, Trescothick was strictly limited to cameo appearances. A few boundaries were thrashed but a nick was sure to follow and he settled in nicely as McGrath's latest bunny. "When Trescothick first comes in, you don't want to go for a pee because you might miss him," wrote Geoffrey Boycott at the start of the series.

But while Hayden flapped and Langer scrapped, Trescothick grew in confidence and stature to become the dominant force in his tussles with Australian bowlers.

After 15 Tests he was still awaiting a maiden Ashes hundred but for the first time Australia had a glimpse of the damage Trescothick can inflict. Standing still and swinging from the hip, Trescothick signified England's fightback with a bruising 90 at Edgbaston. England scored 407 in a day and the Ashes series had changed.

"Maybe I did take a little motivation last year from Shane Warne's claims that you didn't have to be Einstein to work out how to get me out," wrote Trescothick in his Daily Telegraph column.

Innings of 63 and 41 represented a healthy return at Old Trafford but Trescothick should have scored his Ashes hundred at Trent Bridge where on a truncated first day he was bowled by debutant Shaun Tait for 65.

But he stuck to his game-plan. He thumped the ball through the off-side and was a consistent performer in every match along with partner Andrew Strauss. "The 2005 Marcus Trescothick is a different player. Not technically different. Psychologically different," wrote Simon Hughes.

No longer was Trescothick worried about the odd waft and with his inner demons conquered he could turn his attention to the Aussie bowlers.

ENGLAND
A J STRAUSS

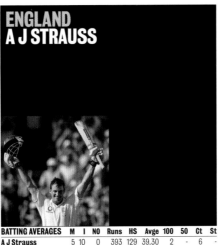

BATTING AVERAGES	M	I	NO	Runs	HS	Avge	100	50	Ct	St
A J Strauss	5	10	0	393	129	39.30	2	-	6	-

If Trescothick was to be McGrath's rabbit then Warne had eyes only for Strauss. Continually goaded by Warne, he called him Daryl after his favourite South African batsman Daryl Cullinan, Strauss rose above the sledging to continue the remarkable start to his Test career.

Warne may have dismissed him six times but Strauss calmly eased his way to two centuries in his first Ashes series. The second, in the final Test at the Oval, will perhaps be remembered as a career defining innings.

"There is something reassuring about Strauss," wrote Simon Hughes. "Like his captain, he is a balanced individual, someone who doesn't get over-excited by success, or unduly concerned about failure."

Scores of 2 and 39 at Lord's were a disappointment and gave the Australians a false sense of security. They had heard all about Strauss but felt they had another Trescothick on their hands – a player who would score runs against everyone else but lacked the game and gall to do it against them.

When Strauss was twice bowled by huge spinning leg breaks from Warne at Edgbaston, he was forced to turn to outside help. Merlyn the bowling machine became the first hulking lump of steel to win an Ashes series. Strauss spent hours in the nets and the result was a second innings hundred at Old Trafford.

"In setting up the endgame, Strauss battled a cut ear (courtesy of a Brett Lee bouncer) and indifferent form to make 106," wrote Derek Pringle. "As he swished his bat and removed his helmet in delight at reaching the milestone, the field dressing on his left ear recalled Van Gogh's harrowing self-portraits, though Strauss did have a smile on his face."

He had an even bigger smile on his face when he provided one of the iconic moments of the series at Trent Bridge. His brilliant one-handed catch at slip off Adam Gilchrist brought a thousand gasps of surprise from the crowd.

Strauss's enthusiasm and approach to the game made him a popular member of the England dressing room. His performances against Australia proved what a rounded cricketer he is.

ENGLAND
I R BELL

BATTING AVERAGES	M	I	NO	Runs	HS	Avge	100	50	Ct	St
I R Bell	5	10	0	171	65	17.10	-	2	8	-

BOWLING AVERAGES	O	M	R	W	Avge	Best	5w	10w
I R Bell	7.0	2	20	0				

A pair of fifties at Old Trafford suggested Bell had the wherewithal to fend off the wily old schemers in Australia's attack but by the end of the series he looked a forlorn rookie.

A pair at the Oval followed single figure scores at Trent Bridge where his second innings hook to deep square leg was the shot of a player cracking under pressure.

Bell's confidence will have been helped by the support he received from the England management who believe his classic technique suggests a bright future. Having faced Warne and McGrath in his first Ashes series, Bell should have filed away plenty of notes for future reference. Under S for slider there will be a whole wad of information. Warne's straight one had made Bell look out of his depth at Lord's.

Boycott was not impressed. "I see that Bell has been quoted saying: 'I've watched it again and again on television and it still looks a leg-spinner to me.' Well, someone should tell him that that's what a slider is – it looks like a leg-spinner but instead of turning, it runs on straight and quicker."

The third Test in Manchester provided Bell with the chance to answer his critics. Warne put him under pressure in both innings and he had to work hard for runs, especially with Australian fielders breathing down his neck waiting for a bat-pad catch.

"But he rode his luck to score 59 and 65 and ignored the Aussie shouts of 'we'll get him soon.'" Bell showed an admirable maturity and played like the man whose career he helped to end – Graham Thorpe.

His sprightly presence at short leg was a boon for England and his eight catches made him the best fielder in the side. Bell also brought an added touch of youth culture to the England dressing room.

ENGLAND
K P PIETERSON

BATTING AVERAGES	M	I	NO	Runs	HS	Avge	100	50	Ct	St
K P Pietersen	5	10	1	473	158	52.55	1	3	-	-

The big talk, coloured hair and in-your-face confidence that earned Pietersen his Test chance was beginning to hang like a boulder around his neck as the Ashes entered its final day. Pundits were whispering about big-headedness and style over substance but in one afternoon, Pietersen silenced the grumbles.

England's king of bling delivered cricket's crown jewels with an innings of 158. The crowd sang about the Ashes coming home and didn't give a hoot that they had been delivered by a player with a South African accent.

The determination that coursed through Pietersen's cricket was honed in the disappointment of having to leave his native country in order to further his career. As Matthew Hayden wrote after the Lord's Test: "I love his aggression and I thought it was a fantastic performance. I simply love the way he plays his cricket. He plays like a true South African."

After two fifties on his Test debut at Lord's Pietersen had vindicated the decision by England to select him ahead of Graham Thorpe. With his aggressive style, ability to improvise strokes out of nothing and will to succeed, Pietersen gave England a new dimension.

"He has catapulted English batting into a post-modern, shot-a-ball era," wrote Simon Hughes. "He has taken it to new uninhibited levels. Some of his shots have defied belief, never mind description. He has helped England to a run-rate in excess of Australia's for the first time since the Eighties."

He took on his great mate Shane Warne and won the early battles. He struck him for six at Lord's and then hit him into the stands at Edgbaston.

But with attack comes risk and Pietersen's luck began to run out. Catches would find the boundary fielder and promising starts were squandered. Watching Flintoff and Pietersen bat together emptied bars, it also did little for the cardiac health of the nation.

He required some luck at the Oval. Being dropped on 15 by Warne was a cruel irony as it had been the Australian who urged England to pick Pietersen in the first place. He was then battered by Brett Lee as Australia sensed a chance of victory. Pietersen hit back. "It was either him or me," he said. It was him and England were grateful. "Monday became Pietersen day," wrote Mark Nicholas after the Oval Test. Pietersen probably expected little else.

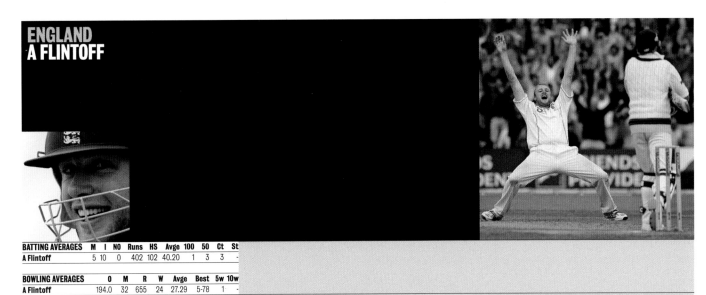

ENGLAND
A FLINTOFF

BATTING AVERAGES	M	I	NO	Runs	HS	Avge	100	50	Ct	St
A Flintoff	5	10	0	402	102	40.20	1	3	3	-

BOWLING AVERAGES	O	M	R	W	Avge	Best	5w	10w
A Flintoff	194.0	32	655	24	27.29	5-78	1	-

If an Ashes series is cricket's kingmaker then Andrew Flintoff enjoyed a glorious reign over the summer of 2005.

His bowling was both awesome and brutal, his batting a blend of maturity and menace. With success against the best team in the world, and possibly of a generation too, Flintoff ascended the throne as the world's greatest allround cricketer. Flintoff also succeeded where countless others had failed and talk now will not be of the next Ian Botham, but of the new Andrew Flintoff. But whereas Botham was loved by the people for his exploits on the field, Flintoff's popularity stretches beyond the boundary rope.

With his wife Rachael and baby daughter Holly, Flintoff is every inch the family man. When he needed an escape from the Ashes cauldron, he didn't turn to nightclubs or go on a bender in Ibiza, instead he settled for a quiet few days in Devon or France with his family. On the open top bus parade through London, he proudly clutched Holly, leaving his teammates to hold the Ashes urn. After his 24-hour binge to celebrate the Ashes victory, there were no stories of late night punch-ups, just pictures of Flintoff chatting with England fans, while looking as dazed as a batsman that had just been struck by one of his bouncers.

Freddie's image as a friendly giant who biffs cricket balls during the day and changes nappies at night may not be entirely accurate but it does ensure he appeals to more than Barmy Army blokes wearing England shirts.

But Flintoff waited a long time for his first Ashes series. In 2001 he was in his own words, "truly awful," as form and fitness deserted him. When he arrived in Australia he was still struggling with his recovery from a hernia operation and was unable to run. England were not about to take any chances this time. Sent home early from England's winter tour to South Africa due to an ankle injury, Flintoff swapped a honeymoon in the sun for February spent fell running around Preston and sessions in the gym.

The result was there for all to see on the penultimate morning of the series. Flintoff bowled 18 overs unchanged as he all but delivered the Ashes for England with a five wicket haul. Australian players looked on from the dressing room in awe as Flintoff ran in, and bowled fast over after over. "Not bad for a fat lad," Flintoff once said. Nobody was about to call Flintoff fat again.

"We have had the most influential player on either side, Andrew Flintoff. At crucial points, he has been able to lift the team and the public with his batting and bowling. Flintoff has been the match-winner," wrote Geoffrey Boycott, a Flintoff fan even in his darkest days of underachievement.

On Australia's last visit to England, Nasser Hussain's bowlers had failed to find a way to bowl to Adam Gilchrist. No shame perhaps considering every other country had suffered at Gilchrist's hands, but this time England were determined to curtail his threat. Flintoff was their key. "Flintoff's duel with Adam Gilchrist is vital," wrote Simon Hughes. "Gilchrist is the samurai sword of the Aussie flashing blades, arriving in mid-innings to apply the mortal strikes to an already wounded opponent. His average is a daunting 61."

This time it would be a far from daunting 22. Gilchrist walked into Flintoff's trap Test after Test, falling to him four times during the series. Australia, and in particular their left-handers, did not know whether to attack or defend. Simon Katich was guilty of leaving him at Old Trafford and had his poles knocked out of the ground. When they attacked Flintoff, catches were flashed to gully or slip. If Kevin Pietersen wasn't around, the catches were held.

"The public now recognise that we have some very good players, some real winners and, in Andrew Flintoff, a cult hero," wrote Boycott. "When Flintoff is bowling well the crowd have this empathy with him. He galvanised the whole England side."

But Flintoff's worst fears were coming true. He was turning into a bowling allrounder rather than a batter who sends down a few overs. He responded with half centuries at Edgbaston that stamped his mark on a fantastic match. His seven wickets, including the dismissal of Warne on the final morning, brought him a man of the match award.

If that was the greatest ever Test, then Flintoff's handshake with Brett Lee at the end was a 'Bobby Moore-Pele' moment. Two men who had spent the previous five days trying to inflict bodily damage on one another had reached an unspoken understanding. There had been a building up of tension between the two sides, but Flintoff and Lee pierced it in an instant. The rest of the summer was to be played out against a backdrop of inspiring sportsmanship.

"Flintoff went to Lee first for one of those spine-tingling embraces that endorses sport's reference to traditional human values," wrote Mark Nicholas. "If governments ever say that competitive sport is a bad thing, they should be sent the tape." If they could find one that is. The DVD for that Test match sold out in days. Ashes fever had truly gripped the nation and Flintoff was top of the bill.

But Flintoff knew if he was to have a great series then runs had to flow. An average above 40 would represent a contribution beyond flashes of breathtaking strokeplay. In the fourth Test at Trent Bridge, England needed Flintoff to be responsible and he played as though Boycott's commentary was being piped direct to his helmet. "Flintoff curtailed his game and played with control, responsibility and great skill," said the Yorkshireman. Flintoff turned 241 for five into 477 through his 106, his greatest innings. "I can't remember the last time I saw an Australian team run for cover," said Boycott.

At The Oval the stage was clear for Flintoff. Simon Jones, his fellow 'reverser' was injured and Flintoff had to take responsibility. Having squandered the opportunity to bat Australia out of the match, England then saw the Ashes imperilled by some resilience from Matthew Hayden and Justin Langer.

But by continually hitting the pitch hard and bowling his combination of yorkers and short balls, Flintoff pulled Australia back. Moments after winning the England player of the series award as well as the inaugural Compton/Miller medal (presented to the best player from either side), Ricky Ponting said: "It would be nice if we could find an Andrew Flintoff from somewhere." It was the highest compliment and confirmed Flintoff's new status.

ENGLAND
G O JONES

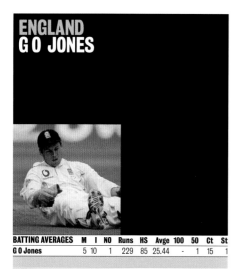

BATTING AVERAGES	M	I	NO	Runs	HS	Avge	100	50	Ct	St
G O Jones	5	10	1	229	85	25.44	-	1	15	1

There were times when it seemed Geraint Jones would be the favourite to drop the Ashes and not Shane Warne. As it turned out Jones missed a series of chances behind the stumps but he clung onto the most important catch in recent English history.

Jones was presented with the match ball from the Edgbaston Test (after it had been wrestled from umpire Billy Bowden's clutches) following his low, tumbling leg side take off Mike Kasprowicz's glove.

But Jones just had one of those series. Tidy work was often overshadowed by ugly errors. In the next Test at Old Trafford he missed a regulation stumping of Warne on 55 and then dropped a catch off the same batsman on 68. Warne made 90 and went a long way to saving the Test. Martin Johnson called Jones a "missed stumping waiting to happen."

The gaffes continued to follow the good at Trent Bride. His partnership of 177 with Andrew Flintoff, when Jones made 85, was the highest of the series and gave England a healthy first innings score. But he then missed another stumping off Michael Clarke after Australia had followed on. "Jones spent so long juggling with what appeared to be a live electric eel that Michael Clarke could have had the turning circle of the Queen Mary and still made it back," wrote Johnson.

But the Flintoff-Jones axis in the lower middle order backed up the selector's belief that a wicketkeeper had to contribute runs. That ability combined with a perky attitude preserved his place. "Jones is a great foil for Flintoff," wrote Simon Hughes. "A ball that Big Freddie will stride towards and thump back wide of the bowler, Little Geraint will lay back and cuff square of the wicket."

The problem was that little Geraint could also be frail. The smear of Warne in the second innings at Trent Bridge could have lost the match and suggested a hot headed approach under pressure.

ENGLAND
A F GILES

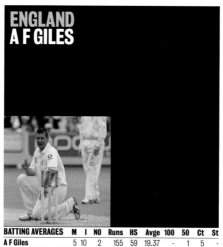

BATTING AVERAGES	M	I	NO	Runs	HS	Avge	100	50	Ct	St
A F Giles	5	10	2	155	59	19.37	-	1	5	-

BOWLING AVERAGES	O	M	R	W	Avge	Best	5w	10w
A F Giles	160.0	18	578	10	57.80	3-78	-	-

So he's no Shane Warne. Comparisons with the great man left Giles feeling inadequate and unloved at the beginning of the series following a disappointing first Test at Lord's.

The coach of the worst county in the country, Derbyshire's David Houghton, said he thought England were playing a man short with Giles in the team. The King of Spain gags were quickly aired again and Giles was the most maligned man in English cricket.

He took on his critics in his newspaper column. The Aussies sniggered behind closed doors and Giles went into his home Test at Edgbaston under enormous pressure. It was time for the whinging to stop and the twirling to start.

"Crikey, the criticism directed at Giles in the last week is nothing compared to what I have had to deal with in my career," wrote Boycott. "So stop being a namby pamby! What you have got to do now is pick yourself up, dust yourself down and get stuck in."

We all love an underdog and Giles is at his best when he's angry. His best mate, Michael Vaughan, was clearly hurt by the criticism and seemed even happier than Giles when he held onto Ricky Ponting's top edge at fine leg to give the left-armer a much needed wicket. "One of his team-mates should tell him to belt up in the future but he was back to his best yesterday," said Boycott after Giles had picked up three first innings wickets.

He went on to take only seven more wickets in the series but Giles dismissed every member of Australia's top eight at least once and the ball he bowled Damien Martyn with at Old Trafford will live with him for ever. Pitching on leg stump it spat and turned past Martyn's bat before hitting the top of off stump.

"If it possessed the romance of Warne's ball to Mike Gatting here 12 years ago, it also got rid of the opposition's best batsman," wrote Derek Pringle.

But it was Giles's batting that was to be crucial in the next two Tests. He scored only seven runs in the second innings at Trent Bridge, but in the maelstrom of Australia's Nottingham fightback Giles's contribution was crucial. At The Oval his highest Test score, 59, enabled Kevin Pietersen to indulge himself and ensure the Ashes.

ENGLAND
M J HOGGARD

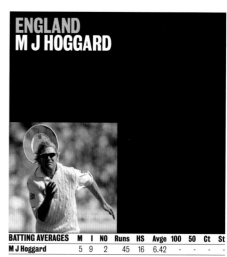

BATTING AVERAGES	M	I	NO	Runs	HS	Avge	100	50	Ct	St
M J Hoggard	5	9	2	45	16	6.42	-	-	-	-

BOWLING AVERAGES	O	M	R	W	Avge	Best	5w	10w
M J Hoggard	122.1	15	473	16	29.56	4-97	-	-

The Australians chuckled before the first Test when Hoggard had the temerity to question their stamina of their aging side.

But as the overs mounted and the Aussie bowlers creaked it was Hoggard who had the last laugh. His 11 over spell in the fourth Test at Trent Bridge swung the match England's way and Hoggard's importance to the cause magnified as the series wore on.

Traditional swing bowling is Hoggard's strength and at Trent Bridge and the Oval he found conditions to his liking. Forget the new fangled reverse swing, Hoggard relies on old fashioned means. Once the leg side four balls had been cut from his repertoire, Hoggard found greater confidence from his captain and was thrown the ball for longer spells.

At Trent Bridge he became the first quick bowler to get Adam Gilchrist leg before and by pitching the ball up and swinging it late, he took 16 wickets in the series. Working in tandem, he and Flintoff proved an irresistible double act for England.

But at Trent Bridge it was Hoggard's batting the nation revelled in. A blocker in the Gillespie mould, Hoggard relies on discipline and a decent forward defensive to protect his wicket. With England requiring 13 runs when he came in, he unfurled a Vaughan-like cover drive off Brett Lee that raced to the ropes and calmed the nerves.

"He showed better composure than some of the more experienced and better batsmen," wrote Boycott, clearly impressed by some Yorkshire steel.

Buoyed by his new found hero status Hoggard, the laid back fell walker with the farmer's stride, stood tall at the Oval. Just as Australia scented a first innings lead he teamed up with Flintoff once more and took four wickets.

"The marauding Freddie one end; the galumphing Hoggy the other. The raging bull and the determined mule. They might have had ideal bowling conditions to work in but they exploited them brilliantly," wrote Hughes. "Australia slumped from 277 for two to 367 all out. The sort of decline that in the past was England's prerogative." Not anymore.

ENGLAND
S J HARMISON

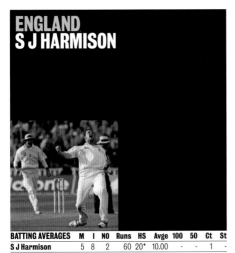

BATTING AVERAGES	M	I	NO	Runs	HS	Avge	100	50	Ct	St
S J Harmison	5	8	2	60	20*	10.00	-	-	1	-

BOWLING AVERAGES	O	M	R	W	Avge	Best	5w	10w
S J Harmison	161.1	22	549	17	32.29	5-43	1	-

He may have failed to scale the adrenalin-pumping heights of that first morning at Lord's but Harmison left an imprint on the series and bruises on Australian skin.

He hit Justin Langer's elbow with the second ball of the series and then cut Ricky Ponting's cheek in a blood curdling opening to the series. "First overs set the tone," wrote Simon Hughes. "And Harmison sent down a humdinger. Nine runs came off the over, but this was Grievous Bodily Harmison, not Ginger Benign Harmison."

He also took five for 43 as Australia were blown away for 190 and the series launched in frenetic style.

The wickets may have dried up as the series wore on but the ones Harmison did take were often crucial. Michael Clarke, for one, was beaten by a glorious slower ball in the final throes of Saturday at Edgbaston. "After two vicious throat jobs came the ultimate slower ball, delivered bravely, convincingly and cleverly off the middle finger of what was surely a trembling hand," wrote Mark Nicholas. "Get it wrong and it whistles to the boundary, releasing the highest and happiest endorphins into the Australian dressing room. Get it right, as Harmison did, and the same endorphins float next door."

And it was of course Harmison's bouncer that brushed Michael Kasprowicz's glove to win that Test. In the course of one delivery Harmison changed the destiny of the Ashes.

Quiet and unassuming, Harmison made a reluctant hero. The Australians began the series teasing him about his problems with homesickness but Harmison earned respect by delivering at the crucial moments.

His close friend Andrew Flintoff eclipsed him for the remainder of the series and Harmison enjoyed his success. The pair partied together on the night of England's Ashes triumph, a fast bowling double act at the top of their game.

ENGLAND
S P JONES

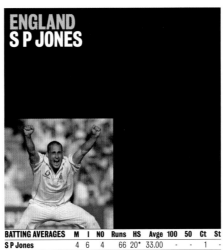

BATTING AVERAGES	M	I	NO	Runs	HS	Avge	100	50	Ct	St
S P Jones	4	6	4	66	20*	33.00	-	-	1	-

BOWLING AVERAGES	O	M	R	W	Avge	Best	5w	10w
S P Jones	102.0	17	378	18	21.00	6-53	2	-

Started the season posing nude for a women's magazine but it was his naked ambition and determination that left an impression on the series.

Topped the England bowling averages with 18 wickets including six for 53 at Old Trafford – the best return of the summer by an Englishman.

The last time Australia saw Jones he was slumped in a heap on the outfield of the Gabba in Brisbane, his knee shredded and career hanging in the balance. The words of Australian supporters who shouted obscenities at him while he was being stretchered off were perhaps ringing in his ears as he set about leading England's attack.

With Jones unearthing prodigious reverse swing, accuracy, and a good outswinger, Vaughan had an unexpected extra weapon at his disposal. Throwing the ball to Jones allowed the other seamers to rest and also cranked up the pressure on the Australians.

The reverse swing had been learned from Waqar Younis, its founder and architect, when he played for Glamorgan in the late 1990s and was honed in the nets over the winter months following England's tour to South Africa. With a scuffed up 60-over old ball and a low slingy fast action Jones graduated to the highest level of Test cricket.

"Confidence accounts for much of the headway made, but despite the bulging biceps and pecs, Jones has an inquisitive mind hungry for improvement, at least as a bowler," wrote Derek Prngle.

It was just a shame an ankle injury kept him out of the final Test and forced England into rethinking their strategy. A bowler who was not trusted by his captain only months previously had become his team's most potent asset. "Simon has definitely come of age," was England coach Duncan Fletcher's verdict.

ENGLAND
P D COLLINGWOOD

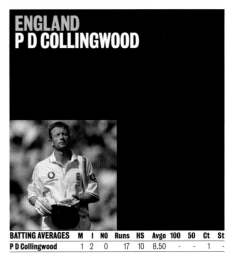

BATTING AVERAGES	M	I	NO	Runs	HS	Avge	100	50	Ct	St
P D Collingwood	1	2	0	17	10	8.50	-	-	1	-

BOWLING AVERAGES	O	M	R	W	Avge	Best	5w	10w
Collingwood	4.0	0	17	0	-	-	-	-

Only one Test match but what a Test to play in. Collingwood eased his way into the England side for the Oval Test in the place of injured Simon Jones.

Picked as an extra batsman he was the one charged with the dirty work – clearing up a mid-innings collapse or holding the hands of the tailenders. Collingwood had earned respect from the Australians for his one-day performances and his tough-talking ways. He was not underestimated despite only two previous Test match appearances.

He bowled only a handful of deliveries but he accompanied Pietersen for 14 overs in a tension-soothing second innings stand on the final day of the series. Collingwood blocked for all he was worth as England finally began to believe they would reach the finishing line. He scored only 10 runs but ate up 52 deliveries and 71 minutes. Time was of an essence for Australia and Collingwood was a nuisance determined to hang around.

The publishers would like to thank all
of the following who gave so generously
of their time, energy and expertise during
the making of this book:

Michael Doggart and Tom Whiting
at HarperCollins*Publishers*

Designers David Hawkins and
Glenn Howard at Untitled along
with the industrious Matt Brown

Keith Perry, Martin Smith and
Morven Knowles at the Telegraph

The contributing writers at the Telegraph –
Michael Parkinson, Derek Pringle, Martin
Johnson, Simon Hughes, Nick Hoult and
especially Simon Briggs for his all night
proofreading efforts and cricketing brain.

Phil Brown – a photographer who managed
to find the time in between his other jobs
as a short-order cook and mini-cab driver
to assemble the images in this book

Sue and Frank Wheeldon for supplying
the scorecards and player averages

All photographs are © Philip Brown,
except pages 14–23, 14 (left) © MCC Library
24–28 © Action images